SWALLOWED

2-8-19

Karen —

God never gives
upon us!

Jim

SWALLOWED

Exposing Trendy Beliefs That
Can Swallow Your Career

RUSS SHINPOCH

Xulon Press

Xulon Press
2301 Lucien Way #415
Maitland, FL 32751
407.339.4217
www.xulonpress.com

This book is dedicated to

9 Kids Who Own My Heart
Anna Kate, Abby, Emma, Callie,
Jessie, Johnson, Caroline, Ruby & Rya

Because they...
laugh when I act goofy,
run when they get to the beach,
listen when I tell bible stories,
scream with excitement when I walk in the door,
want me to read books to them,
wear Georgia Bulldogs fan gear on game days,
always want one more push in the swing,
make monkey sounds with me at the zoo,
give world-class hugs,
bring me drawings to put on the wall,
can't wait to open presents,
love to FaceTime,
never touch my "medicine" (chocolate candy),
pray with me,
can't wait for me to write the Alligator book,
sing "Riding Down the Bike Path" song on our bikes,
like to talk about Herschel the big black dog and the Armadillo,
dare to dip vegetables in ketchup,
AND sneak snacks...
God has given me an awesome life with the Crew!

Acknowledgements

❖ *My wife, Carol, has never quit believing in God and me.*

❖ *My children and their spouses—Joanne & Trey, Joel & Jen, Jonathan & Janelle— have encouraged me and honored me with the way they live for Christ.*

❖ *My parents, John and Barb, have inspired me with their desire to enjoy every moment of the simple things of life and experience all God has given them.*

❖ *Buddy Perstrope, awesome pastor and friend for nearly 30 years of ministry whose joy in Christ and encouragement has sustained me many times.*

❖ *Jim Perdue, bold preacher and long-time friend whose generosity and prayers have refreshed my ministry.*

❖ *David & Debbie Settle, who have hosted us and our furniture, shared scripture, prayed over us, laughed, and cried with us.*

❖ *Larry & Janice Rutledge, faithful friends who love God and family better than almost anybody.*

❖ *Ken & Carolyn Hood, whose laughter and hopeful spirit are traditions with us.*

❖ *David & Linda Hancock, whose faith and integrity encourage us.*

❖ *Chris Grant, "marketeur" and corporate missionary, husband, and father of two amazing preschoolers, whose biblical insight on issues and relationships deepened my faith for these past several years and whose coming book will be huge!*

❖ *Scott Enzor, one of the boldest preachers that will not compromise, has been a faithful friend.*

❖ *Ralph Carter, legendary pastor who has believed in me when others didn't and given wise counsel through all our Chick-fil-A sessions.*

❖ *Mike Hamlet, big church pastor who has taken time to intentionally pour encouragement into my life during this ministry transition.*

❖ *Jim Goodroe, Pastor & retired Director of Missions, enthusiastically gave friendship & wisdom.*

❖ *Paul McKee, Director of Missions, whose big heart for pastors found me at a critical moment.*

❖ *Al Phillips, Director of Missions, whose wisdom and prayers have been solid guidance.*

❖ *Randy Bradley, Director of Missions, who befriended me and was the first to support this book.*

❖ *Woody Oliver, Director of Missions, who has encouraged Carol and I since the Bluffton lunch.*

❖ *Brett Selby, pastor to untold thousands of pastors through Lifeway and the Oklahoma Convention, who has encouraged me with texts, calls, & Starbucks meetings.*

❖ *Harry Black, Director of Missions, whose first prayer over me and lunch at the German deli kept me going.*

❖ *Preston Collins, Director of Missions, whose contagious faith and friendship has been timely.*

❖ *Terry Rials, the ChurchRevitalizer, who took the time to encourage me over that steak lunch @ Cattleman's in Oklahoma City's Stockyards City.*

❖ *Dr. Greg Ayers, whose fellowship in all the breakfast/lunch meetings and example of "fiery-furnace faith" has inspired me.*

❖ *Reggie Choplin, who does more than coach basketball at Wade Hampton High School—he shapes the next generation of leaders and invited me to be a part of it.*

Table of Contents

Trendy Belief No. 1:   It's okay to quit if things get tough 1

Trendy Belief No. 2:   If you want to be happy,
follow your passion. 12

Trendy Belief No. 3:   God uses imperfect people. 18

Trendy Belief No. 4:   Your ability determines
your success. 23

Trendy Belief No. 5:   God will never ask you
to do something hard. 29

Trendy Belief No. 6:   It doesn't matter what
you believe. 38

Trendy Belief No. 7:   God doesn't want
you to go through trials. 49

Trendy Belief No. 8:   You can't succeed without a vision. 60

Trendy Belief No. 9:   Other people are
your biggest problem.. 65

Trendy Belief No. 10:   You are free to do
what you want. 74

Trendy Belief No. 11:   You can't please everybody.. 82

Trendy Belief No. 12:   It takes a long time to get past failure. 96

Trendy Belief No. 13:   Keep believing and the
breakthrough will come! 106

Trendy Belief No. 14:   There's always a
second chance. 114

Trendy Belief No. 15:   Some situations are
impossible to turn around 120

Trendy Belief No. 16:   Your potential is unlimited. 132

Trendy Belief No. 17:   Serving others is the
best way to live your life. 140

Trendy Belief No. 18:   You can't know God's
will with 100% certainty. 148

Trendy Belief No. 1:
It's okay to quit if things get tough.

I'm quitting to pursue my dream of not working here anymore.
—Anonymous

97% of the people who quit too soon are employed by the 3% that never gave up.
—Daymond John, Shark Tank Multi-Millionaire Entrepreneur

The hardest part of parenting is when I'm with my kids. I don't know what's more exhausting about parenting: the getting up early or the acting like you know what you are doing....The hardest part of parenting is when I'm with my kids.
—Jim Gaffigan, Dad Is Fat

The Lord gave this message to Jonah: "Get up and go to the great city of Nineveh. Announce my judgment against it because I have seen how wicked its people are." Jonah got up and went in the opposite direction to get away from the Lord.
—Jonah 1:3, NLT

Quitting is risky. Avoiding God for any reason equals running. And running equals quitting. You've tried running from God. Everybody does it. Nobody's good at it. Mostly because it becomes a survival game.

Kevin Farzad tweeted: *"I'm sorry if I don't wave back or smile at you while I'm running....I'm trying very hard to not die."*

Jonah was waving at God...*waving goodbye!* And was trying very hard not to die while running.

All of us have tried to avoid God's voice on some issue. And sometimes we don't hide it well. Like the emotional and quirky Jewish prophet, Jonah, who heard God's call to rescue a terrorist capital and then booked a cruise in the other direction. God's Nineveh project was inconvenient. It conflicted with Jonah's sense of justice. In fact, it made him crazy angry. Jonah quit.

Quitting *never* works out like you think.

The moment God told Jonah to go speak to the capital city of a terrorist nation, he became accountable. When God asks you to do something on any level, He's not *challenging* you to be a leader. He's *choosing* you to be a leader.

Once God speaks, nothing can ever be the same. Your commitment either grows or shrinks. Trying to escape God's presence with a Mediterranean cruise equaled quitting ministry for Jonah.

The most miserable people in the world are not non-believers. It's believers who are running from God.

Alyssa Kramer tweeted: *"I always hope that when people see me outside running they think, 'Wow, an athlete!' but instead it's probably more like, "Aw, good for her."*

Nobody wants to talk about why they run...but it could keep you from getting swallowed.

Quitting means you don't want to trust God or anybody.

Sometimes quitting is okay—like when you do it to stand for truth or put family first or pursue higher goals. But frequently, the real reason anybody quits is because they don't want to trust God on some issue. Like when God asks you to forgive someone, stay in a job or marriage, or be pure even though you are miserable.

Rather than believe God has big purpose and big power, you opt for stress-free. Voices everywhere tell you stress is wrong, and you have a right to a happy, conflict-free life. Sometimes you are just too afraid to face the person or the situation because you know God could change them too.

What if staying or working through it created a breakthrough for the other person?

Stress is multiplied by quitting. Jonah was still covered in "whale" vomit when he realized that God's purpose was to *change his heart*, not remove the challenge. Every task and trial are designed by God to drive you to trust in Him alone.

My friend, Pastor Gary, and his wife, tragically lost their 8-month-old daughter. He felt helpless as his wife cried for months. Almost a year later, without answers and desperate for relief, he told God he thought the only way to survive was to quit ministry. He chose a specific Sunday. At the service the week prior to his scheduled resignation, he poured out his heart about their loss to the church for the first time. Tears poured and brokenness swept the congregation. A member came to him and confessed: "We saw you dying and couldn't stand it so we had stopped coming." They knew Pastor Gary and his wife needed to open their hearts to survive the loss. Healing began.

Obeying creates stress. Opting out creates more.

Quitting creates "whales"!

We create our own "whales"! If your plans marginalize God, you make yourself bait! The moment Jonah decided to run and bought his cruise ticket, God released a huge fish to meet the ship and booked the storm on Jonah's calendar.[1] Nobody but Jonah could be blamed for his near-death experience of being in a fish belly for three days and nights...and he knew it. Instructing the panicked and desperate crew to throw him overboard before the waves and wind wrecked the ship, he confessed, "This terrible storm is all my fault".[2] Even the pagan crew said they knew the storm and violent sea was the result of Jonah's "sin".[3]

The reason we *feel* guilty is because we *are* guilty. We're not lost because we sin. We sin because we are lost. People are condemned before God not because of what they have *done* but because of what they have <u>not done</u>, which is to believe on Jesus.[4]

You don't run from God because you're *scared*.

Nobody is looking for a place to hide. There isn't any.

You run from God because you want to *sin*...

Or *keep sinning*...as in, hang on to attitudes and addictions that you know mess up God's plan.

Everybody knows it's impossible to escape God's presence or the consequences of breaking His rules. You know in your heart that you reap what you sow. *And yet...*

God didn't want Jonah to die...just his plans.

Though technically impossible, the outlier preacher had a *divided heart*. Jonah left room in his heart to pursue other plans if God's plan was ever inconvenient. Hard to be committed to a marriage if you won't give up your girlfriend. Jonah scheduled a getaway. So, like a rogue dictator playing with nukes that deserves a response, Jonah learned more about God than he planned!

Think...before you ask for a sign about God's will. You may get one. Jonah did! The big fish sent for Jonah represented God shutting down his plans. It was God's grace that Jonah's plans would be stopped, and he would be swallowed. That intervention saved his life! Sometimes the limitations you endure are God's mercy to protect you from loss or grace to purify you for leadership.

Be grateful God does send storms and big fish.

Storms don't mean God has *abandoned* you. Just the opposite. God is *attacking* toxic beliefs that could kill you. Getting swallowed by something doesn't mean God has *forgotten* you. God is shouting that He is *following* you!

There's something worse than God *redirecting you through a trial*. God could *remove you with a trial*. He targets pride.[5]

Quitting is a BIG sin because it's really unbelief.

Walt Deptula hosts *Road Rage* on 105.5 FM, *The ROAR*, the premier local sports radio station in South Carolina. After hearing a nationally known college quarterback stumble through a post-game media conference talking about how huge their win was over a team that didn't have a chance anyway, Walt said, "He's living in his own private Idaho!"

Jonah was "living in his own private Idaho"—out of touch with God and reality. You can't be sold out to God *AND* quit.

All sin is conflict with God. Some consequences are big.

What if quitting *is* actually a bigger sin than other things?

Not adultery. Not addiction. Not lying. Not killing innocent people with drunk driving. Not hate speech. Not stealing retirement funds. Just intentionally walking away from God's plan for your life.

Avoiding what God has told you to do is definitely a sin.[6]

When Israel pushed back on God's command to go fight for the Promised Land, God labeled it *unbelief*: *"How long will these people reject Me? How long will they not believe Me, with all the signs which I have performed?"*[7] Israel's fear of giants in the new land was just a cover for their decision to draw a line. They had reached their limit of what they would tolerate with God in that situation. People today still put limits on what and how they will obey God.

Quitting is a deeply personal offense to God. He won't let you get away with thinking it's okay...normal....justified...or the *right* thing to do in your pressure-filled situation! Like a woman choosing abortion because of fear and pressure.

Jonah's refusal to go to Nineveh was proof that his issue was really with believing God, not just hating the bad guys. To Jonah, Assyrian terrorist baby-killers weren't worth saving. No way should a just God erase all their sins! So just label Jonah's ship, "Unbelief"! Jonah didn't want to be connected in any way with mercy for the original terrorists.

That meant Jonah didn't want God.

And that's the *classic definition* of unbelief.

When you're not in control, you discover your security.

When three Hebrew millennials refused to worship the golden image of Babylonian King Nebuchadnezzar and were threatened with a fiery furnace, they believed God would deliver them. Even if God chose not to intervene, they vowed not to back down from their stand against evil.[8]

When you can't control what's happening, you discover what you've been trusting for your security...and maybe your identity. Quitting on God's call to Nineveh exposed Jonah's security was in his career and country, not God. The only real security is surrendering to God, never in this temporary world. If your security is in your career, when you lose your job, you'll lose your identity.

People normally try to cover up quitting.

Taking a trip is pretty innocent. It hid Jonah's decision temporarily. Like friends and family of mass shooters typically say *after* the tragedy...there were "no obvious signs" Jonah was out-of-control at war with God. The cruise was his cover.

You can quit on God without changing locations. You can let God's vision die while you keep your schedule. It's possible to abandon responsibility without appearing running. Lots of husbands and wives quit but go through the motions, *enduring but not enjoying*, marriage. Some ministry leaders fake it...until their "whale" swallows them!

Because ministry is a spiritual commitment, leaders can quit in their heart long before anybody suspects they are running from God. How? Usually because it's easier to *fake* commitment than to *follow-through* with it.

And it feels easier *initially* to quit than change. What if the only thing holding back a blessing was an attitude shift? What if a miracle you have prayed for can only be triggered if you agree to trust God *through* something you don't want to do?

Remember, the sins you cover, God uncovers.

The sins you uncover, God covers with his grace.

Multiple faith heroes, like Abraham, Samson, and David, got busted by God. Their adultery went public and their attitude went south.

Cover-ups don't work.

Running from God is always linked to a single incident.

Like the specific call Jonah rejected, running from God can *always* be traced to a single incident when you decided it wasn't worth it to trust God any longer. People look for loopholes in their commitment all the time. But there's always a specific moment when you pull the trigger to go in the opposite direction and start the *running mode*.

Quitting can always be traced back to an original disagreement with God.

God wanted to forgive the terrorist Assyrians. Jonah refused. Running officially started.

It's not your ministry. It's God's ministry.

One of the most popular and scary and spiritually dangerous beliefs trending in Christian culture is:

You get to choose your own level of commitment!

Jonah obviously felt entitled to decide when he should be committed and what his commitment should look like. If God's plan was illogical or irritating, he could opt out. This sense of entitlement was drowning Jonah long before his doomed ship was hit by hurricane force wind and waves.

Biggest mistake? Jonah believed it was *his ministry* and *not God's ministry* given to him! God's not going to give grace for that belief to survive! Because God calls you to ministry, the map belongs to Him. It's not about you. It's all about Him.

We exist to glorify God. Yes, it is *that* simple.

Everybody quits. Nobody has to stay there.

Quitting is an option...a ticket out of the pressure.

But hold on to that option, and you will eventually use it.

Quitting is *not* an option for people sold out to Jesus.

A powerful leadership axiom is that successful leaders never quit. It still happens. But it doesn't have to be final.

After denying Jesus three consecutive times just hours before the crucifixion, Peter labeled himself unfit for ministry and unilaterally made the decision to quit and return to his former career. After His resurrection, Jesus confronted Peter—*and his three historic total failures*—in a conversation at the beach with three questions about commitment. Nobody can say that didn't work because the flawed follower became an unashamed advocate for Jesus.[9]

Jesus obviously thought it's right and good and healthy to confront people who have messed up their commitments!

Everybody calls time out for some lame reason. What determines long-term happiness and usefulness to God is how long you camp out in the "I quit" zone and pretend not to be running. Avoiding God for any reason equals *running*. And *running* equals quitting...even if the attitude only lasts minutes.

The big question is when will you let God wreck your heart to reconnect with Him? Give up the crazy belief that you can escape God's presence or avoid what He's asking.

That's what atheists believe—if *you* decide God doesn't exist...then God doesn't exist. You can deny the law of gravity, but you will die if you jump from 10,000 feet without a parachute. Refusing to believe does not make God go away.

Jonah pretended unbelief intimidates and limits God.

God is bigger than your mistakes...*but*...

God will bug you about them until you try things His way.

There's no hiding.

Nobody quits when things are good.

Quitting usually happens at low points.

The universal belief? *Commitment is good. Quitting is bad.*

But all of us eventually mess up and give up. At some point, you decide you've given enough and deserve a break from responsibility. The call of God that once energized you has now emptied you. There's real disillusionment with God because things happened that left you with more questions than answers. Admit it. You're angry. There's zero passion left for another battle. Nothing's in it for you.

But rather than question *why* you don't want to do ministry, or marriage, or serve chick-n-mini's any more, you start to separate from your commitment. Rather than investigate *when* you feel most like quitting, you just want it to be over.

Jonah internally blamed God for tolerating terrorists. Sort of like thinking, "If God can heal, why doesn't He remove the cancer?" Nothing had changed from Jonah's perspective. The evil Assyrians were still in control. Intellectually, if you know you can't change a situation, why keep fighting at all?

Jonah was wrong. God was right. Jonah quit in the face of an impossible situation. What he didn't know was that God's breakthrough was next.

We quit. God doesn't.

Sometimes quitting is cover for secret sin.

Hidden attitudes can take you under.

A California couple knew something was terribly wrong with their brand new, 22-foot boat. The boat barely made a wake even at full throttle. After an hour of fighting it, they puttered to a nearby marina, hoping somebody could rescue them. The marina guys checked everything, including the engine and propeller. Perfect. Then one of the marina guys jumped in the water to check underneath. He came up choking on water because he was laughing so hard. Under the boat, still strapped securely in place, was the trailer!

Underneath the image of a successful ministry, Jonah's heart was strapped to an attitude that would take him under.

His *idol* was entitlement.

His *indulgence* was resentment.

Tim Keller, American pastor and Christian apologist, said, "When anything in life is an absolute requirement for your happiness and self-worth, it is essentially an 'idol,' something you are actually worshiping. When such a thing is threatened, your anger is absolute. Your anger is actually the way the idol keeps you in its service, in its chains. Therefore, if you find that, despite all the efforts to forgive, your anger and bitterness cannot subside, you may need to look deeper and ask, 'What am I defending? What is so important that I cannot live without?' It may be that, until some inordinate desire is identified and confronted, you will not be able to master your anger."[10]

Jonah simply didn't want to trust God's plan. That's fatal for leaders, especially those in ministry. Maybe he had never been tested with having to trust God in a big way. Did he hate the Assyrians because they had captured and tortured a family member? What's the benefit in serving God if He is not going to punish people who have hurt you or your family?

There's a reason for every person God puts in our lives...including Assyrians!

Jonah's real fear? That he would actually have to start being the leader God expected. By calling him to care about real souls in a specific city—not just *pray for the world*— God was targeting his secret sin of bitterness.

Battles won't kill your ministry. **Bitterness** will.

Ministry is not a <u>label</u>. It's a <u>life</u>!

If ministry is the overflow of a loving relationship with a living God, then quitting means your relationship with God is broken. Your heart has become dysfunctional. Your motivation for ministry is messed up. Ministry is not merely a label to identify a career. Nor is it a label reserved exclusively for church leaders.

Ministry is you pursuing God's purpose for your life, in any career.

Former seminary professor, Howard Hendricks, was on an American Airlines flight during a very long delay. A man who had too much to drink was being rude to other passengers and abusive with the flight attendants. Hendricks watched one flight attendant treat this out of control passenger with class, dignity, and professionalism. She was unruffled. When he was offensive, she was polite. Howard was so impressed that he walked to the back of the plane to commend the flight attendant. He told her what a good job she had done and that he was so impressed he was going to write a letter of recommendation to her boss at American Airlines. So, he asked the name of the person she worked for. The attendant replied, "Thank you sir, but I don't work for American Airlines." Hendricks was briefly confused until she added, "I work for Jesus Christ." She didn't quit because she was called to show Jesus to people. Especially the crazy ones.

Whether you are employed at Chick-fil-A, ESPN, Target, Amazon, Apple, Delta Airlines, Starbucks, the University of Georgia, the NFL or the FBI, you don't work for them. Your ministry through your career has a higher ultimate accountability as a leader. A believer serves with excellence because that's who they are. Ministry is the overflow of loving Jesus radically.

Quitting was an option for Jonah because ministry wasn't sacred. Ministry ceases to be sacred when it's not all about making God known. Running proved it was his *work*, not his *worship*! It was his *career*, not his *conviction*. If you can run and relax on a ship like Jonah, maybe you aren't committed...*or maybe you were never called*. Either way, like Jonah, you'll have to refresh your definition of ministry.

Ministry done God's way will always be scary.

God's call is never safe. Jonah quit when threatened.

But before you join the cyberbullying on Jonah, have you run from responsibility as a leader? I know pastors who haven't confronted the sin in their own church for fear of losing their income and lifestyle. I know politicians who won't fight for some legislation because they're afraid of losing the next election. I know parents who avoid setting boundaries for their kids because they don't want the conflict. On the other hand, there are corporate leaders who have taken a controversial stand on biblical truth that forwarded God's message to our post-Christian culture. Chick-fil-A and Hobby Lobby leadership have defended the biblical marriage model.

Sometimes a leader is the *first* to stand.

Sometimes the *only one* to stand.

It's never easy. It's always scary.

Do it anyway. Do it afraid.

God never apologizes for hard choices. He likes them.

Big challenges require big trust. Challenges force your faith in God to grow. Hard choices grow healthy commitment. Hard choices help you identify what you really believe and what you will stand for.

It doesn't bother God to force you to make hard choices. Why? Because He wants your exclusive and total devotion. That's what the 10 Commandments are all about—to remind you God is the unchallenged sovereign of the universe, He alone deserves your worship, He's holy and we're not, family and promises matter to God, and His values can save your life, so you need Him—not the other way around.

Boundaries exist to protect blessings. God always has a good reason for expecting believers to rise to a higher standard than the rest of the culture. Even taking a risk to reach the Assyrian terrorists was a legitimate purpose.

Choices exist to create commitment. As a leader, Jonah knew God doesn't apologize for calling you to bigger challenges. Hard choices grow commitment...and reveal it.

God knows your heart. You don't. But you need to know. Knowing your "spiritual heartbeat" may be humbling but can be healthy. That's heaven's real purpose in every crisis.

Quitting means your heartbeat for God has collapsed.

You don't have to like God's call. You just have to do it!

God didn't apologize for expecting Jonah to obey immediately and completely (i.e., all the way to Nineveh), even though Jonah got mad and acted out. As with any call from God, you don't have to like it, you just have to do it!

Jonah had hidden sin when God called him to do the Nineveh project. God doesn't hold up His projects waiting on perfect people. Most of the time, God calls you and adjusts your attitude *during* the mission!

Did you notice Jonah wasn't talking on board the ship headed for Spain? You don't talk God much when you are running.

God didn't ask Jonah to love Assyrians. God expected Jonah to love Him. At least enough to obey. God is more concerned about your *obedience* than your *opinion*.

God strengthens faith by stretching faith.

Trust is never a 100% intellectual thing. There will always be logical reasons *not* to take risks. Trust is not a *feeling*, because circumstances change your emotions. Fear wins if you let it overwhelm your thinking. On the scale of emotions, fear always dominates. Faith is a choice of the will. When God tells you to do something, and you do it, that's trust. Until then, your faith is all talk.

Faith only grows when you have to actually risk something and depend upon God.

Quitting kills the process of making faith stronger.

The more you trust, the bigger God becomes to you.

Fear doesn't disappear! If you expect your fear to go away, it never does. You never really get free of fear. Obeying God is normally trusting Him despite the paralyzing fear you feel. Live your faith, not your fear. That spirit of fear is never from God![11]

What big thing is God asking you to do right now? Normally, you can be sure it's God's voice if it is bigger than what you can handle. And...if it's something that scares you.

God does want you to be afraid...not of the scary stuff He is calling you to do... but of the scary life you'll have when God is opposing you if you don't follow-through.

Elisabeth Elliot, whose 28-yr-old husband was killed along with four other missionaries in the jungles of Ecuador, confessed that her life was owned by fear. Every time she tried to do something for God, fear stopped her. Then a friend spoke a challenge that set her free, "Why don't you do it afraid?" Elisabeth accepted the counsel. Together with Rachel Saint, the sister of one of the martyred missionaries, they boldly took the gospel to the Auca Indian tribesmen who had killed their husbands.[12] Elisabeth observed, "Faith does not eliminate questions....faith knows where to take them."[13]

Quitting doesn't remove fear. It rewards fear.

The 2017 Oscar-nominated movie, DUNKIRK, relived a turning point moment for British morale in World War II that defines leadership. In May 1940, a surprise German blitzkrieg had crushed Belgium and Holland, resulting in their surrender. British troops in France were pushed back and pinned down on the beaches at Dunkirk. Surrounded by the Nazi's and near shallow beaches that could not reached by the Royal Navy, only a miracle could save the British, French, and Belgium soldiers from inevitable surrender. Newly elected British Prime Minister Winston Churchill issued a call for all available civilian watercraft to rescue their army. About 1,200 boats, including many fishing boats, headed for Dunkirk under fire from the German Luftwaffe. More than 300,000 troops were miraculously rescued, and England survived.

Days later, on June 4, 1940, Winston Churchill's now famous speech to Parliament rallied the will of the British people to fight, giving them hope that the war could be won:

> [We] shall not flag or fail. We shall go on to the end, we shall fight in France, we shall fight on the seas and oceans, we shall fight with growing confidence and growing strength in the air, we shall defend our Island, whatever the cost may be, we shall fight on the beaches, we shall fight on the landing grounds, we shall fight in the fields and in the streets, we shall fight in the hills; we shall never surrender...

You always have a choice.
Fear can't make you quit. It can only make you feel hopeless.
Fear is only conquered when you move forward in God's purpose.
Quitting doesn't *remove* fear. It *rewards* fear.

God's call always leads to battles before breakthroughs.

Not sure why our current Christian culture has also bought into the fake belief that God owes you a blessing without a battle. Everything of value to you and God— your children's purity, your health, a safe school, a bible-believing church, trust in your marriage, a good job, a friend's salvation, the success of your company, freedom—are all things you have to fight for to possess and preserve.

God doesn't call you to lead where wars are already won! We're called to a spiritual war.[14] Leaders face real threats, but the conflict is with internal fear and invisible forces trying to separate us from what God has called us to do.

Satan wins when you quit.

If you fear God's purpose, then your God is too small.

If you hold back on commitment, your God is too safe.

If you can't give up control, then your God is your servant.

God is in control. Don't quit.

Even in the face of career change, critics, cancer, cheating, credit theft, or cyber-bullying...

...Don't quit!

Trendy Belief No. 2:
If you want to be happy, follow your passion.

My life feels like a test I didn't study for.
—Anonymous

Passion is energy. Feel the power that comes from focusing on what excites you.
—Oprah Winfrey, Entrepreneur

Jonah got up and went in the opposite direction to get away from the Lord.
—Jonah 1:3, NLT

Following your passion is a mistake. So is going through the Starbucks drive-thru during rush hour but chasing *your* dream might have bigger consequences.

Passion rules our culture. Judges tell American Idol contestants to keep chasing *their dreams*. Commencement speakers challenge graduates to lock into *their passion*, not a position. College football fans tailgate and paint their bodies to show *their passion* for their teams. When Mark Zuckerberg tells the Facebook journey—from dorm room idea to global social media wave—following *your passion* is inspiring. *Following your passion* is America's newest idol.

Following your passion is selfish. Jonah's passion took him in the wrong direction—away from God. The trendy Christian culture now says if you want to know God's will, just follow your passion. Deciding God's will by how passionate you feel about something is the wrong benchmark.

When Jesus approached four fishermen struggling to keep their small business alive, He didn't say *"Follow your passion"*. He had two words: *"Follow Me"*.[1]

Focus on destination, not desires.

"Happiness is a moving target", according to Maureen Henderson in the *FORBES* article, "Why 'Do What Makes You Happy' is The Dumbest Advice".[2]

Desires change quickly. The average U.S. consumer spends a whopping $5,400 each year on impulse purchases! Family credit card debt went north of $1 Trillion in 2018, with the average person using three credit cards running a balance of more than $6,000![3]

A shocking 84% of all shoppers make impulse purchases; impulse purchases represent 40% of all e-commerce; and, millennials are more likely to make impulse purchases than any other generation.[4]

Our generation is easy to track—we follow desires! Whether it's one click on Amazon or candy in the Walmart check-out line, feelings at the moment drive decisions.

God's plan is never boring! He has a specific will, full of risks and surprises. And you are *not* going to like some of those twists and turns. Like calling out a terrorist capital city.

God's will is never random. There's always a specific purpose. He didn't tell Noah to just go build a boat and start an animal rescue zoo, or Moses to practice rock climbing and learn to hydrate, or Jonah to do more traveling and expand his cultural awareness. God told Jonah to speak in Nineveh.

God has a perfectly designed plan.[5] You deal with issues, encounter people, experience trials, and move at pre-selected times. It's always good for you,[6] but simultaneously *radical* because you *will* have to choose against the tsunami of cultural trends.[7]

Believers should be controlled by God's *destination,* not confused by *desires.*[8] In other words, be obsessed with finding out what God is doing, not chasing what you want.

Jonah's desire was escape. God's destination was east.

Jonah was energized by his plan.

The plan got him swallowed.

Passion is about what energizes you.

Emotions are the juice.

No guarantee of success...or happiness.

Passion fades. Purpose finishes.

Having passion doesn't prove you're in God's will.

Passion is totally overrated.

I'm a Guy Fieri fan. Amazing food creations are his passion. He gets me fired up to sample outrageous eats at diners, dives, and drive-ins across America, like Guy's favorite classic chili cheeseburger at the Beacon Drive-In in Spartanburg, South Carolina. In another adventure, I developed a fresh respect for conservation from Australia's Steve Irwin, "The Crocodile Hunter", because of his passion for wildlife: *"I have no fear of losing my life. If I have to save a koala or a crocodile or a kangaroo or a snake, mate, I will save it....I believe that education is all about being excited about something. Seeing passion...helps push an educational message."*[9] 2018 Super Bowl MVP quarterback, the Philadelphia Eagles' Nick Foles, almost quit the NFL two years before during a season of failures in St. Louis: *"I had to take a step back and say, am I doing this for the right reasons? Because if I can't do it with my heart, I can't do it. When you have your heart in something you give it everything you have, and that's the important thing."*[10] So impressed by Foles' faith and transparency. Many believe passion *alone* proves you're in the right place.

Passion may work for chefs and crocodile hunters and champion quarterbacks but not as the ultimate indicator for confirming God's will.

There was definite passion when Jonah paid for his cruise.

Just because you are passionate about your plan doesn't mean it is even remotely lined up with God's plan for your life. Passion can take you in a direction that competes with God's plan. If some college fraternities could follow their passion, they'd graduate with a degree in *macro partying*.

There are some places God doesn't want us to go...period.

And if you go, it triggers fast, frequent, and full intervention.

Yes, God does work in us to create a desire to His will.[11] Trusting your desires can be a good thing if it's consistent with scripture and what God has been speaking into your life through circumstances. Passion may flavor commitment but doesn't guarantee to finish it.

Following your passion can be totally selfish. If it aligns with God's will it's sweet. Even if your passion is to dig wells in Africa, if that's not God's specific will now, it's selfish and it steals energy and funds from something even better.

Jonah had zero passion to be a missionary to Nineveh. His passion was to wipe Nineveh off the map. That was in direct conflict with God's plan.

God's call required Jonah to give up his passion, not chase it. Sadly, even today's Christian culture urges you to dream big. Not in scripture. Daniel had visions and dreams. The difference is that they all originated with God, not him.

Always check the source before believing a sign.

Prayer gives passion a direction.

Passion without prayer is like an airline boarding pass without a destination on it. God gives direction, just not normally through emotions. Being fired up—even for a spiritual cause—isn't a reliable indicator of being locked into God's will...according to Jesus.[12]

When I read scripture, I often ask the obvious, "What's missing?" In Jonah's story, it's prayer. There's no mention of Jonah having a record of wearing God out in prayer to save Nineveh, worried that their sins would trigger God's judgment. Nothing in his past about begging God to forgive and flip the terrorist nation of Assyria back to righteousness.

Don't just pray over the basics but pray over the big stuff in your life and their lives! Why not believe God for a whole city to repent? Who sees the *BIGGER* picture?

One big reason we don't pray is that we don't want to hear God saying "NO" to our desires. Worship is an intentional choice to honor God. Worship may stir emotion but can't start in emotion. Prayer is the intentional choice to submit to God. Prayer done right does create passion—a desire to love what God loves, and hate what God hates. Prayer's best outcome is that you quit fighting for your plan and follow His plan.

It's not like it's weird or unprecedented to be passionate. Abraham was passionate begging God to spare his nephew's family and the city of Sodom from judgment.[13] Moses pleaded passionately with God not to annihilate Israel for worshipping a golden calf.[14] David was passionate about killing Goliath to save his nation.[15] Jesus wept over Jerusalem rejecting Him as Messiah and cried out passionately from the cross repeatedly for the Father to forgive His enemies.[16] In each case, passion was prompted by prayer.

Prayer is more than begging God to give you the perfect FastPass time at Disney World. Leonard Ravenhill *wrote,* "Prayer is not an argument with God to persuade him to move things our way, but an exercise by which we are enabled by his Spirit to move ourselves His way."[17] At the core, prayer is the humbling process of bending your will to God's will—your attitude agreeing with God's view of circumstances—like Jesus' prayer in the Garden of Gethsemane: *"Not as I will, but as You will".*[18] We are expected to let God change our mind to conform to His perfect will.[19]

All parents can relate to Tricia Goyer's car seat battle:

> *My toddler...doesn't like...getting strapped into his car seat. "Down. Down please, Mommy!" he cries. He doesn't like to be restricted. He doesn't like sitting still in his car seat. It takes energy to strap him into the seat, and I try to calm him with my words. "I know you don't like this now... but just wait and see where we're going!" There are times I have to fight to strap him in to go to the park or the zoo. I'm hoping the stage will pass, and [he] will learn to trust me—trust that I have his best interest in mind, even if it feels confining for a time.*
>
> *I've found the same true in my own life. There are times when I feel God confining me and shutting doors I wish were open. I pray. I plead. I cry, "Please, God." But with no avail. Usually I'm too busy complaining to hear His reassuring voice, "I have something good in mind for you... trust Me." It's not that God isn't answering my prayers...He has something better.*
>
> *I can either struggle with Him, question His motives, and plead for my own desires, or I can pray, trust His motives, and listen to His heart.*[20]

Jonah got "strapped into his car seat" and didn't like it!

God doesn't exist to keep you happy.

Here's a controversial statement: **following your passion is not in scripture.** From Eve lusting after fruit in the Garden to Demas chasing more money, the bible discounts passion.[21] Take the embarrassing case of the Jewish patriarch and the maid. Instead of waiting on God's promised timing for a son and heir, Abram and Sarai gave in to their surging passion for a child. The outcome of his sex with an employee was an unwanted pregnancy and a hated single mom.[22] Total disaster.

Life with God is about following His purpose, not your passion. If following your passion is the ultimate guarantee of happiness, it didn't work out for Jonah. Getting swallowed by a huge fish and forced to finish the Nineveh project proved God didn't exist to keep Jonah happy. We exist for God and His glory.[23] Jonah was created to worship God and make Him known—to all tribes and cities.

What motivates you? Is it the size of the spiritual need, the risk involved, what you would stand to lose, how you feel, what you can get out of it, fear of failing God, or saving a career?

God called Jonah to be *His voice* to the terrorist capital city.

It was not about Jonah *finding his voice.*

God's plan isn't waiting on your passion.

A really crazy belief is that what God wants to do is on hold until you become passionate about it. God's plan actually started before you had a clue and doesn't depend on your energy or vision. An angel had to be sent to Daniel to explain God's vision for the last days that was already determined.[24] God revealed his ultimate plan in a dream for Joseph to become a ruler over his brothers, but Joseph had zero passion to start his career in Egypt. Slavery definitely wasn't ever a career strategy.[25]

God's plans exist long before we're interested and whether we're excited about them or not.

God planned to rescue Nineveh regardless of Jonah's attitude. Jonah's approval was not required. The plan was dropped on Jonah for a reason—God controls stuff.

Whether you are passionate about doing God's will or push back on it, is totally irrelevant. God's call doesn't change. It is set up independent of your reaction or your circumstances.

God is not interested in what you feel, only what you do.

In a rant against Vice-President Mike Pence's statement that God speaks to him, *The View* co-host, comedian Joy Behar, proclaimed, "It's one thing to talk to Jesus. It's another thing when Jesus talks to you. That's called mental illness, if I'm not correct, hearing voices."[26]

Behar doesn't get to decide that. God really does speak to believers. The experience is real and verifiable.

We're in a relationship, not a religion. He speaks to us.

And when He speaks, God's plan is not optional. A believer's relationship to Jesus is not a democracy where your opinion or vote changes anything. Jesus is Lord. Therefore, a call carries judgment or blessing, depending on which direction you go.[27]

Life with Jesus is all about listening to Him—not following your passion.[28] Emotions are for NFL end zone celebrations, weddings, and protests.

One of the biggest lies in our generation is that Christians are only real when they live by emotions. One pastor told me if you aren't loud in worship, you're dead! Some believe if you can't feel God, you are not saved. I had a friend who argued if you love somebody else it's okay to leave your mate, regardless of what the Bible says. God's not interested in what you feel or whether your heart is in it—He wants obedience, based on His word.

What if that same crazy belief that your heart has to be in it was the standard that had to be met for you to enjoy married life and stay committed? You would never love or submit on the bad days! Breaking News: Marriage is not like the fairy tale Wedding of Prince Harry and Meghan Markle!

What you feel or what you're going through is not a surprise to God. His call is more important than any existing commitment or crisis you have. Since He controls everything from storms to someone's sense of guilt, you can overcome any difficulty.

God's call is not *linked to* or *limited by* anything. If He calls you to do something, He becomes totally responsible for you. He can use Afghanistan veterans with artificial limbs or NFL veterans who win Super Bowls...or, *leaders who run.*

Passion becomes all about your voice, not God's voice.

God's voice should be the only one that matters—the Orca whale in the ocean of voices—totally dominating. Nobody escapes the Voice.

God's voice was more urgent to Noah than the voices of those partying until the flood. God called Noah to build an ark to exact detail. Noah got it done by perseverance, not passion.[29]

God's voice was clearer to Joseph than his boss' wife begging him to commit adultery.[30] Joseph ran from her out of fear of committing sin, not just passion for being the best slave.

God's voice was bigger than Moses' memory of his past sins because Moses had zero passion to confront the most powerful global leader.[31]

God's voice was more intimidating to David than facing Goliath.[32] David was passionate in calling out Goliath but killed Him to honor God's name.

God's voice was so real and unmistakable, Jonah's passion took him in the opposite direction.

Nobody just runs. We have other passions, other stuff we chase. Sin is as much about substituting our idea of happiness as it is refusing to submit to God.

How passionate are you?

Trendy Belief No. 3:
God uses imperfect people.

I don't even believe myself when I say I'll be ready in 5 minutes.
—**Anonymous**

I'm not arguing. I'm simply explaining why I'm right.
—**Anonymous**

"Fries or salad?" sums up every adult decision you have to make.
—**Aparna Nancherla, Comedian**

Jonah...found a ship...bought a ticket and went on board, hoping to escape from the Lord.
—**Jonah 1:3, NLT**

T he **"nobody's perfect" line is an excuse.** Getaways can swallow you. Vacations can turn into nightmares that cost in more ways than you imagined. An American Express survey found the average per person vacation splurge is $1,145, or $4,580 for a family of four.[1] Financial advisor Dave Ramsey posted some vacation nightmare stories from his Facebook page on his blog. One vacation victim, Sabi, confessed: "We went to Disney World...and trying to impress my parents, we overspent by nearly $6,000 in four days! Each time we had to pay for something, I held my breath waiting to see if the card was going to be approved or declined." Chris and his wife had vacation hangover from Cabo: "I got caught in a moment of weakness and bought a $12,000 timeshare, and we spread it out over three credit cards!" Chris *fixed* their mistake by selling the timeshare—for only $2,000: "That's $10,000 in stupid tax. Sure wish I had a do-over!"[2]

That's true for pretty much everybody.

Because nobody's perfect, right?

Sorry. That's not the issue.

None of us are really victims. Substitute your plans for God's plans and you have just scheduled a getaway nightmare. We create our own storms. Jonah did.

Nobody escapes God's voice...or His presence...or His timing...or His intervention...not even on vacation. God doesn't casually stand by and let you throw away His amazing plan for the next step in life or ministry without consequences.

But then, that was Jonah's biggest mistake.

And maybe yours too.

He assumed it was *his* life...*his* ministry!

Yesterday's worship just expired!

The shelf-life of worship is minutes! Loving God and living right yesterday doesn't give you a pass today. Past obedience doesn't entitle you to sin, any more than making last month's car payment entitles you to skip the next!

Being in control is an illusion. Jonah "found a ship", so it looked like he was in control for a while. He knew what God wanted of his life and intentionally created his own plan.

It wasn't a *weak* moment. It was a *wicked* moment. Pre-meditated defiance. A sort of *"I'm-going-to-do-this-and-I-don't-care-what-happens"* moment of wrecking his life and ministry. Jonah would rather drown than save one terrorist.

How was his decision any different than the evil of Nineveh? No matter how legit Jonah's cruise looked, both were aggressively and openly in the act of rejecting God. Just because you've obeyed God in the past doesn't give you the right to break the rules now. Past faithfulness doesn't entitle you to do what you want. Someone else's evil doesn't give you permission to "go evil". Their sin is not an excuse for you to sin. You don't have the right to sin because somebody else is doing it.

Since when does God have to cut you some slack for wanting to indulge your desires? Nobody can excuse sin because you were hurting or stressed or overwhelmed. You can't take a break from being a Christian like you've earned some time off. There's never an excuse for telling God "No". Believers live by grace, not good works.

Jonah wasn't perfect. Nobody is. Which, of course, is an argument used to excuse really bad decisions...like this one. But this was intentional. Jonah's plan was in direct competition with God's plan. God always wins.

The reality is that God owns Jonah's story...and yours.

So, the big getaway question is not "Who's in control"?

Because you and God both know *He* is.

The question becomes, "Why test Him?"

Don't poke the bear and complain about getting mauled.

God doesn't use imperfect people—only invested people.

The big lie about living for God is that you don't have to be 100% sold out to be used by Him.

The argument goes like this. Not only is being 100% committed a totally impossible goal, but it's not even necessary. Why? Because God loves us but He is stuck with our sins, mistakes, and weaknesses. Meaning...He's got to work with *our* attitude and *our* choices. We're imperfect, so God's got to get over it. Sounds good. Too bad it's wrong.

Jonah chose a ship going in the opposite direction.

An "imperfect" choice. Why is that bad? Nobody's perfect.

People use "nobody's perfect" as an excuse to keep sinning and postpone changing as long as possible. And it's always cover for chasing something else. Nobody just runs. We have other "ships"—competing plans. Sin is as much about *substituting* our idea of happiness as it is not *submitting* to God. But God doesn't negotiate. Life is either centered in Him or chaos.

God doesn't use imperfect people.

He uses imperfect people *who want to obey.*

He uses imperfect people *who want to keep commitments.*

Recently, my family and I spent our Christmas holiday at a huge popular water dome indoor park with 17 water slides! I opted to sit at the edge of one landing pool in my beach gear and watch suicidal kids launch themselves down a nearly 6-story drop through water slide tunnels and loops at about 60mph! Sitting next to me was a middle-aged couple who looked like they had just come from a wedding. She was still dressed in a shiny black, full length, formal sequined dress. Her husband was in a tux. He sat briefly but bolted away quickly without explanation. Then, without any warning, she exploded with screams and laughter as her husband, still formally dressed, came shooting out of the tunnel on a water tube, creating a small tidal wave as he crashed his tube into the landing pool, soaking her and me! When I dried off, she was gone. Minutes later, I saw a huge, yellow double-8 tube *rocket* out of the water slide tunnel and land with a giant splash. It was that couple, still in formal attire, the wife in front freaking out, rolling overboard and going completely under, thrashing around desperately...not for her *husband*, but for her *hair*! She grabbed her floating wig with one hand, spit out a gallon of water, adjusted her dress, tipped up her bare feet, and screamed with delight! I nearly fell in laughing. *And*...I knew immediately they were going to do it again!

This couple was all in!

You don't sit on the sidelines for what you want.

God uses people who see what He's doing and jump in!

And God only has one level of commitment—surrender. God's minimum commitment is total surrender. All rights waived. No sliding scale of commitment. God doesn't offer credit card-type levels for commitment like Gold, Platinum, World Elite, or Black, based on how much you want your faith to impact your lifestyle.

You can fake anything for a while, *except* surrender.

Total abandonment to God's plan is a radical choice. Everybody knows what you believe when you don't care what you're wearing and lose your hair! Everybody knows what you believe when you are flying down the water slide. And everybody knows what you believe when you aren't.

You can't board a ship and not participate in the trip!

Commitment is choosing one priority and rejecting all the others. Jesus said it's impossible to serve two masters.[3]

You can't be on a ship and serve God in Nineveh at the same time. One priority always wins.

How close are you keeping your other options? If it doesn't bother you to board the wrong ship, then you're in a dangerous place. And the delusional part is that Jonah believed he could board the ship without becoming guilty.

We're so crazy deceived we think it's possible to board a ship and not participate in the trip. Plenty of believers are living compromised lives. Not because they are outwardly immoral but because they are in a place God doesn't want them to be. Peter knew he wasn't supposed to go back to his former career after denying Jesus.[4]

So the issue is not that you're imperfect. We're all sinners. You know it. God knows it. That's why Jesus died for us.

It's about outcomes. It's never "I can be on a ship and not sin". The truth is that being on the ship *IS* the sin! So the issue is, where is your ship taking you?

Don't make God have to come get you.

What you are doing right now is what you really believe.

God knows your heart better than you. He not only knew *when* Jonah boarded the ship but *why* he did it.

Country music star, Brett Young, delivered his 2017 platinum hit, "In Case You Didn't Know", with a line that said, "You had my heart a long, long time ago, in case you didn't know." Well, God *knew* He *didn't* have Jonah's heart.

Jonah found a ship going in the direction he preferred.

It wasn't random or reckless. So many times, what appears to be *careless* behavior is actually *calculated*. Choices are rarely *unguarded*, just *underestimated* in consequences.

Jonah wasn't conflicted. He was committed...to *his* plans.

Your choices reveal what's in your heart.

Your real beliefs are exposed when what you have to choose what you love most. We only sacrifice for what we really believe. Our time and energy flows toward what we value as important. Regardless of what someone *says*, just watch what they *do*. That's what they really believe.

Once you start running, you can't stop.

Once you start running, only God can stop you.

Jonah bought a ticket and boarded the ship. Once he had "found a ship", it was easy to rationalize the timing, ticket, trip, and the temptation. The longer you linger in sin, the harder it is to recognize what's right and wrong and the less desire you have to remove yourself from the situation.[5]

If going near boats tempts you to buy tickets and run from God, don't go near boats! Boats aren't bad. They don't *make* you sin. Just because you are tempted doesn't mean your situation is not unique. Every temptation you feel has happened before. God knows your limits and will always offer you a way to opt out and escape.[6]

But if that's your weakness, live a *boat-free life!* Just because you have freedom to do something, doesn't mean it's right, good for you, or that you will be free after you do it. Having access to something doesn't mean you have God's approval.[7]

Nothing wrong with being on a cruise, unless God has already told you His will is in another direction.

If you can *leave* your ministry (i.e., put it on hold to cheat on God for a while or avoid leadership on an issue), then you don't *love* your ministry! A friend told me a family member wanted God *plus* this other thing he loved—a relationship he knew was outside of God's will. He put his relationship with God on pause, so he could test what was out there, but there was a cost. You can't play around and not get burned. Nor can you decide at what point you want to change.

There's actually a group of hot peppers called *7 Pot Jonah*, originating in Trinidad (an island near the Venezuelan coast), with some strains up to 480x hotter than a typical jalapeno pepper! They are so hot that gloves and goggles are recommended when handling them to avoid chili burn.

FACT: You can't swallow the world's 5th hottest pepper without getting burned! And when you walk away from God, even for a moment, for any reason, you will get burned. You lose the ability to decide at what point you want to opt out. Once you get involved, you're no longer in control.[8] You are a slave to whatever controls you.[9]

Some things swallow you and only God can get you out.

Believing you can get in or out of commitment whenever you want is as crazy as believing you can eat a *7 Pot Jonah* and not feel it. God doesn't let you expand the definition of commitment to include random running when you feel like it.

Trendy Belief No. 4:
Your ability determines your success.

First rule of leadership: Everything is your fault.
—A Bug's Life

*If our identity is in our work, rather than Christ, success will go to our heads,
and failure will go to our hearts.*
—Tim Keller, American Pastor & Christian Apologist

*Jonah got up and went in the opposite direction to get away from the Lord. He
went down to the port of Joppa, where he found a ship leaving for Tarshish. He
bought a ticket and went on board, hoping to escape from the Lord by sailing
to Tarshish.*
—Jonah 1:3, NLT

God controls success and you. Comedian Jim Gaffigan, author of *Dad is Fat*, reports, "With five little kids, there is no ending to bedtime. There is always one awake...like they are taking shifts. I imagine they have scheduling meetings: 'All right, I'll annoy Dad from midnight to 2 a.m. Who wants the 3 to 6 a.m. shift?'" Ninety percent of parenting is just outlasting kids.

God outlasted Jonah.

God's plan is different than a free-range chicken. No roaming allowed. God's plan has boundaries. And His patience has limits. Jonah decided to test the limits.

Jonah went to Joppa and booked a ship.

Didn't panic God.

Jonah tried to wait out the deadline on board the ship.

Didn't prevent the storm.

I'm pretty sure Jonah's cover up was impressive, like maybe booking a *Save the Planet* conference in Tarshish. You can be running from God while doing something good.

A 5-yr-old girl prayed, "Thank you Jesus for dying on the cross and thank you for our sins."

Running away was like Jonah being grateful he could sin. He wrongly assumed that testing the limits of God's plan doesn't have consequences. That God only gets mad if you actually break a *big* commandment—like murder or adultery. Otherwise you can exit His plan or tweak His call to fit your feelings, *whenever*...like an Amazon order. Then Jonah pretended that boarding the ship would make his call go away—disappear like it never happened. That God would give up on His idea and just forget about the whole crazy episode.

Like success has nothing to do with God or His plan?

Oswald Chambers, author of *My Utmost for His Highest*, wrote, "It is easier to serve or work for God without a vision and without a call, because then you are not bothered by what He requires. Common sense, covered with a layer of Christian emotion, becomes your guide....Our ordinary and reasonable service to God may actually compete against our total surrender to Him."[1]

Jonah's common sense and emotions took him away from God. His argument? He was more effective by *not* going to Nineveh. Serving God was his substitute for surrender.

Most of what you learn about leadership is from mistakes.

Most mistakes are made while ignoring the rules.

This was Jonah's biggest. All leaders make mistakes.

Successful leaders don't repeat them.

Calls don't have expiration dates.

Currently, the highest paid player ($33M) in Major League Baseball, is Los Angeles Dodger pitcher, Clayton Kershaw. His believes career and call are connected: "You're not doing it for yourself, you're not doing it for the coach, you're not doing it for your teammates—you're doing it to glorify God."[2]

Every believer has a specific call from God. Your call is God's plan to use your gifts, experiences, personality, and relationships to serve people in the career and locations He chooses.[3] God speaks to you and sets up situations to lead you to people who need to see He is real.[4]

God's call is basically what He expects you to do with your life on a moment by moment basis. It's about the next step in your journey with Him, not just building a career. Your life belongs exclusively to Him: "*...do you not know that your body is the temple of the Holy Spirit who is in you...and you are not your own? For you were bought at a price; therefore glorify God in your body and in your spirit, which are God's*".[5]

Leaning into God's call makes your life meaningful.

Avoiding His call makes your life miserable.

Once you are tagged with a call, it follows you for a lifetime: "*God never changes his mind about the people He calls and the things He gives them*".[6] God never takes back His call. No escaping. No breaks from the responsibility...ever.

And that's not a threat to your happiness.

It's an honor to be chosen.

A lot is riding on getting it done.

But reject His call and you've rejected God. It's personal. God personally designed an amazing life and ministry around you. He wants YOU, not somebody else! He doesn't make mistakes. You weren't randomly selected. God chose you before you were born to be a leader in the unique ministry role He designed for you: *"Before I made you in your mother's womb, I chose you. Before you were born, I set you apart for a special work. I appointed you as a prophet to the nations"*.[7]

He'll never stop loving you!

And He'll never stop expecting you to live up to His call...even if you would never have chosen it...even if you hate it...even if you run from it.

Successful leaders obsess with God's purpose.

Some argue leadership is all about *passion*. Passion drives political campaigns, ninth inning rallies, teacher walk outs, stock market surges, car wash fund raisers, and even recruits people to terrorism. People are inspired when a president, soldier, coach, teacher, CEO, or dad is emotionally obsessed with getting things done.

Others make the case that leadership is all about *performance*. Performance requires ability, either inherited or coached. It's simple. Leaders get results. If a leader performs, they succeed. The proof cited is legislation passed, team wins, higher test scores, bigger profits, or more followers. Leaders motivate through the charisma of passion and move things forward with the ability to perform.

But leadership can't be totally defined as *passion*.

Nor is it exclusively driven by *performance*.

Success in leadership is explained by *purpose*. Purpose is the heart of leadership. Purpose is not emotion. Purpose doesn't come from salary or social media, or celebrities would be happy. More than the temporary sizzle of passion or the adrenalin-rush of performance, purpose means something bigger than you motivates and sustains you.

My friend is the best high school basketball coach in our state. Not because he can develop raw talent or fit players to roles or motivate players to their full potential better than anyone I've ever seen. Not because he has won a 5A state championship and is year after year in the playoffs with new teams. It's his heart. And Coach Reggie Choplin can name the date his heart...his life...and his coaching...was changed forever—November 2, 2009. Early that Sunday morning he was flooded with calls from players, coaches, and parents in the community reeling in shock from the news. A popular and gifted sophomore, a rising star that the whole team loved and had just earned varsity playing time in the tournament that Saturday night—*was found dead!* Around 1am the well-hidden tension in his home between his mother and her new husband had exploded. Jealous of the mom's closeness to her son, the stepfather walked into the boy's room in a rage and shot him in bed. All the players were asking Coach the tough question: "Why?" That senseless loss and the questions have haunted him ever since that fateful morning. Coach Choplin told me he realized in that moment that knowing the players and what was going on in their lives was everything! Coach Choplin was called by God, not to *coach basketball*, but to *coach players*.

Knowing your purpose explains why you get up in the morning.[8] *Having a purpose* motivates you to take on any challenge to reach the goal.[9] *Living your purpose* influences and inspires others.[10] *Guarding your purpose* protects you from losing your soul in our temporary existence.[11] *Sacrificing for your purpose* enables you to rescue others.[12]

God gave Jonah a leadership test. Sell out to His purpose.

Jonah failed. No trust.

Leadership is not a position. It's purpose in motion.

What matters is where your purpose will take you.

His live shows have a *lounging-on-an-island-beach* feel. Fans wear Hawaiian shirts and call themselves "Parrotheads". He's the *other* legendary singer from Mississippi, Jimmy Buffet. With a razor-sharp business purpose, the ageless entertainer with the beach-bum image has built a $550 million empire on books, resorts and casinos, beach-wear and a custom label. Best known for his mega hits "Margaritaville" and "Cheeseburger in Paradise", he's also become a passionate sailor, pilot, and environmental activist. When NBC talk show host Megyn Kelly asked Buffet how piled up his fortune, he smiled confidently: "I watched all those who were losing money."[13] Entrepreneurs worship that attitude!

Regardless of what you think about Buffet and the Coral Reefer's Band no-boundaries partying reputation, there's zero confusion about what he believes or what he wants in life. When asked who he thought Jesus was, he replied, "I don't know and I don't care."[14] His purpose is public. He committed to building an image and an empire and succeeded!

What seems crazy is that if Jimmy Buffet is sold-out to his purpose, why aren't believers sold out to God's purpose? Maybe it's because they think God will somehow overlook their dysfunctional beliefs about commitment. And the most dangerous one is saying you believe in God but don't buy in. It's been said a *Christian atheist* is someone who believes in God but lives as though God doesn't exist.

Anybody can chase a really cool life purpose. What matters eternally is where your purpose takes you. Jesus said your heart will be linked to what you treasure.[15]

Chasing a purpose that keeps God in the margins of your life is fake. Chasing a purpose that leaves God out is fatal. Jesus explained that with a Twitter-sized story of a businessman who used huge profits to plan a big expansion and retire, only to die the night before the launch![16]

Leadership is about abandonment, not ability.

Major League Baseball Hall of Fame coach, Tommy Lasorda, fired up his teams for years with this: *"There are three types of baseball players: Those who make it happen, those who watch it happen and those who wonder what happened."*[17] Who wouldn't have wanted to leave it all on the field for him? Coaches universally demand *all in*! They know ability alone doesn't make a winner.

If ability determines success, then Jonah was a hero. Awesome intellect and timing created what he thought was a perfect escape and alibi on board the ship. But without God!

Launching anything is crazy hard. Less than 3% of new consumer products succeed, according to Joan Schneider and Julie Hall, coauthors of *The New Launch Plan*.[18]

Jonah launched without God! Leadership flop!

Leadership is not all about *ability*.

Leadership in any career or ministry is totally about *abandonment*. Abandonment is selling out to your purpose. People who are all in shred their return flight ticket. Nothing else matters but getting it done. They typically don't talk about anything else but their goal. It requires disciplined obedience.

Leadership is not performance sustained by *ability*.

Its purpose sustained by *abandonment* to God.

Jonah had a purpose. It was to let Nineveh be destroyed.

Too bad it was the wrong one. God wasn't in it.

Leaders make a commitment.

Jonah was assigned by God to go to Nineveh and *"call out against it, for their evil has come up before Me."*[19] Jonah wasn't selected because of superior *ability* but because of *accountability*. God simultaneously targeted His leader and the Assyrians, holding them *both* accountable for a heart change.

God does judge lifestyles. And these people qualified as evil. The word "evil" isn't used much anymore...even by preachers.

God made this ridiculously simple for Jonah. The whole project was just, *go there and say something!* If you do what God says, when He says to do it, then you will be an effective leader, regardless of results or response.

Leaders obey God. They commit to do God's revealed will. Whether anybody else cares or participates or follows or agrees or commits, leaders move with God. It normally means you have to get out front and risk something. It starts with an initial surrender and is sustained by daily submission to whatever God asks you to do.

Leadership is taking on the God-task in front of you, stepping up and getting it done. Others see you and your boldness influences them. They think that if you got involved it has to be important. And people who follow-through on what God expects make a difference. God uses them.

Leadership is giving your best even when asked by God to do something even if you don't like it or agree with it.

There is no sliding scale of commitment. You're either committed to live for Jesus or not. You're either in His will or out of it. Nobody wears an *Alabama Crimson Tide* shirt *and* a *Georgia Bulldogs* cap. You've got to choose.

Commitment means you gave up your rights on the front end. You don't get to choose where God takes you. You don't get a vote on what God expects you to do. You just do what He wants.

That's not scary—it's *security!*

Leadership equals ability PLUS responsibility!

Just before the final exam in a college finance class, an under-performing student approached the professor: "Can you tell me what grade I need on the final to pass the course?" The teacher gave him the bad news: "The final is worth 100 points. You need 113 points to earn a D." With a goal in mind he asked, "And how many points would I need to get a C?"

Some plans are never going to work!

Why is it people make their own plans and then are shocked when God doesn't bless them with success?

God's purpose was to change the terrorist nation and he wanted Jonah not just to *be there*, but to *buy in*. Jonah was ultimately willing to walk through Nineveh shouting God's warning of coming judgment, but he hated every minute of it!

That's the point of the book.

Jonah's heart was never in it.

God wanted Jonah to have a heart for rescuing the invisible casualties of war—120K people in spiritual darkness, including children.[20] Jonah was so self-centered he chose a cruise over moms and dads and children who were 40 days out from dying! Becoming the leader God intended is about having your heart broken by the things that break the heart of God.

For Columbus Day, an elementary school teacher assigned her third-grade class the task of drawing one of the three ships used by Columbus. She had no sooner sat down when a boy came up with his paper. He had a lone dot in the middle. "What's that?" she asked. He replied, "That's Columbus, way out to sea."

Jonah was a dot in the middle of the sea...far from God...or so he thought.

Accept *responsibility*. Go beyond the minimum required. Do whatever it takes! Even if you don't want to be there. Take on God's challenge. Give everything you've got to succeed. You are called to make a difference. Be part of the solution.

Ability means you *show up,* but ability alone can also make people *throw up*! Ability without a heart purpose leaves the Down syndrome student out of the basketball game. *Responsibility* rallies the basketball team around that student and gives him minutes and shots in a real game.

Committed leaders take responsibility for what they do...even the mistakes.

Not Jonah.

At least until *after* he got swallowed.

Trendy Belief No. 5:
God will never ask you to do something hard.

Something is wrong when our lives make sense to unbelievers.
—**Francis Chan, Author and Preacher**

The first time I see a jogger smiling, I'll consider it.
—**Joan Rivers, Comedian**

Jonah got up and went in the opposite direction to get away from the Lord.
He went down to the port of Joppa, where he found a ship leaving for Tarshish.
He bought a ticket and went on board, hoping to escape from the Lord
by sailing to Tarshish.
—**Jonah 1:3, NLT**

Obeying Jesus *is* hard. It's harder than being President. It's even more controversial. Presidents only have hard choices about things like nuclear war for two terms max. Committing to Jesus is for life...or it's fake. You get hope while you become a target. Life with Jesus is life in a war zone.

The Bible identifies three sources of extreme, unrelenting tension for believers: a seductive culture,[1] a strategic devil,[2] and your secret desires.[3] Nothing about living for Jesus in that mix is easy.

God loves us enough to include us in His amazing plan. God can choose to do it all by Himself, but He wants you...with Him...in the adventure.

God wants your full surrender precisely because it is hard. Avoid what He has planned, and you do become *special*—a *special* target for His anger at messing with the plan!

Do you really believe God should never ask you to do something that is hard? Like forgive a terrorist or risk your reputation on an impossible project? Rethink what you believe about people? Take a bigger risk with your life and career? Jump into something that will either break your heart or break your pride? Take on something that will require more love and sacrifice than you think you have left to give?

Oh yeah, He will. That's normal. That's who He is.

Because God *knows more*...and *loves more* than you.

God doesn't need to apologize...or explain...or wait on you to agree. And that's exactly what made Jonah mad enough to board a ship. Jonah knew that was God's character and he wanted to give God as much grief as he could over it.

Everybody is a believer.

Some are fans. Fewer are followers.

Jesus forces you to choose a cross or culture.

Obeying God's call to go to Nineveh meant Jonah had to reject the political correctness of his culture. His nation hated their nation. Sure they were evil terrorists and a legitimate threat to Israel's security. But nationalism crossed the line into racism. Hatred was culture. God wanted to change that. Following Jesus will make you anti-culture.

Nobody is neutral about Jesus. It's impossible because he didn't offer that option. Jesus said if you are not with Him you are against Him.[4]

Four of the world's largest tech platforms say the same thing, so Jesus is not an outlier on the issue of choosing sides. Amazon, GOOGLE, Facebook, and Twitter work with a nonprofit group to police their platforms for "hate speech" or "hate groups" and have shut down Christian legal groups.[5]

America's post-Christian culture is against Him. There are movements, groups, and political organizations right now applying pressure to silence your voice or kill your faith. Colorado baker Jack Phillips was sued for discrimination when he refused to create a wedding cake for a same-sex couple's wedding because it conflicted with his Christian beliefs. He won the 2018 Supreme Court case but not before nearly losing his entire business.

A godless culture is now in full push back mode...or is it "Shut Up!" mode? People of faith are expected to *scale back* their beliefs, not *speak* their beliefs. A scary battle rages over the line between religious freedom and discrimination. Christian beliefs are already labeled hate speech. We're one court case away from criminalizing Christian beliefs as discrimination.

Jesus challenged a wealthy young leader with his hardest choice ever, to give up his wealth and follow. He chose to keep his portfolio intact and walk away.[6]

Known to be the hardest training in the world with only 6 out of 100 candidates becoming a Navy SEAL, their training is not designed to get you in shape. You have to pass the extreme 5-event timed SEAL PST (Physical Training Test) before even being considered as a SEAL candidate. Life as a SEAL is so demanding, families are at risk: "The Air Force has the highest divorce rate among enlisted troops of any military branch at 4.3 percent. The divorce rate among U.S. Navy Seals is over 90 percent."[7] A tragic cost.

Raising the bar separates the crowd. You discover who loves Jesus when the choices are hard. What God asked Jonah to do was legitimately hard. It definitely raised the bar with an unprecedented mission.

God expected him to risk his life to save people he hated.

He would have to give up his lifestyle...and racism.

Jonah didn't want to do the hard thing. So he chose a cruise over moms and dads and children who were 40 days out from dying!

Jesus said if you want to follow him, give up your plans and take up your cross (Matthew 16:24). A cross is for dying—the price you pay for being different than everybody else.

The cruise was an easy choice. The cross is not.

You can't have a Savior without suffering...

If you think you're special, you're not.

In Wellesley High School English teacher David McCullough's "You're Not Special" graduation speech that went viral, he defined reality for the next generation:

You are not special. You are not exceptional.

Contrary to what your U-9 soccer trophy suggests, your glowing seventh grade report card, despite every assurance of a certain corpulent purple dinosaur, that nice Mister Rogers and your batty aunt Sylvia, no matter how often your maternal caped crusader has swooped in to save you...you're nothing special. Yes, you've been pampered...helmeted, bubble-wrapped....we've been to your games, your plays, your recitals, your science fairs....smiles ignite when you walk into a room, and hundreds gasp with delight at your every tweet....And now you've conquered high school....But do not get the idea that you're anything special. Because you're not. The empirical evidence is everywhere, numbers even an English teacher can't ignore....Across the country no fewer than 3.2 million seniors are graduating about now from more an 37,000 high schools. That's 37,000 valedictorians...37,000 class presidents...92,000 harmonizing altos...340,000 swaggering jocks...2,185,967 pairs of Uggs.[8]

If *everybody* is special, then *nobody* is special.

Jonah actually believed he was special. That he deserved an exemption from a really threatening assignment. God had no right to expect him to offer rescue to a bunch of terrorists that hated him and his nation.

Feeling entitled is a ministry-killer. Entitled people believe they are owed special treatment because they are simply special. That they should get a break when stressed.

An employer interviewing a new university graduate recently, said that before he could ask the millennial a question, she told him the salary she expected and assured the prospective boss that she could do what he couldn't—take his company and turn it around! That's why it's a shock when they get hit with something hard.

If hard stuff is a shock, then change your expectations.

Following Jesus is wild and unpredictable. It makes swimming with sharks feel routine. It's about getting out of boats to *step* on water, not being thrown out of boats to be *swallowed* like Jonah.

If God expects you to do something that's out of your comfort zone, you have to change, *not Him. Recklessly Alive* blogger, Sam Eaton, confessed:

> *I don't want to come face to face with the areas of my life I could improve; I'd rather just go on believing I'm awesome. Yet following Jesus means constantly means working on improving the way you live and recognizing where you could step up your game....I think if Jesus is at the heart of your life, you'll want to be the best follower you can be and that requires vulnerable things like apologizing, admitting sin and asking for help.*[9]

Jonah definitely didn't want to be vulnerable with God. No discussing his struggle with resentment and racial bias.

If it bothers you that God leaks your sins, you don't know how God works.

If it bothers you that God is consistently leading you into high risk situations, then you don't understand God.

If you are angry at God because life is unfair, get over it. God is not going to change. Life gets more complicated, not less. Life **IS** unfair. God is **not**. He will eventually make things right unless you fight. What God expects you to do to love people is going to crush you. So get excited about people who will be saved, even though you sacrifice.

But then, loving you got Jesus got crucified.

I'm pretty sure He thinks you were worth it.

When Pastor Tim Keller asked a girl what was so scary about undeserved free grace from God, she said: "If I was saved by my good works, then there would be a limit to what God could ask of me or put me through. I would be like a taxpayer with rights. I would have done my duty...and would deserve a certain quality of life. But if it is really true that I am a sinner saved by sheer grace—at God's infinite cost—then there's nothing He cannot ask of me."[10]

Until you let God be God, you are going to be as miserable as a guy choking in fish vomit.

By definition, living by faith will never make sense.

No way you can please God without faith.[11] Faith is *raw, radical, reckless* trust. You say ***"YES!"*** before you even know what God is asking. Why? Because He *owns* you. He doesn't *owe* you!

Again, Sam Eaton knows faith doesn't make sense:

I've found in my years of chasing Jesus that my life is just going to look a lot different than the way people expect. From finances to waiting to have sex until marriage, to how I spend my time—a life lived with Jesus will always stand out....But with that comes almost certain attacks from the outside....God sometimes calls us to make the illogical choice: to choose a lower paying job or give away more money than seems socially acceptable. Sometimes God calls us to do something reckless like befriend a homeless man or be a missionary to Zimbabwe. When we listen to God's plan for our lives, we have to walk in faith even if the world doesn't understand.[12]

Jonah and I agree on one point. It didn't make sense to even attempt to change a terrorist nation. Keep your defenses and keep your distance. These were the guys that ripped open pregnant women just to kill the babies of their enemies. But God sovereignly chose to give them one last chance to change their hearts. Nobody could have predicted the miraculous spiritual reversal.

Yet God expected Jonah to trust Him enough to go call them out right in the nation's capital. Surrounded by terrorists who would kill him instantly just for being a jerk, much less Jewish, he was supposed to save people who didn't believe in the Jewish God with an 8-word warning?

Makes zero sense. But faith means doing what God wants, even if you don't get an explanation before it happens. And it still doesn't make sense to show up for church, read the Bible at the beach, forgive your enemies, serve the poor on your day off, be baptized publicly, pray for your boss, give crazy amounts of money away, or sing worship songs with your kids in the car. At least it doesn't make sense to people who don't believe.

Faith creates an awesome life. Some thought Katie Davis was crazy when she gave up a comfortable life and friends at age 18 to pursue God's call to Uganda. Five years later, God's purpose seemed obvious looking back. Her faith was rewarded with meeting her future husband, Benji (while teaching in Uganda), adopting 13 girls, starting Amazima Ministries, and writing her first book, a New York Time's Best Seller, *Kisses from Katie*. When she left Uganda to return home to Tennessee, she confessed she was forever "ruined for comfort and convenience", instead opting for "challenge, sacrifice, and risking everything" to do something she believed in.

Why live on the edge, without explanations, just because God expects it?

Katie answered that: "You see, Jesus wrecked my life!"

You don't have to know everything...just God.

When is the last time you did anything that required faith?

What is there in your ministry that can't be explained except that God did it when you stepped out in faith?

When you stop believing in God, you'll believe anything.

During his first year at Harvard Medical School Charles Krauthammer was injured in a diving accident that left him a quadriplegic. Confined to a wheelchair for life, he made the hard choice not to become bitter or allow the accident to define his life. He overcame the limitations, graduating medical school to practice psychiatry, and became one of the most powerful forces in American conservativism through his roles as columnist, commentator, editor, and panelist, for *The New Republic, The Washington Post, The Weekly Standard, TIME,* and most recently on *FOX News.* On June 8, 2018, Krauthhammer announced that he had been suffering from cancer and had only weeks to live. In his best-selling book, *Things That Matter: Three Decades of Passions, Pastimes, and Politics,* he observed, "The trouble when people stop believing in God is not that they thereafter believe in nothing; it is that they thereafter believe in anything."

Jonah stopped believing in God. Because, by definition, believing in God is actually trusting Him...even when it's only interrupted belief. Hurricane-level winds, record waves, and a huge fish proved God was still in control, even if Jonah didn't believe. In the meantime, he had started believing it was possible to escape God's presence. That you only have to obey God when it works for you.

That's believing *anything*!

You can't always choose your circumstances.

You can always choose your attitude.

You can't always choose your opportunities.

You can always choose to believe God.

Jonah didn't...for a while. Mistake.

When you don't like the task in front of you, do it first!

Mark Twain said that if the first thing you do each morning is eat a live frog, you can go through the day with the satisfaction of knowing that is probably the worst thing that is going to happen to you all day long. Business consultant and motivational speaker, Brian Tracy, said your "frog" is the hardest, biggest, ugliest or irritating thing you face but is also the key to success. Tracy's "second rule of frog eating" is that you should not avoid it but do it immediately.[13]

Jonah definitely didn't like the task God put in front of him. Just because you run, avoid, or postpone doing something that is difficult or disgusting, doesn't make it go away. Especially when God has already decided to pour out His love and forgiveness on somebody who needs it.

Even after boarding the ship and taking the trip, he was still going to have to go to Nineveh. After wandering in the desert for 40 years as God's punishment for not stepping out in faith to fight the giants in the promised land, Israel was brought right back to the original place where they disobeyed God 40 years before to get it right the second time!

Why put yourself through the misery when you are going to have to face the problem at some point again anyway?

Take on the hardest thing first. Do what you can't stand.

It'll be over quickly. You'll live. God will be happy.

What else matters?

Reject God and life gets more complicated, not less.

When you reject God's plan for your life and substitute your own, life doesn't get easier. Life gets more complicated.

Why? Because to stop you from going the wrong way and messing up more of your life, God starts hurling storms to scare you and sending fish to swallow you and spit you out where you needed to be in the first place.

A whole lot of problems are solved if you just do what God originally told you to do.

We need to learn God's Word...and His ways. Knowing how God reacts to your choices just might save your life at some point. 1 Peter 5:5-7 says, *"God opposes the proud, but gives grace to the humble. So humble yourselves under the mighty power of God, and at the right time he will lift you up in honor. Give all your worries and cares to God, for he cares about you"* (NLT).

Running from God's will is like begging God for a storm!

Worried about what will happen? Trust God. Don't run.

The life God has designed for you will be rocked with challenges but rewarded with contentment. There's only one place on the planet where you'll be happy—in the center of God's will. Obeying Jesus makes life simple, even though it means sacrifice. You know where you're going and why.

There are really rich and famous people who don't know and can't cope. They search for meaning in the wrong places. That's one reason for suicide. That's also why Mexican drug cartels keep smuggling drugs into America. Jesus said you can gain the world but lose your soul in the process.[14] In the center of God's will--that's the only peace.

What would cause an 18-year-old senior class president and homecoming queen from Nashville, Tennessee, to disobey and disappoint her parents by skipping college, break her little brother's heart, lose all but a handful of her friends (because they think she has gone off the deep end), and break up with the love of her life, all so she could move to Uganda, where she knew only one person and didn't even speak the language, just to become adoptive mom to thirteen girls? In Katie J. Davis' own words: *A passion to follow Jesus.* Katie adopted thirteen children in Uganda and has established a ministry, Amazima, that feeds and sends hundreds more to school while teaching them scripture. Her book, *Kisses from Katie: A Story of Relentless Love and Redemption,* recounts a journey of radical love down the red dirt roads of Uganda. She got God's will right: "It may take place in a foreign land or it may take place in your backyard, but I believe that we were each created to change the world for someone. To serve someone. To love someone the way Christ first loved us....This is the dream, and it is possible....People who really want to make a difference in the world usually do it, in one way or another... They hold the unshakable conviction that individuals are extremely important, that every life matters. They get excited over one smile. They are willing to feed one stomach, educate one mind, and treat one wound. They aren't determined to revolutionize the world all at once; they're satisfied with small changes. Over time, though, the small changes add up. Sometimes they even transform cities and nations, and yes, the world."[15]

Jonah didn't want to make a difference.

God's will didn't matter to Jonah because people didn't matter to Jonah (Jonah 4:3, 10-11).

So glad God didn't allow Jonah to win that one.

Nineveh wouldn't have been saved if it depended on him.

So glad it depended on God.

Is your life complicated? Think we both know why...

God's definition of success is doing what He expects.

Most people define success with terms like wealth, fame, or power. Others capture it in very personal ways.

Famed WWII British Prime Minister, Winston Churchill, was kept out of office for ten years, but believed, "Success is going from failure to failure without losing enthusiasm".[16]

Founder of the Virgin Group which controls over 400 companies, billionaire Richard Branson said, "Success should be measured by how happy you are."[17]

The NBA Dallas Mavericks owner and Shark Tank Entrepreneur, Mark Cuban, observed, "I was happy and felt like I was successful when I was poor, living six guys in a three-bedroom apartment and sleeping on the floor. I was going to work hard to get somewhere, but I was having fun."[18]

For Oscar winning actor, Matthew McConaughey, it's about priorities: ""How do I define success? For me, it's a measurement of five things: fatherhood, being a good husband, health, career, friendships. These are what's important to me in my life. So, I try to measure these five each day, check in with them, and see whether or not I'm in the debit or the credit section with each one."[19]

Billionaire investor, Warren Buffet, has a long-term view: "When you get to my age, you'll really measure your success in life by how many of the people you want to have love you actually do love you. I know people who have a lot of money, and they get testimonial dinners and they get hospital wings named after them. But the truth is that nobody in the world loves them. If you get to my age in life and nobody thinks well of you, I don't care how big your bank account is, your life is a disaster."[20]

World Champion NBA star, LeBron James, was brief: "You can't be afraid to fail. It's the only way you succeed."[21]

Facebook founder and CEO, Mark Zuckerberg, offered this: "The question I ask myself like almost every day is, 'Am I doing the most important thing I could be doing?'"[22]

God's defines success as gaining His approval. Living by *faith* pleases God. Abraham is a model: "*He didn't doubt God's promise out of a lack of faith. Instead, giving honor to God for the promise, he became strong because of faith and was absolutely confident that God would do what he promised. That is why Abraham's faith was regarded as the basis of his approval by God*".[23]

By that definition, Jonah was a failure. God didn't approve of his new definition of ministry that omitted *faith*. No faith required to board a ship and avoid the biggest risk of your life.

In comedian Amy Poehler's book, *Yes Please,* she compares a career to a bad boyfriend: "Here's the thing. Your career won't take care of you. It won't call you back or introduce you to its parents. Your career will openly flirt with other people while you are around. It will forget your birthday and wreck your car."

Creating a big career is *not* her idea of success.

Jonah was focused on saving his career, not taking the next step in faith. His definition of success didn't include rescuing people different from him. Jonah didn't want to depend on God for anything, especially ministry career decisions. He didn't *follow* God. He *fought* God.

Justin Timberlake, the 37-yr-old mega-famous singer/songwriter, has sold 32 million albums: "I think the first half of my 20s I felt I had to achieve, achieve, achieve....I'm looking around now and I'm like, Where am I running?"[24]

When faith is not in the mix, you'll look around at some point and wonder what your life has been all about.

Success is gaining God's approval, not building a career.

Jonah was successful...briefly...in taking a cruise. At that point, he still had a career, but not a ministry. There was still evidence that God was working in his life...*working to shut him down!*

Jonah knew that career choice was empty. He didn't care.

Are you successful?

Trendy Belief No. 6:
It doesn't matter what you believe.

Everything happens for a reason. But sometimes the reason is that you're stupid and you make bad decisions.
—Anonymous

You know what it's like having a fifth kid? Imagine you're drowning, then someone hands you a baby.
—Jim Gaffigan, Comedian

The Lord hurled a powerful wind over the sea, causing a violent storm that threatened to break the ship apart. Fearing for their lives, the desperate sailors shouted to their gods for help and threw the cargo overboard to lighten the ship. But all this time Jonah was sound asleep down in the hold.
—Jonah 1:4-5, NLT

What you believe creates a life for you. Author of *Dad is Fat*, comedian Jim Gaffigan has five children: "Sometimes going to bed feels like the highlight of my day. Ironically, to my children, bedtime is a punishment that violates their basic rights as human beings. Once the lights are out, you can expect at least an hour of inmates clanging their tin cups on the cell bars."[1] Jim obviously believes in family...and is now paying the price!

Nobody can hide what they believe...and most people don't want to.

I'm going straight to hell. That's what country music mega star, Darius Rucker and friends, Luke Bryan, Jason Aldean, and Charles Kelley, sang in Rucker's latest hit single from the album *When Was the Last Time*. That single, "Straight to Hell", ends with the words, "Help me Jesus." Don't know if that's entertainment or entrepreneurship, but the lyrics are clear.

Beliefs matter. Especially to the business world.

A study concluded we speak about 16,000 words per day.[2] Listen to people for a few minutes and you'll know what's important to them. *Flurry Analytics* reports U.S. consumers spend 5+ hours per day on mobile devices.[3] Google, Facebook, Amazon, YouTube, Twitter, Instagram, Verizon, American Express, Spectrum, and other companies track things like physical location, posts, calls, texts, sites visited, viewing and spending habits to market everything. They don't guess. You are profiled. They know where you live and what you like. They know your age, lifestyle, political tendencies, vacation preferences, favorite shows, bank account balances, credit score, and when you are likely to have your next child, buy your next car or retire! They know more about you than your mom or first girlfriend. If you have children, it's no accident they've been begging to go to Disney World.

What you believe is already out there!

Jesus said your words reveal what's in your heart and your lifestyle is what you really believe.[4]

Jonah was sleeping below deck while the violent storm God sent to stop his cruise was threatening to flip the ship and drown the crew. That explains everything we need to know about Jonah's beliefs. He didn't try to hide his escape from God or his effort to protest God.

Choices expose your priorities, pain, and passions.

And because you live what you believe, every belief takes your life in a specific direction.

What you believe has a destination.

What you believe has consequences.

What you believe has real impact on others…and eternity.

By the way, hell is real…and you have choose it.

God doesn't send anybody there.[5]

Being sincere doesn't make your beliefs true.

That makes about as much sense as saying the reason 72% of Americans eat fast-food for lunch is because they believe that will make them better parents.[6]

Jonah was totally sincere in his rebellion against God. So sincere, he resisted God as long as he could. He didn't willingly jump out of the boat to save the crew, he waited until he had to be tossed overboard.

Jonah wasn't right because he was sincere.

Jonah was just serious about his belief.

The trendy belief in our culture is that you can believe anything you want—*about God, morals, afterlife, or Marvel Superheroes*—as long as you are sincere. And the more vocal and passionate you are about your beliefs, supposedly the more legitimate they are.

After 9/11, Osama bin Laden vowed to kill Americans and Jews because they were evil. He was sincere in his beliefs. But terrorists killing 2,977 innocent people is evil to the USA.

Both beliefs can't be simultaneously right.

In *Reason to Believe*, R.C. Sproul argues, "Can classical Islam have a valid ethic that endorses the killing of infidels while at the same time the Christian ethic of loving your enemies be equally valid?"[7]

All beliefs aren't equally true.

A pro-abortion woman who supports federal funding of Planned Parenthood, wrote in an online chat, "I know that there are a lot of religious perspectives in which I don't measure up but I have just as much faith in my own beliefs, in which trying your best to be a good person and doing your best to balance the effects of good and evil that seem to always exist in our world count for something."[8]

Okay, then who gets to decide what is good and what is evil? And where does the whole idea of good and evil come from? How do you know how good you would have to be, to have peace or assurance about heaven, hell, or God?

Identity thieves are successful in stealing someone's personal information every 2 seconds, creating 15 million shocked consumers in 2017.[9]

Thieves are sincere...and evil.

Some sincere beliefs take you in the wrong direction.

There's always a reason for what you believe.

There's always a starting point for your beliefs. Beliefs aren't contagious like a disease you can't stop from taking over your body.

Researchers at MIT found that we expel sneeze particles at 93mph and they can travel up to 200 feet![10] Scary. Germs are easily spread. According to research published in the journal *BMC Infectious Diseases*, those gray plastic trays in the airport screening line for your wallet, cell phone, shoes, sun glasses, laptops, and keys are covered with more bacteria than your average airport toilet.[11] You get exposed to all beliefs but you choose what to embrace. Which also makes you totally responsible for what you believe.

Jonah's belief? Assyrians deserved to die.

Jonah ran from God's plan to redeem a terrorist nation because of those beliefs. Where did that hatred come from? It had to start either because terrorists hurt his family/nation or the teaching in his family/nation inspired racism.

Hatred isn't contagious—it's chosen.

Israel was God's chosen people. God chose them to serve and to set-up the coming Messiah. But they believed that made them superior and invulnerable...that they could practice any lifestyle and participate in any sin and still be immune from judgment. That's the same insane belief American culture rides today—*since we're special we can believe in God, break any rules, and still be blessed.*

All beliefs have a starting point. Beliefs are normally linked to *experiences* or *education.*

CNN founder and billionaire media mogul, Ted Turner, was openly hostile to Christianity mostly because when his teenage sister tragically died decades ago he felt God ignored his prayers to heal her.[12]

Chad Williams, now a nationally known Christian speaker, was once failing most of his classes at a California college because he was more interested in surfing and drinking with buddies. Searching for peace, he decided to become a Navy SEAL (Sea—underwater assignments, Air—halo jumps, and Land—direct assaults) while watching an ABC News war report. ABC had showed the bodies of his mentor Scott with three other SEAL Team members (that had all been murdered on security detail in Fallelujah) being dragged through the streets and then hung upside down from a bridge over the Euphrates River. Chad was 1 of only 13 that survived the grueling competition to serve on SEAL Teams 1 and 7 in places like the Philippines, Saudi Arabia, Bahrain and Iraq. One of the toughest men in the world, Chad could not even find peace as a SEAL until 2007. When he heard Greg Laurie speak about God requiring Commander Naaman to remove all his armor (as a symbol of no longer depending upon his own strength) to find healing (2 Kings 5), Chad accepted Jesus Christ as his Lord and Savior.[13]

One man chose to believe God *abandons*.

One man chose to believe God *accepts*.

There's always a reason for what you believe.

Some reasons lead you in the wrong direction.

Every belief has a price tag.

Whatever you believe, it will cost you something.

A friend was fired because he believed integrity matters and would not lie for his boss. On April 30, 2018, Spc. Gabriel D. Conde, 22 of Loveland, Colorado gave his life in Afghanistan because he believed in freedom. USA Today said believing in the American Dream (*a family of four, owning a home and SUV, including taxes, education, gas, medical bills, food, etc.*) now comes with a price tag of $130,000! Microsoft creator, Bill Gates, has donated $35 billion to charity because he believes in promoting global healthcare and reducing poverty.[14]

Postponing confession costs more than you think.

If you believe in covering up sin until you are forced to take ownership of what you've done, you'll pay a price...and so will others around you. Sometimes innocent people suffer for someone else's sins.

The fact that Jonah slept while the ship rocked in the storm, and the panicked crew prayed to their gods and tossed valuable cargo overboard to survive, proved he was delaying confession of his sin as long as possible. Jonah even admitted to the crew that the sea would be calm only if they threw him overboard.[15] His intentional delay had a price tag. It created extreme fear in the crew that God would blame them and kill them too![16]

Sometimes the price tag is emotional. Occasionally it is physical. But there's *always* a spiritual price to pay.

Her blog, *TrueLoveDates.com*, reaches millions of readers each year. In one blog, counselor Debra Fileta shared personal stories to prove price tags exist:

One evening, I was on a walk with a prostitute....

We'd become good friends over the course of my ministry to this specific inner-city location. That evening, I had pulled into the street to make some visits and happened to see her camped out on the street corner, looking for some business.

I got out of the car and walked over to her, and we started to chat. If you know me, you know I'm not much for small talk, so I quickly got right to the point. I knew she had been working at letting go of this particular "job", and so I wondered what she was doing here today. "So...What's going on?" I said. She looked down at the ground and replied, "Well, I'm in another bind, and it's a way to make some money." I don't remember too many details of our conversation that evening, but there is one thing she said through the course of our talk that I will likely never forget, because it made my stomach churn, my heart sink, and my spirit ache. **"50 bucks is real good money"**

A few months ago, I was having a conversation with another young woman. *She had been sexually involved with a guy who had now cheated on her. But the problem was, they were never even dating to begin with. Their interactions in friendship started crossing the emotional and physical lines, until one thing led to another. Shortly after that they were regularly having sex and fooling around, with no commitment, no conversation, and no real relationship. She came to chat with me after 4 months of this "relationship" left her with a broken heart, and a broken sense of self. I can't help but see a theme that connects both of these stories together. Two different women from totally different parts of the country, from different socio-economic status, different races, and different ages. But with one thing in common:* **They each come with a price tag.**[17]

Every belief has a destination.

Every belief matters because of where it takes you.

Delayed gratification is not an American value. Financial advisor Dave Ramsey says nobody likes being told "No", especially when it comes to overspending. Ramsey identifies three reasons for the emotions that lead you to spend money you don't have: trying to impress, avoiding a budget, and shopping to feel better. Is retail therapy an actual disease?[18]

If you believe in uncontrolled spending, you get debt. When you can't even wait 30 days to buy something, maybe there's a bigger problem than budgeting? Guilt has never really been a good lifestyle choice.

Every belief has an outcome—a specific experience God has pre-designed as a reality check. God wants you to know who's in control and what your belief will cost you.

Myth: If God doesn't kill you the moment you sin, you've escaped.[19] Like jumping out of a plane without a parachute, just because you are enjoying the experience doesn't mean it will end well.

Consequences are normally delayed. There's a natural time gap between the pleasure and the problems. Usually it's because God is merciful and giving you a chance to realize your sin and repent.[20] But "the gap" is a big reason sin is appealing. You don't see or feel any bad effects until it's too late and you're in over your head. Who thinks about pregnancy in the moment of passion? King David wasn't thinking *consequences* when he seduced Bathsheba. Who thinks about cancer when smoking a cigarette? My uncle didn't. Who believes they'll become addicted when they're drinking? Answer: Nobody. My brother-in-law didn't.

Jonah's cruise was awesome…until the storm hit.

Galatians 6:7 (MSG) says, *"Don't be misled: No one makes a fool of God. What a person plants, he will harvest."*

So when a couple tells me they are living together, I usually start by asking "How's that working out for you?" because there are natural consequences you can't reverse.

First Things First (FTF) is a non-profit organization that provides healthy relationship skills through classes, events and multimedia outlets—a huge community resource created by civic leaders in Chattanooga, Tennessee, in response to family crises like divorce, pregnancies outside marriage, and absentee fathers. They're on the front-lines, know the war, and confront 7 lies about living together that go like this: it's an easy way to *test drive* marriage, it makes you stronger, sharing finances makes relationships easier, sex gets boring in marriage, marriage is just a piece of paper, it's only temporary because they plan to marry, and it benefits children. FTF labels it "pretend marriage" without commitment, because 60% never marry and there is a 50% higher divorce rate for couples who have lived together.[21]

Psychology Today reports (See: *Knot Yet* National Marriage Project*)* the typical cohabiting couple breaks up in less than 5 years and kids are victims. Barbara Ray wrote:

> *Heather, a single mom who has been on her own since she had her son at age 18 and recently married at age 31, told me, "Kids are very hard on any relationship. If you're not with someone willing to make a commitment, then the chances of that relationship being able to withstand the stress is pretty slim. If a guy can just get up and walk away and go somewhere without the stress, he probably will"….Evidence shows that children in cohabiting relationships have more behavioral problems and cognitive problems than those in married-couple families.[22]*

Every belief has embedded consequences.

What Jonah wanted—*to interrupt God's rescue of Nineveh*—was more important to him than anything happening to the crew or in Nineveh. That *belief* prompted the ridiculous cruise escape plan. God made sure he got thrown overboard and swallowed.

Every belief has built-in, unavoidable results.

Trying to mess up God's plan is actually a belief in motion. And that belief was dangerous. If you don't care that you put other people's lives at risk, then you're selfish… actually, *you're sinful!*

Beliefs are not casual emotions—something you like or feel good about in the moment or you have to have when it just pops up. Beliefs aren't created while you stare at the McDonald's menu or send a text or select the next golf club. Beliefs are something you've decided *before* what you do on the cruise, *before* you go to your first college party, *before* you speak in the courtroom, *before* you get fouled on the basketball court, and *before* you teach in the classroom.

Jonah had already decided the limits of his forgiveness. The cruise just confirmed to a pagan crew that Jonah wouldn't bend to God's will unless it was his only option to survive.

Beliefs are heart commitments that give you identity.

Beliefs are convictions that you fight for.

Choosing not to believe in Jesus *is* a belief.

There are consequences for belief...or unbelief.

Worst case scenario for consequences is the belief that you can reject Jesus all your life and it doesn't matter. When that happens, then God gives you what you always wanted...*separation* from Him...*permanently*...in a fiery hell...for *eternity*.[23] God is compassionate, a perfect and fair judge,[24] who knows what's in every person's heart with all their hidden secrets.[25] The bible says He will one day judge people from record books of their lives kept in heaven.[26] Hell was created initially to burn Satan and demons alive forever but tragically will be the destination of millions despite God's multiple offers to save.[27]

Heaven and hell exist precisely because God is loving. Because He loves sinners so much, Jesus died on a cross to pay the sin penalty we deserved and offer the gift of eternal life.[28] That sacrificial love demanded an option for those who refuse to ask forgiveness.

Many believe good people go to heaven and bad people go to hell because they need to be punished—that some justice has to exist in eternity. The bible teaches people don't go to hell because they're bad. *Nor do good people go to heaven*...because nobody is good enough to deserve forgiveness. They will spend eternity in heaven because they accept Christ's death for their sins as their only hope. Or they will be in hell because they reject Jesus as Lord and Savior.

That's the one belief that matters the most.

A Pew Research Study found 72% of Americans believe in heaven, and 59% believe in hell.[29] A shocking 100% will believe in both immediately after death.

In a Lifehack Blog, Craig Harper argued that religion is emotional, not spiritual—that believers won't give up on the "whole Messiah thing" because "They have too many years and too much emotion invested to even entertain the notion that they could possibly be misguided, misinformed or even completely wrong in their thinking." So he would label belief in a Savior as an "incidental belief", like believing a BMW is better than a Toyota.[30]

Even crazy beliefs have a purpose.

Every belief matters because it's connected to a purpose.

Some say it doesn't matter what you believe as long as you believe in something. The idea is that what you believe in is not as important as just believing in something!

Sounds cool but so does socialism...and that's failed 100% of the time. Some beliefs are good. Some are bad.

Everybody believes in something. And those beliefs drive the choices you make. If you don't believe in camping, you stay at Holiday Inn. If you believe in beaches and that melanoma is deadly, you spray on something like Banana Boat SPF 100 sunscreen. If you believe in protecting the environment, you won't use plastic straws. If you believe in Georgia football, you tailgate and celebrate!

One blogger, who leans on the writings of Emanuel Swedenborg, argues, "If I drive on a road that goes to Denver, it is not necessary for me to believe in the governmental entity that built and maintains that road, or even to have any idea at all about who built the road. It is sufficient for me to drive on the road, and I'll get to Denver. Similarly, if the Son has provided a pathway to the Father, that doesn't necessarily require that we intellectually believe in the Son; only that we travel the path that the Son has provided."[31]

Sounds impressive, but it's not in the bible. And your life is not a road trip to Denver. Jesus didn't offer the option of getting to heaven by rejecting Him but trying to live a good life. Just the opposite. You are saved by believing in Him: *[16] For God so loved the world that He gave His only begotten Son, that whoever believes in Him should not perish but have everlasting life. [17] For God did not send His Son into the world to condemn the world, but that the world through Him might be saved. [18] "He who believes in Him is not condemned; but he who does not believe is condemned already, because he has not believed in the name of the only begotten Son of God.* (John 3:16-18, NKJV)

Beliefs are only worth what they are based on. Jonah believed in making his own decisions. Sadly, that's why some leaders go down.

Faith is a label...not their life.

You are accountable to God for what you believe.

The trendy belief in our culture is that what you believe is your own business. Not true. What you believe is what you live. How you choose to live affects others.

Even more controversial?

You are accountable to God for what you believe!

Culture says: *Don't impose any moral standard because everybody is entitled to their own lifestyle...and their own truth, of course.* They argue nobody has the right to label anybody else's choices as right or wrong. And the logical outcome of that trendy belief is that Christians don't have the right to share the gospel because by definition it means other beliefs aren't legitimate. Just being a believer equates to attacking them.

Our culture's gods are diversity, inclusion, and equity.[32] Bundle those three idols and their beliefs can't be challenged. Just having values equals hating others. Secular culture is hostile to Judeo-Christian values precisely because those with faith actually have values. People of faith really don't have the right to speak their opinions!

You ought to be more afraid of what God thinks than what non-believers think.

God hurling the hurricane winds at Jonah's ship was proof that what you believe matters to God! He will make sure you own your beliefs. You can choose your beliefs, but God has the final word on what you do with that belief and how it impacts *His* plan. Some sins will be judged in *this life.*

Jonah slept below deck while the panicked crew fought for their lives in the storm. He exposed his heart. So what did Jonah really believe? Simple. He didn't care if they died or God's plan to save Assyrians died!

Case closed...or better, ship's cabin door closed.

You are right now doing what you think is important.

Bishop Fulton Sheen said, "If you do not live what you believe, you will end up believing what you live." Look what people are doing right now. Those are their real priorities, regardless of what they say they believe.[33]

While the raging storm tossed the ship around and the crew was in panic mode, Jonah was sleeping through it! Jonah believed he had the right to ignore people and problems he thought weren't deserving of his time. That choice alone meant he cared nothing for the crew, the children in Nineveh, or a commitment to God.

Jonah was willing to die and take the crew down with him, before trying to save the hated Assyrians. Booking this cruise opposite God's destination meant his real battle was with God, not Assyrians. What he really believed was that Israel deserved *prosperity* and Assyrian deserved *punishment.*

Jonah was the small town prophet who became famous in Israel's northern kingdom under King Jeroboam II, speaking for God.[34] Jeroboam led national expansion and an economic resurgence, diversifying international trade in key markets like Egypt and Assyria.[35] But God called Jeroboam "evil" for also leading the nation to worship giant golden calves as their gods.[36] One of Jonah's prophet peers, Amos, said their prosperity had led to crazy extravagance and scary pride that made Israel believe nothing could bring the nation down.[37]

No different in American culture today. You can have anything you want. Take the Burger Brasserie at *Paris* in Las Vegas. Their famous perfectly cooked *best-cut-in-the-world* Kobe beef burger is topped with Maine lobster, pancetta, imported Brie cheese, caramelized onions and a 100-year aged balsamic vinegar. Complimented with fine drink, it's only $777 per plate! Prosperity leads to pride.

No record of Jonah speaking out against the perverted worship and the prosperity that was ruining Israel spiritually. So he ignored the sins of his nation but was angry that God might ignore the sins of Assyria?

If you are building a Habitat for Humanity home when you could be mowing your lawn, you believe people deserve a hand up. If you are mentoring fifth-graders when you could be playing golf, you believe every child deserves a chance to succeed. If you are coaching a rec football team instead of watching football on TV, you believe every child deserves an opportunity to be part of a team. If you are fighting insurgents in Afghanistan when you could be fighting for tickets to a college football game, you believe every person deserves freedom. If you are working through disagreements with your spouse instead of leaving, you believe marriage and children are worth sacrifice.

You are right now doing what you believe is important.

If you are not 100% committed, you are not committed.

When you're committed to something, you'll find *energy* to make it work. When your heart isn't in it, you'll find *excuses* to avoid it. *That's what Jonah did.*

I bought a case of bottled, PURE LEAF real brewed sweet tea. It's 100% black tea. No artificial additives. Anything less and the label is fake. The flavor is amazing when you grab a bottle out of the cooler. Grocery stores sell curvy, stackable things that aren't 100% potato chips, flexible orange things that aren't 100% cheese, yellow creamy spreads that aren't 100% butter, and white stuff with red streaks that's not 100% crab. The products are a blend of artificial ingredients, flavorings, and chemicals.

Let's stick to the stuff we know is real—*hot dogs!*

If it's not 100% cheese, it's not cheese.

If you're not 100% committed, you are compromising.

If you're not committed to working out, you eat out. If you're not committed to writing a book, nothing gets published. If you're not committed to campaigning, you lose elections.

People do crazy things when they are not fully committed to what's in front of them. Like take cruises...

Taking a step of faith makes your beliefs real.

Beliefs aren't real until they are risked.

God told Jonah to go to Nineveh. A Jew confronting their most feared and hated enemy, a terrorist state, would seem insane. But rather than believe God and take the step of faith to head to Nineveh to save a nation, Jonah ran.

The reason you struggle is not because you lack *answers* but lack *ambition*. People don't struggle with choices because they are confused about what God is saying. They struggle because they won't commit to what God is saying.

There are things you don't want to face. Life is good so why invite crisis by stepping out in faith to obey what God had told you to do? A step of faith to obey what you don't want to do requires an intentional choice to separate and start something new. You can't get anywhere without breaking from what you fear, what is familiar, and what needs forgiveness.

In fact, if you are waiting to get over your fears before you obey, you will never step forward in faith. God promises His presence, but never promises to protect you from fear.

You will miss God not because you don't *love* Him, but because you *limit* Him!

The amount of time it takes for you to obey a fresh word from God is a function of the distance between you and God. If you are already surrendered, there's no struggle to catch up. Jonah struggled because he believed he could *serve* God *without surrendering* to God.

To have gone to Nineveh immediately without questioning God would have been right but looked ridiculous.

Why is it that a faith step looks crazy or weird to most Christians? When God told Jonah to lead a million people to cross a raging river, they were scared but packed up and crossed immediately. But it was not until they got to the edge that the miracle happened—the waters parted, and they *ran* across on dry ground.[38]

It may not feel right at that time.

It may not look right at that time.

It may not work out right at that time.

But taking that step of faith will make your beliefs real.

Following Jesus is radical. Friends thought we were crazy to leave our big church and comfortable life in St. Louis to lead a small, declining church in north metro Atlanta that had just been rescued from bankruptcy, suffered from a well-deserved bad reputation in the community, served by a staff that didn't want me to be the Pastor, and offered zero promise that I would get paid. Friends said NO, but God said GO! With three children and faith, we packed up and left immediately! Less than five years later, thousands of people had come to that church and scores were being called into missions and ministry. It was the greatest work of God we had ever seen! Without that initial step of faith, we would never have experienced that miracle.

It's not the typical lifestyle for many Christians.

Faith looks crazy to people who aren't committed.

It's impossible to please God without faith (Hebrews 11:6).

Without faith you have to have answers before you answer His call. Without faith you have to know the outcome before you obey. Without faith you have to have a plan before you can proceed. Without faith you will only attempt what you can conceive instead of experiencing what God can create.

When God speaks, that's all you need to know.

Nothing else matters. You've got to *believe* that.

Trendy Belief No. 7:
God doesn't want you to go through trials.

Every trial has a purpose. Sometimes you even get to find out why things happen like they do. Or...questions may haunt you until heaven. Still not sure why my friends' sweet little 10-year-old daughter died of a heart defect or why my cousin and two others were the only survivors when his combat unit of 150 was ambushed by the enemy.

After losing a baby, Hillary Scott, from country music group Lady Antebellum, courageously shared her struggle to understand God's plan in the lyrics of her hit song, "Thy Will Be Done":

> *I'm so confused. I know I heard You loud and clear.*
> *So I followed through. Somehow I ended up here.*
> *I don't wanna think I may never understand,*
> *That my broken heart is a part of Your plan.*
> *When I try to pray, all I've got is hurt,*
> *And these four words: Thy will be done.*

Through tears in a *Good Morning America* interview, she confessed, "there's pressure...to walk through life like it never happened."[1]

Life is a roller coaster. Everybody has trials.

Some people even create their own...*like Jonah!*

We get hurt and need healing. We get disappointed and need direction. Trials can be self-inflicted wounds or shrapnel wounds. There are no easy answers for the evil Parkland School shooting that stole the lives of 17 innocent victims. There *are* easy answers for swiping your Visa more times than you can pay off! Divorce isn't an accident...it's avoidable. Cancer isn't a choice...it's a consequence of living in a diseased world.

Either way...*nobody* is exempt from suffering.

A trendy belief says nobody should have to suffer. That's scary theology because it implies what doesn't kill you *can't* make you stronger. And it assumes God is unpredictable or unfair, ready to crush you for a totally innocent mistake. The truth is 180-degrees in the other direction.

The world is messed up. God is merciful.[2]

Because God is in control *and* cares, nothing touches your life without a pre-designed purpose.[3] *Nothing*!

Trials don't interrupt God's plan. They are the plan!

Trials *are* God's plan...*to change you.*

Best time to change? Now.

It was *intentional*. The source of Jonah's storm was clearly God. There are no accidents or random events with God. This was God's response to Jonah's rebellion.

It was *intense*. Scary high winds and waves that could make splinters out of the ship, slammed it with a fury. What God starts, He finishes. No way is the outcome different. Both Jonah and the crew would know God started the storm!

It was *individualized*. Nothing short of a storm could have ripped Jonah off that boat. God didn't send food-poisoning or a big chariot repair bill to discourage Jonah. He sent a storm. Challenging circumstances are delivered at differing levels, depending on your level of responsiveness to God. From the plagues on Egypt to crush Pharaoh's hard heart[4] to the prison cell earthquake for Paul to convert a hard-hearted jailer,[5] God matches degree of difficulty with degree of defiance.

It was *isolated*. No record of the storm hitting anywhere but Jonah's ship. God had a specific target. He didn't want to destroy Israel's entire west coastline or the cruise line, just toss Jonah's boat around until he got tossed around by the crew. God was so precise that Jonah was *wrestled* from the ship without *wrecking* the ship! And the storm ended the moment Jonah was thrown overboard.[6] Trials don't last forever...even if it feels like it. One day, when God shuffles people to the places He wants and squeezes hearts to the position He wants...it will be over. You will get through!

It was *infallible*. The timing was perfect. Jonah had run but could still recover. He had sinned but had not totally separated from God, so the damage of Jonah's escapade could be limited. The storm didn't happen *before* the trip to *delay* his plans but *on* the trip to *destroy* his plans. It set him *free* from bondage to the ship so he could eventually speak, and created enough *fear* to make Jonah hesitate the next time he tried to run from God. The storm didn't happen after Jonah spoke in Nineveh because of the risk of him twisting the Word of God without caring what happened. It happened before he walked into the city, so redemption could be his fresh, personal experience.

It was *instruction*. We need to learn something from every trial. The storm hit at the peak of Jonah's rebellion—not after he could cool down—so he could learn God's power is greater than our worst sin.

Trials teach you more about yourself than God.

Trials are for you, not God.

He's limitless. We're limited. He's Lord. We're learning.

"You learn ten times more in a crisis than during normal times," says Geoff Colvin, author of *Talent Is Overrated.*[7]

God didn't promise a *vomit-free* ministry and life! God allows trials to purify faith and push us toward genuine worship.[8] God uses difficult circumstances to get you from Point A to Point B spiritually—to move the needle on your level of trust. The goal is to move you from defiance, past denial, over debate, through delay, beyond desperation... to dependence.

When His disciples were caught in a violent storm on the sea and failed to call out for Him, Jesus calmed the storm and called out their hard heart and unbelief.[9] Jesus strategically put them in a storm to break that cycle of unbelief! He used *waves* to start *worship*. Like Jesus was saying, "I put you in this storm to learn submission. What's it going to take for you to trust Me?"

The storm God threw at Jonah exposed something missing in his life—forgiveness. Without a willingness to forgive your worst enemies, there's no passion to obey the God whose heart is pure forgiveness. Jonah had something in his heart that had to be confronted or it would swallow his ministry...or his life!

Without the storm, Jonah's sin stayed secret.

Without the swallowing, Jonah's rebellion stayed alive.

Without the swimming—being sucked into a fish belly to fight 3 days for life—Jonah never starts down the path of brokenness.

This trial exposed Jonah's heart as the barrier to changing an evil city...*not* the people of Nineveh!

Jonah's *not-so-secret* sin was his hatred for the people of Nineveh. For the angry preacher, there was no legitimate reason to forgive the terrorists. Knowing God chooses to forgive anyone who repents, Jonah saw the Nineveh redemption story coming and didn't want to be a part of it. Jonah was willing to die to hang on to his bitterness.

God knows what's in your heart. Every secret will ultimately be revealed at judgment (Romans 2:16). But until then, the sins you cover, God uncovers, and the sins you uncover in repentance, God covers with redemption. Nobody gets away with anything!

Your view of trials IS your view of God.

What we learn from Jonah's severe weather threat is that God is in control and can set up a situation where He owns your attention. You *will* start talking to God if you are floating in a fish stomach! You can't go through a trial without *admitting* your view of God and *adjusting* your view of God.

God sent Jonah's storm.

His signature was all over Jonah's trial.

Not every crisis is *created* by God...just *controlled* by Him.

If you view trials as random accidents, you'll view yourself as a victim and God as unloving. God knows your pain.

If you view trials as spiritual attacks, you'll view your situation as hopeless and God as undependable. Satan can set you up, but he can't bring you down. You do that. God warns you.

If you view trials as relentless adversity, you'll view your life as a battle and God as unfair. God is with you.

If you view trials as rare opportunities, you'll view your future as blessed and God as merciful. God is good.

Ever wondered why believers go through trials and non-believers prosper? Maybe trials are blessings...

Laura Story asked the questions in her song, *Blessings*:

> *What if Your blessings come through raindrops?*
> *What if Your healing comes through tears?*
> *What if a thousand sleepless nights*
> *Are what it takes to know You're near?*
> *What if trials of this life are Your mercies in disguise?*
> *What if my greatest disappointments, or the aching of this life*
> *Is the revealing of a greater thirst this world can't satisfy?*
> *What if trials of this life...the rain, the storms, the hardest nights...*
> *Are Your mercies in disguise?*

Trials happen for reasons other than punishment.

It's not always true that trials are punishment.

Trials can bring *redemption*.

Jesus said one man was born blind, not as punishment for his or his parent's sin, but so Jesus glorify God by healing him.[10]

Trials can bring *redirection*.

September 17, 2006. Amazing how one moment can change a life. Georgia Bulldogs star defensive edge rusher and the 2005 Cincinnati Bengals' first-round pick, David Pollack, played his final snap in the NFL. Pollack collided with a Cleveland

Browns running back breaking his C-6 vertebrae. It ended his career. Now an ESPN college football analyst, Pollack has a fresh perspective on the fateful day of his injury:

> Twitter (9-17-18): *12 years ago today my world was forever changed. Everything I grew up wanting to be was taken away in one hit. Never doubt what God can do! So thankful he took football away and brought me where I am today.*

The life you want may not be the life God has planned. Never fear. It's going to be good because God is good. Every trial is another step closer to discovering your God-given purpose in life. God arranges all circumstances for good.[11]

Jonah was swallowed for *both* redemption and redirection.

You can actually become stronger through a trial.

Trials are used by God to make you *stronger*, not *skeptical*: "*when your faith succeeds in facing such trials, the result is the ability to endure*" (James 1:3, GNT). Believe that and you'll see God as *Savior*. Reject it and you'll feel *separated*.

God put Jonah in the fish belly not to *end* his life but to *enlarge* his life. God wanted to use Jonah in a greater way but that couldn't happen unless Jonah faced his anger.

Bart Millard, with the award-winning Christian group MercyMe, made history when his song, *I Can Only Imagine*, logged 2 million digital downloads, as the first Christian song to go platinum and double-platinum in the digital domain. At the tender age of 10, Bart came home from camp only to find his mom had abandoned him, and his dad would abuse him.

> *His dad switched from a razor strap to a wooden paddle halfway through the beating. Bart...was terrified. He'd been beaten before, often. If dad got cut off in traffic, Millard might get a beating. If the Dallas Cowboys lost, another beating. The whippings came as often as three or four times a week, and the boy lived in constant fear, and yet...after the beatings, Millard's father would hoist the boy onto his lap, apologize for losing his temper and hold him while the two watched TV.*

> *But this time was different. His father ambushed him and grabbed the boy with one arm, [hitting] away with the other with a growing rage his son hadn't seen before. "He beat me like a dog on a leash," Millard said. "When I made eye contact with him, I thought: He's going to kill me." After that, the boy missed two days of school—it hurt too much for him to put on clothes.*[12]

Bart later suffered a football injury that sidelined him and redirected his life toward music. When his music career hit a wall, he attempted a rocky reconciliation with his dad, discovering his dad had become a Christian but was dying of cancer. When his dad died, it was the first time Bart got mad at God: "I finally got the dad I wanted, and he left."

At the gravesite, Bart's grandmother, a believer, remarked, "I can only imagine what Bub's seeing now." Bart became obsessed with the phrase "I can only imagine" for years, but finally wrote the song in 1998. *I Can Only Imagine* was written as Bart's message of hope to see his dad again in heaven. After his father became a believer, he had set up a fund for Bart to receive $600 per month to help him pursue his music dream. The last $600 check arrived the week the song hit No. 1 on Christian radio charts.

Recently, Bart and MercyMe released a K-Love award-winning hit, *Even If*, to make another statement about trusting God in trials:

> *I know You're able and I know You can*
> *Save through the fire with Your mighty hand*
> *But even if You don't, My hope is You alone.*

God won't schedule a trial without speaking in that trial.

If you believe trials are random accidents or rigged attacks, there's zero *leaning* on God or *learning* from God. You'll miss the point that God loves you. God loves you so much that He won't leave you alone!

You may not *like* what you learn from God in the storm, but you will never be *left* by God in the storm. God may never explain His *purpose* for what you feel is crushing you to the breaking point, but He will extend His *protection* before you crash at the breaking point.

God will make Himself known.

If you believe God is not in control, or out of control and trials are random, you're going to be anchored to that incident for years to come without the revelation from God that you needed to give you hope.

Listen to God. Look for God in the storm.

The storm was God speaking in a way that couldn't be misinterpreted. Even the pagan captain and crew knew God was sending a message and told Jonah to get up and pray[13] when the storm hit, and begged the Lord not to kill them![14] Jonah finally explained God had set up the storm to stop his sin.[15] Yet Jonah's "confession" never really translated into a passionate commitment. Explanation is fake confession—the *Splenda* of repentance.

Billy Graham's grandson, Tullian Tchividjian, was fired as Pastor of a Florida mega-church after an affair was disclosed. He disqualified himself, ending his career with his own sin, but his apology and confession was a seminar in truth:

Repentance is progressive and often painful. It involves disclosing and dealing with the darkest places of our hearts and lives.[16] *Nothing grieves me more than the fact that people are suffering because of my sins....I take full responsibility for this....God has increasingly been settling my heart and mind by meeting me in the deep places...exposing my idols and replacing them with a fresh assurance of His love and grace....I could tell you a thousand stories of the ways God has sweetly met me very specifically in my darkest and most despairing moments...God has met my guilt with His grace, my mess with His mercy, my sin with His salvation.*[17]

If the loss of his family and his firing was his trial, he definitely caused it, but God definitely spoke through it.

God spoke clearly through Jonah's trial.

God hates exits...and explanations.

If God wants to use you, He disrupts your life.

All great changes start with chaos.

New York Times Best Selling author and corporate motivational speaker, Andy Andrews believes, *"Adversity is preparation for greatness....The greatest pressure yields the most valuable diamond."*[18]

Adversity is: *life disrupted* and *expectations disappointed.*

Adversity puts things in perspective: Life is fragile, so maximize faith. We fail. Others fail us. So choose forgiveness.

God told Abraham to leave his religion and country. Joseph was sold into Egyptian slavery. Joshua was told to take 6 million people across the Jordan River and start a war. Goliath bullied David. Peter got out of a boat and walked on water. Jairus' 12-yr-old daughter died before Jesus got to the house and raised her from the dead. The Rapture will trigger the emergence of the Anti-Christ and 7 years of tribulation.

When chaos starts, don't leave like Jonah...listen! Our problem is not that we can't hear God. It's that we usually don't agree with what we hear.

Until you go through a trial, God isn't that important to you because He isn't real to you. Pastor Tim Keller stated, "One of the main ways we move from abstract knowledge about God to a personal encounter with him as a living reality is through the furnace of affliction."[19]

The late pastor, Adrian Rogers observed, "The opposite of truth is not error—it's sin.... When you're saved, God doesn't fix it so you can't sin anymore. He fixes it so you can't sin and enjoy it."

Jonah sinned, but he didn't enjoy it. You can choose your sin, but you can't choose your consequences. And the storm, the fear, the resentment of the crew, and getting tossed overboard were just the appetizers for the really big consequence.

God was going to use Jonah...period. The Nineveh assignment started the chaos. The storm was the disruption to start a new direction Jonah didn't want to go.

You can't go where God is not. No matter what you believe or how hard you try to shut God out of your life, He keeps showing up and messing up your plans.

Someone said the First Rule of Holes is: Quit digging! Jonah kept resisting what God told him even in the initial stages of the storm. When the storm hit, he stayed in his cabin. No movement toward God or repentance. That's why the storm got worse and didn't stop until Jonah was thrown overboard to make his next appointment.

God's discipline is scary. It should be even scarier when God stops speaking. What happens after that is never good. A big mistake is assuming when God starts to change something it always happens slow and sweet. His discipline can happen *Star Wars-fast*.

Storms are scary. Storms do damage. Storms downsize confidence. Storms maximize listening. Because you are already locked into a comfort zone, God disrupts your life to:

1) **Shake your confidence in your plans.** *Because radical change was needed to get Jonah involved in this risky ministry to Nineveh, the ship had to be rocked. God shakes you to create* **listening.**

2) **Separate you from whatever owns you now.** *Because Jonah couldn't do God's will from where he was, God removed him. That's why getting fired from a job or sidelined from an injury could be God redirecting you to His real plan. God separates you to create* **liberty.**

3) **Shock you with truth you don't want to hear.** *Because God was actually going to do something about the terrorists, Jonah had to face his evil attitude. It could only happen in Nineveh. God shocks you to create* **learning.**

Don't resist trials. It's lazy theology to label change or loss as *crisis* and not a *call*. Your most recent and biggest interruption may be God's voice!

God delights in *disrupting* lives...to *save* lives. He is not intimidated and doesn't get worn down by your arguments or apathy. God doesn't hesitate to make things inconvenient and frustrating to change you! He's more concerned about your soul than your success, your humility than your happiness, and your confession than your career. If it takes losing your job to make you confess, God can arrange that!

A military officer confessed he had neglected his marriage but wanted to save it. I prayed God would make him follow-through with that commitment. Days later he was seriously injured on patrol and brought home for recovery. The couple was forced to spend the next several weeks together as she helped in his recovery. Their marriage became awesome again! Was that trial in God's plan?

You need to fear God...AND His discipline. Since God opposes pride,[20] He often has to *crush* before He can *convince*. But His discipline is only to teach dependence.

A hard heart can only be broken by a trial!

It saves a lot of grief to see circumstances like God does.

Booking a cruise after a project was supposed to be launched was *running*. The storm God sent was a *rescue*. The fish God sent to swallow Jonah and keep him alive for three days was *redemption*. Being vomited out on the beach was a *restart*. Walking through the city yelling judgment was a *reckoning*. Sitting on a mountainside threatening suicide was pure *resistance*.

The thread through all those situations was a *hard heart*.

Running was technically not the sin, even though you call that a sin—it was a *symptom*.

The *sin* was a hard heart.

Hard hearts can only be broken by trials. It takes something harder than the hard heart to break it. Something more unexpected and uncontrollable. And it has to last long enough to exhaust—to drain all the energy out of running.

People aren't lost because they sin.

They sin because they're lost.

God's plan is: worship or be wrecked!

The truth to be learned through the storm was *worship or be wrecked!* The single most obvious sign of running is absence of worship. The entire pagan crew tried worship when nothing else was working[21]—in fear, every guy cried out to "his god".

In his best-seller, *In the Eye of the Storm*, Max Lucado had some insight on a storm that rocked Jesus' disciples:

> *Before your rescue, you could easily keep God at a distance. Comfortably dismissed. Neatly shelved. Sure He was important, but so was your career. Your status. Your salary. He was high on your priority list but He shared the spot with others. Then came the storm...the rage...the fight... the ripped moorings...the starless night. Despair fell like a fog; your bearings were gone. In your heart, you knew there was no exit. Turn to your career for help? Only if you want to hide from the storm...not escape it. Lean on your status for strength? A storm isn't impressed with your title. Rely on your salary for rescue? Many try...and fail. Suddenly you are left with only one option: God. And when you ask...genuinely ask...He will come. And from that moment on, He is not just a deity to admire, a teacher to observe, or a master to obey. He is the Savior. A Savior to be worshiped. That's why I'm convinced that the disciples would do it again. They'd endure the storm another night...a thousand nights...if that's what it took. A season of suffering is a small price to pay for a clear view of God....Worship is the awareness that were it not for His touch, you'd still be hobbling and hurting, bitter and broken. Worship*

is the "thank you" that refuses to be silenced. We have tried to make a science out of worship. We can't do that anymore than we can "sell love" or "negotiate peace". Worship is a voluntary act of gratitude offered by the saved to the Savior.[22]

Lucado is right. Being swallowed by a fish and forced to finish your most hated ministry is a small price to pay for a clear view of God...and maybe your own hard heart.

If you aren't worshipping, God will make you explain. You can't reject Him without voicing reasons. Man-up about your choices or jump off the boat and try to fight God.

Believers can't go days or even hours without worship. Sin kills worship like no other force. So God used the storm trial as an alert that sin had to stop!

You are either *worshipping* or *being wrecked* right now...

Regretting sin must evolve into removing it.

Some say Jonah's vision was too small. That the purpose of the whole "Storm and Swallowing Trial" episode was that God wanted him to not only *care* about the spiritual condition of entire cities but *capture* entire nations with His Word. That's valid because this was God's way of calling out Israel as a failed international witness—they were only exporting pride and prejudice. The real issue was that Jonah's sin of pride had shifted his vision—downsized it to only love, lead, and lift up his group!!! Do that long enough and God will start using somebody else.

He's not obligated to any nation, ministry, church, or leader.

There's nothing more offensive than telling God who He should love! He loves the world.[23]

What is God doing right now to stretch your vision of who needs Him?

Adrian Rogers taught, "Sin isn't just breaking God's *laws*. It's breaking His *heart*." Jonah was rejecting the love of God for the Assyrians *and* himself. Inside the fish belly, facing death forced him to call out to God with regret[24] but Jonah didn't take the next step of repentance. It's one thing to regret your sin. But that stops short of removing it. In the movie FIREPROOF, a firefighter named Caleb had been involved in internet porn and regretted what it had done to his marriage. Moving past regret, he took his computer outside and started whacking it with a baseball bat!

If there is real regret, real conviction of sin, you don't just feel bad about your sin. You don't just say you are sorry. You take action to change.

Start with **confession**. Confession is why God does trials. Label your sin. Call it what it is. Confess means to agree with God about what you've done and that it cost the life of Jesus to pay for it. Regret does not equal repentance. Tell the truth without excuses, blaming, or explanations.

At the 2018 Golden Globe Awards, Oprah Winfrey said, "Speaking your truth is the most powerful tool we all have!" Talk show host Ben Shapiro nailed it: "There is no such thing as 'your truth'. There is truth and your opinion."

Confession is agreeing with God's truth about your sin.

- ✓ **Confess *biblically***—what does God's Word say about it? A church leader with a wonderful wife and children, who was a friend of mine, casually announced in my office, like he was talking about where to go for lunch, that he was in love with another woman. As if to give the affair credibility, he said they had prayed about it and God had confirmed it was His will! I didn't hesitate. I picked up the bible on my desk, and firmly said, "This is God's will! You don't have to pray about it. You don't have God's permission to commit adultery!" He divorced his wife and married the other woman anyway. Dennis Prager, who is Jewish but respects people of faith and the bible, commented: "But what we have today is worse than ignorance of the Bible. It is contempt for it. Just about anyone who quotes the Bible, let alone says it is the source of his or her values, is essentially regarded as a simpleton who is anti-science, anti-intellectual and sexist."[25]
- ✓ **Confess *immediately***—a postponed confession is a cover up.
- ✓ **Confess *fearfully***—admit your sin was a personal attack on Holy God.

Move to **confrontation**. Assess the damage from your choices. There is *connection damage*—additional sins that happen afterwards, like lying. There is *collateral damage*—what is the impact on others? Ask God to show you specifics of how you sin, when you sin, where you sin, why you sin, and against whom you sin. There is *cross damage*—remind yourself of the price Jesus paid with His life and blood to buy your forgiveness. Author Jerry Bridges challenged, "Preach the Gospel to yourself every day." Donald Whitney raised the bar: "The closer you get to Christ, the more you will hate sin; for nothing is more unlike Christ than sin. Because Jesus hates sin, the more like Him you grow the more you will grow to hate sin. And the more you hate sin, the more you will grieve whenever you have embraced that which killed your Savior."[26]

Close the deal with **change**. Adjust your lifestyle choices. There must be *separation*—avoid sin with simple distance. You also need *saturation*—immerse yourself in bible study and fellowship with other believers. Pray through scripture (e.g., Psalm 51), until you know your heart is broken. And don't forget *substitution*—create a replacement habit so you don't fall back into the same cycle of sin.

Trash pickup is weekly on most streets.

In your heart it has to happen moment by moment.

Trendy Belief No. 8:
You can't succeed without a vision.

First rule of leadership: Everything is your fault.
—A Bug's Life

The key to being a good manager is keeping the people who hate me away from those who are still undecided.
—Casey Stengel, Baseball Hall of Fame Manager

You have enemies? Good. That means you've stood up for something sometime in your life.
—Winston Churchill, WWII Prime Minister of England

The Lord hurled a powerful wind over the sea, causing a violent storm that threatened to break the ship apart. Fearing for their lives, the desperate sailors shouted to their gods for help and threw the cargo overboard to lighten the ship. But all this time Jonah was sound asleep down in the hold.
—Jonah 1:4-5, NLT

Vision is overrated. At least the *vision-trafficking* in our generation's churches. It's been hyped in corporations and churches for the last generation as the secret to leadership success. Having a vision doesn't make you a leader any more than having a basketball makes you LeBron James.

Vision gives you platinum leadership status. The corporate world expects leaders to create and communicate a vision—a dream and direction inspiring others to excel. Some in the faith community have flirted with big dreams as their key to success. It's a killer cycle that rewards leaders for results—crowds, celebrity, and cash—and rejects the *controversial, costly,* and *uncool* as momentum stealers!

Here's a sample of the trendy thinking:[1]

> *Good business leaders create a vision, articulate the vision, passionately own the vision, and relentlessly drive it to completion.*
> *—Jack Welch, Former General Electric CEO*

> *The very essence of leadership is that you have to have a vision.*
> *—Theodore Hesburgh, President, University of Notre Dame*

Leadership success always starts with vision. John F. Kennedy famously dreamed of putting a man on the moon. Eleanor Roosevelt envisioned a world of equal opportunity for women and minorities.
—*John Ryan, Former U.S. Naval Academy Superintendent* [2]

You start the vision. *You* sell it. *You* innovate. *You* inspire!
Don't get sucked in.

Vision exists. It just starts with God.

At the age of 10, Steven's dad gave him a toy electric toy train set. He created train wrecks until the cars broke. His dad repaired it but warned if it happened again the train would be taken away. Steven's imagination kicked in. He used the family video camera to record the crashes so if the big wreck happened he could relive the scenes. It led to bigger ideas and productions. Today, Steven Spielberg is the wealthiest and most powerful moviemaker in the world, with his 50+ films grossing $9 billion globally, including classics like JAWS, E.T., the Indiana Jones series, Jurassic Park, Schindler's List and more. The entertainment genius confessed, "My imagination won't turn off. I wake up so excited I can't eat breakfast. I've never run out of energy.... I dream for a living. Once a month the sky falls on my head, I come to, and I see another movie I want to make....You have many years ahead of you to create the dreams we can't even imagine dreaming."[3]

There is such a thing as vision but it's different than the dreams of a genius like Steven Spielberg.

Life is about whether God gets to define who you are and where you go or whether we create the life you want.

That's the simple point of the book of JONAH.

Jonah's vision *vs.* God's vision.

The secret of leadership success is not passionately communicating *your big ideas.* Success in leadership is exclusively about chasing *God's big instructions.* A legitimate vision is the transfer of God's plan from His heart to yours.

Dawson Trotman, founder of the *Navigators* discipleship ministry, said, *"Vision is getting on your heart what has always been on God's heart."*

That's why Jonah is so relevant. The entire book is an epic struggle over whose ideas win—God's or Jonah's?

You are creating your dream or chasing God's dream.

God already has a plan. Vision is what He does really well.

He has *all* the facts...and controls *all* the future.

God's vision to Peter was to get over his racial prejudice and get innovative by taking the gospel to a Gentile military officer whose heart God had already prepared.[4] Not a vision Peter started...but it totally succeeded with Cornelius!

God's visions for Joseph included following through with his planned marriage to Mary *because* of her unexpected pregnancy,[5] and later providing steps to save Mary and Jesus from the threat of the evil Roman King Herod.[6] Without that information, that family is another statistic.

When God revealed to Jonah His vision for the next stage of Jonah's ministry—rescuing the rogue Assyrian nation—Jonah faced a choice. And that same choice today determines whether you will *be successful* or *be swallowed*.

You can't have it both ways. Either you create your own dream, or you commit to God's dream for your life.

Vision is the packaging for God's call.

Vision is never just God handing you really cool insight about what's going to happen. It's God trusting you with *information* that is linked to an *expectation*. He speaks to get you to do something. Basically, it's a call.

Biblically, vision is the process of capturing God's heart and word for the next step in your life and the lives of those you lead. It's the packaging for God's call.

Jonah had a vision. Or at least he had a plan for his ministry career should look like...*BUT*...it competed with God's call. Jonah's vision was to keep his ministry career goals intact by avoiding God's Nineveh project. Like any vision *you* create, it was a substitute for God's plan.

Jonah's vision looked impressive—a clear purpose (*headed to Tarshish*), benefit to the cruise line (*booked a trip*), a passionate commitment to something **bigger** than himself (*check the box that says "Defy God" which was definitely over his head*), effective communication (*the crew discovered his escape from God prompted the violent storm*), and a big challenge for the crew (*they lost cargo and rowed for their lives*)!

And yet...God wasn't in it.

Nothing about his vision was *approved* by God.

Everything about his vision was *attacked* by God.

The 2019 definition? Still the same.

There's a huge difference between vision and call.

Vision has become a dream you create. It's *your* big picture of what your life, ministry, or career should be about next. You are in control, driven by an adrenalin rush of expectations.

Can you imagine the energy in the room when Walt Disney first sketched Disney World, when Steve Jobs proposed the iPhone or Dr. Martin Luther King visualized the 1963 March on Washington rally and his "I Have a Dream" speech?

Those moments were real. History was made. Dreams were forwarded. Great things happened. Culture changed.

Vision is exciting...*just not biblical*. Before you tweet about my insanity, work through it with me. All I've heard for the past two decades of ministry is that a pastor has to cast a vision for a church to move forward, or an organization will fail unless there is a leader inspiring people with a vision.

Sounds scary...actually, impossible and overwhelming.

Unless you let scripture define leadership success.

The biblical strategy is to embrace God's call, not create and cast a vision. Moses had a desire to end the suffering of his people and set them free, but his vision was to *kill an Egyptian a day!*[7] God's preferred method for Israel's miraculous deliverance from Egyptian slavery started with a burning bush conversation. It ended with a call that forced an argumentative and reluctant Moses to just show up and speak up![8]

Pressure gone! Leadership success is not determined by some special ability to be creative or charismatic in moving your group forward. Moses would never have thought to pray and ask God for a big stick that turned into a snake or for 10 plagues to crush Egypt's economy and Pharaoh's power.

Just have courage to obey what God tells you to do.

A call is a direction God gives for you to commit to follow. It's God's revelation of the next step in *His* plan for your life, ministry, or career. Here's some differences.

A vision is your *idea*. A call is God's *instruction*.

A vision gives you a *plan*. A call gives you a *purpose*.

A vision requires *strategy*. A call requires *submission*.

A vision is about *imagination*. A call is about *inspiration*.

A vision is *temporary*. God's call is *permanent*.

A vision makes you responsible. A call means God is.

A vision is about *momentum*. A call is about *ministry*.

A vision is about *feelings*. A call is about *faithfulness*.

A vision *follows you*. A call means *you follow* God.

A vision means *you fight*. A call means God *fights for you*.

God's call must become your vision!

The key issue is always the *source*. Where your plan started is the difference between the Spirit and the flesh...success and failure. Where did you get your *big idea*? Did God speak it through *scripture* or did your idea surface as the best *strategy*? Did the plan come from huge *prayer* or huge *positioning*? Does it depend on your *personality* or the *power* of God for success?

God explained competing sources to Jeremiah the prophet: "*Thus says the Lord of hosts: Do not listen to the words of the prophets who prophesy to you. They make you worthless; they speak a vision of their own heart, not from the mouth of the Lord*".[9]

There's zero in scripture about God expecting a leader to come up with a vision or dream big, or punishing leaders who can't think big! Jesus didn't' wait for the disciples to get a passion and a 3-part sequential strategy to forward the gospel to the world. As He ascended to heaven, Jesus labeled the followers as "His witnesses" and commanded them to start in Jerusalem, launch stage 2 in Judea and Samaria, and then spread out all over the world. What part of that did Peter sketch on a whiteboard? Or beg Jesus to approve his plan?

In fact, 100% of the time people chased their own vision the result was disaster. Sarah told Abraham to have a child with her servant and he did. Big mess![10] Peter cut a guy's ear off with a sword trying to stop the arrest of Jesus.[11] Bloody mess!

The plan for your life starts with God. He initiates a call to get you involved where He is already working. If there's a vision, it should be God's vision for you, not your vision for your ministry.

Successful leaders function through a call, not a vision.

Life with Jesus is totally about hearing His voice and doing His will.[12] Noah would never have thought about building an ark unless God had spoken the reason—a flood—and the rules for construction.[13] When Paul launched his second missionary journey, his plan was to take the gospel to Asia. The Spirit shut down that plan and instructions came that redirected his team to Macedonia where people came to Christ and a church was started![14] Nehemiah specifically said that his plan to rebuild Jerusalem was "what God had put in my heart to do"[15] not *his* vision of restoring the walls and morals of the capital city.

The process in scripture is that leaders are expected to wait on a word from God, not create their own vision. Daniel said God revealed to him the secret to solve King Nebuchadnezzar's problem.[16] Joshua was overwhelmed facing the battle of Jericho until the Lord appeared and revealed detailed instructions for how to win the battle.[17] David admitted that facing Goliath was God's purpose to make His name great, not something David had been dreaming about doing since he was a kid: "Is there not a cause?"[18] Joseph viewed his journey from slavery to Pharaoh's vice-president in Egypt as God's destiny, not *his* strategic dream.[19]

Sometimes God does allow our "vision" to succeed briefly if it fits His purpose—like Pharaoh chasing the Israelites to the Red Sea or Pilate handing Jesus over to be crucified. Daniel 2:21 (NKJV) says God *"changes the times and the seasons; He removes kings and raises up kings."*

But in every case, God's plan wins.

In one sense, even your sin can't mess it up. All the evil plans of the Roman governor and the Jewish religious elite succeeded but they actually fulfilled what God had already planned for Jesus' sacrificial death on the cross for our sins.[20]

So...pray. Ask God what He wants you to do next.

It will be important, even if it's not noticed by the world.

Jonah had a call. It was *God's vision* for him and Nineveh.

He thought *his vision* would work better.

It didn't.

Trendy Belief No. 9:
Other people are your biggest problem.

As a child, my family's menu consisted of two choices: Take it or leave it!
—**Buddy Hackett, Comedian**

Don't be distracted by criticism. The only taste of success some people have is when they take a bite out of you.
—**Zig Ziglar, Motivational Author**

Ability is what you're capable of doing. Motivation determines what you do. Attitude determines how well you do it.
—**Lou Holtz, Famous Football Coach**

"Throw me into the sea," Jonah said, "and it will become calm again. I know that this terrible storm is all my fault."
—**Jonah 1:12, NLT**

You are not a victim. It's an inconvenient truth.
Other people are *NOT* your biggest problem.
Just because Walmart sells Pringles and you are gluten-free, doesn't make you a victim or Walmart evil.

Recently, an elementary school teacher caught a child deliberately destroying a musical instrument belonging to the school. His mom had come to the school for an event and dropped in the classroom in the middle of this scene. The mom watched him but said zero. When the teacher told the child to stop because it was wrong to misuse property that didn't belong to him, the boy ignored her and the mom interrupted. The mom told the teacher she did not understand her son and to stop victimizing the child. According to the mom, her child had just not had an opportunity to express his emotions that day and needed this outlet!

What do you think he needed? *More understanding?*

And while that kid is getting *more understanding*, who pays for the broken instrument? Taxpayers. No such thing as a family having their own problems. It always impacts all of us!

Cultural forces want to label everybody a victim. You have bought in to the victim mentality when you start blaming others for making you unhappy, believing everybody is against you, and feeling powerless to change your circumstances. That's total selfishness, believing everything has to revolve around your needs to keep you happy and nothing bad should ever happen to you. Basically, that attitude says you don't have to take responsibility for anything.

We're in *Generation Snowflake*. When the smallest thing doesn't go their way, there's a meltdown. Easily offended. Quickly upset. Feeling attacked when somebody disagrees. Lots of fear. Believing everything is falling apart.

WOW. Maybe this real Twitter list of Millennial's New Year's resolutions could help: [1]

- ❤ *Limit my "I'm a vegan" announcements to three times a day.*
- ❤ *Looking up from my phone 30 seconds every day.*
- ❤ *Get my own Netflix account.*
- ❤ *Get the Starbucks barista to properly write the name.*
- ❤ *Get my parents better jobs to support me.*

Jonah believed he was a victim.
He got angry. He argued. He avoided responsibility.
He thought God and Assyrians were his biggest problems.
God corrected that. *Jonah was Jonah's biggest problem.*

Everybody has challenges, so get over it!

Life can change instantly. Here's a sample from the lead in to the book, *Love Him Anyway*, by our friend, Abby Banks:

> *Abby Banks put her healthy, happy infant son to sleep, but when she awoke the next morning, she felt as though she was living a nightmare. Her son, Wyatt, was paralyzed. There was no fall, no accident, no warning. A rare autoimmune disease attacked his spinal cord, and there was no cure. In an instant, all her hopes and dreams for him were wiped away. The life she envisioned for her family was gone, and she was frozen by the fear of a future she never imagined. As she struggled to come to grips with her son's devastating diagnosis and difficult rehabilitation, she found true hope in making a simple choice, a choice to love anyway—to love her son, the life she did not plan, and the God of hope, who is faithful even when the healing does not come.*

I was with Jason and Abby that next morning in the hospital to pray for Wyatt and them. I saw their tears and their faith. Since the heartbreak of that moment when 7-month old Wyatt was paralyzed from the chest down by Transverse Myelitis, God has restored hope. Jason and Abby share Wyatt's journey with thousands. He is one of the youngest people to ever propel his own wheelchair. His story has been featured on Fox Carolina and CNN Headline News. I've watched 5-year-old Wyatt fly past me in our church lobby in his custom wheel chair with a license plate that says, "Eat My Dust!", play in a local wheelchair basketball league for kids, and wipe out lots of McDonald's biscuits before kicking-off the annual *FIGHT Like WYATT 5K*. Costs of medical expenses and equipment for paralysis are staggering, estimated by *The Reeve Foundation* to be more than $66K annually.

Not once have Jason and Abby ever whined or complained that they are victims! In fact, they are honoring God by bringing hope to thousands of families.

Jason and Abby believe God *covered* their problems.

Jonah believed God *caused* his problems.

That's scary. Believe God causes your problems and you'll push God away.

SWALLOW ALERT: *Misery is the result of marginalizing God and minimizing His love. God allows you to get swallowed to shift you toward hope, not steal your hope.*

Jesus died on a cross to cover what you've done wrong.

God targets you...*for forgiveness!*

Jonah confessed he caused the storm that threatened to kill the entire crew.[2] Yet he still believed God was unfairly targeting him when the terrorist Assyrians were the real problem. The Assyrians were evil, and God did target Jonah...because Jonah needed to change first!

You can either go through life as a *victim* or *victorious.*

What if your greatest challenge was your greatest call?

Self-pity is a big mistake.

Jonah believed he was a victim because God forced him to go to Nineveh when he didn't want to go. He believed getting hit by the violent storm, the ship's crew turning against him, being swallowed by a huge fish, fighting for his life three days in the fish belly, being vomited on the shore, and forced to complete a Nineveh rescue project proved he was a victim!

> [10] *When God saw what they had done and how they had put a stop to their evil ways, He changed his mind and did not carry out the destruction He had threatened.* [1] *This change of plans greatly upset Jonah, and he became very angry.* [2] *So he complained to the Lord about it: "Didn't I say before I left home that you would do this, Lord? That is why I ran away to Tarshish! I knew that you are a merciful and compassionate God, slow to get angry and filled with unfailing love. You are eager to turn*

back from destroying people. ³Just kill me now, Lord! I'd rather be dead than alive if what I predicted will not happen." (Jonah 3:10-4:3, NLT)

Life will never be perfect. Bad things happen even when you do what's right. Trials hit everybody.

It was called the "Swing Set Standoff". A Farmers Insurance customer parked his RV in his backyard next to a swing set...in moose country. A moose decided the swing set looked like fun and managed to get his antlers entangled. In an effort to untangle himself, the thrashing moose dragged the swing set against the RV, damaging it and gouging the motor home. They covered it. Their claim? "We've seen almost everything, so we cover almost anything."

Nobody is covered for everything. Some moose may wander into your life.

Add stupid choices to that mix and life can be crazy. What about the 12 publishing firms that rejected J.K. Rowling's "Harry Potter and the Sorcerer's Stone"? I don't endorse the books, but the fact is that since the 1997 release, Harry Potter books are the fastest-selling books ever. They probably regret missing that opportunity...and fired somebody!

Life is rock-climbing, not resting in an ENO hammock. You won't always get your way.

Complain about adversity and you will become a victim. Feeling sorry for yourself is spiritual suicide.

You have a choice...not about *outcomes* but *opportunities*. Victims believe they are never to blame, never responsible.

If you think you'll finally be happy *when*...then **you won't!**

Adversity can't steal success. It can only steal spirit.

God didn't create you to fail. You are limited only by believing the wrong things about God.

YOU are your biggest problem!

In Hillary Clinton's book, *What Happened*, she lists 15 things that cost her the 2016 presidential election including: *Russian influence, the DNC, sexism and misogyny, President Obama, Bernie Sanders, WikiLeaks, a traditional campaign, the debate questions, biased media, a democrat predecessor, lack of tv coverage, low-information voters, women under pressure from men, and FBI Director James Comey.* Hillary regrets her emails, promising to put coal miners out of business, and calling Trump supporters "deplorables."

I'm confused. Who's to blame?

Jonah clearly confessed the storm was all his fault! But even then, his attitude didn't change.

SWALLOW ALERT: *Confession changes nothing. Like the lawyer joke: What do you call 100 lawyers at the bottom of the ocean? A: A good start. It's a good starting point for getting real with God, others, and yourself. Confession is like saying you know you need to lose weight. So? What will you do?*

Rappelling solo down an abandoned 100-foot mine shaft in the Arizona desert, 62-year-old John Waddell's search for gold turned scary. When his carabiner broke, he fell 50 feet into a rattlesnake pit, breaking both legs. No cell service, food, or water. To survive he had to kill three rattlesnakes and endure severe dehydration for 48 hours before a friend found him. A team of 12 rescuers worked six hours to pull him out of the shaft for the airlift (10-18-18 Report, KDVR Fox31, Denver, CO). He searched for gold. They searched for him. He was the problem, not the rescuers.

Jonah got thrown overboard not because the crew was crazy out of control, but because he was crazy to rebel against God's control.

The crew was never Jonah's problem.

It was his commitment.

You can't live by blame or comparison. If so, Jonah loses. Jonah *ran*. The crew *repented*. During the storm, the crew decided to get right with God immediately and worshiped, even when Jonah, who wore the *BIG BELIEVER* logo on his golf shirt, was not worshiping!

Nobody else can worship for you.

Nobody else is responsible for motivating you to worship.

Nobody else can limit your passion...but you. And like the crew, you can worship God even if people who pretend to be sold out...*aren't!*

Don't ever let someone else's *junk* steal your *joy*!

Circumstances are never the reason for anyone's lack of success. Neither critics or bullies or their words or stunts or threats can stop you. The only thing that shuts you down is *heart failure*—losing the heart to keep going. And that's totally your choice! It normally happens when you shut God out because your energy...your ability...your endurance...can only take you so far and you'll collapse. Just like Jonah's big bragging got drowned out inside the fish belly.

You are your biggest problem.

What's in your heart determines success or failure.

It's what's in your heart that determines whether you succeed or fail. The loudest voices in our culture scream that you are a victim and need "safe space" so you won't be emotionally damaged on a college campus or in the classroom or at Starbucks. There is no "safe space" when you are trying to shut down God's plan...and His voice!

Jonah was INSIDE the fish belly when he and God finally started talking! The shocker was that Jonah admitted he had not been praying or praising God. Amazing what's in a heart.

Three guys are fishing when an angel appears. The first guy said, "I've suffered from back pain for years. Can you help me?" The angel touched the man's back, and he felt instant relief. The second guy pointed to his thick glasses and begged for a cure for his poor eyesight. When the angel tossed the glasses into the lake, the man gained 20/20 vision. As the angel turned to the third fellow, he screamed, "Don't touch me! I'm on disability!"

Your biggest problem is what's happening right now in your own heart. It's either your greatest asset or your greatest weakness and threat. Quit blaming your mate, boss, staff, team, kids, competitors, community, church, or critics for crushing you or keeping you from reaching your goals or causing your bad attitude.

Jesus said what you talk about is what's really in your heart.[3] Discussing another job? You're not totally committed to where you're at. Had a recent conversation about how the other person gets the breaks? Jealousy is in your heart. Questioning why your kid is in ER? Maybe anger at God has taken over your heart. Talking about a woman other than your wife? There's lust in your heart or resentment toward your wife or both.

What did you say?

Hesitation to obey means you love something else!

If there is *hesitation*, that's the *explanation*. If I ask you if you love your wife and you hesitate, that is the explanation.

Jonah hesitated to obey God. He postponed doing what God specifically told him to do, maybe hoping God would drop the issue or move on to something else or somebody else. If you hesitate to obey—no matter the excuse—it can only be explained as a heart full of rebellion. It's not obvious at first.

Cleansing the Jewish Temple was a huge controversy that helped seal Jesus' fate for execution. The shock was not that He cast out the corrupt money changers, but that immediately afterwards outcasts came in, were healed, and started worshiping![4] Jewish elites resented who Jesus threw out. God in heaven rejoiced over who started filling it up! The Temple was filled with corruption.

Same with your heart. It's full right now with a passion or a problem. There's no such thing as an empty heart...or a divided heart. You are already sold out to something. Everybody is already a worshiper. The only question left is: What do you worship? Only one god, loyalty, priority, or commitment exists at a time. Jesus said it's impossible—*not stressful or difficult or challenging...but impossible*—to serve two masters.[5] Why? Because you will always love one thing more than the other. Simple human nature. Olympic athletes can't simultaneously represent two countries in a competition. Supreme Court justices don't wear red and blue jerseys. All priorities are NOT equal. God doesn't just *expect* you to choose. He *demands* you choose.

That's what getting thrown overboard was about.

God put Jonah in the fish belly to make him choose.

It was a big deal!

Sometimes it's not Satan attacking. It's God against you!

The only reason Israel stressed about crossing the Red Sea or agonized over packing up and fighting for the Promised Land or felt tension over a decision is because their heart was still linked to Egypt and pagan gods.[6] There's always one pivotal choice that finalizes where you're headed and why.

People think they can live in two worlds—successfully manage a double life—honor God's standards and participate in a non-Christian lifestyle. WRONG. What you are living now is who you are and what you've chosen.

It's trendy to blame difficult circumstances for lack of joy or lack of results, and easy to blame trials as Satan launching a spiritual attack. Like Russia wants to meddle in U.S. elections, Satan always wants to mess up our intention to live right.

But sometimes God is against us!

SWALLOW ALERT: *If you want to know if God is driving a situation, try to stop it! If you can stop it, God didn't start it. Jonah couldn't stop the storm or the swallowing or the scene in Nineveh. God is in ultimate control.*

God answered Jonah's heart rebellion big time: *"the Lord hurled a great wind upon the sea, and there was a mighty tempest on the sea, so that the ship threatened to break up"*.[7] Circumstances aren't random. There's a reason your life is being shaken...and it can be your attitude!

SWALLOW ALERT: *God deals exclusively with the heart.*

When Jesus' disciples were rowing for their lives on the Sea of Galilee in a storm that lasted for hours past midnight, Jesus walked on the water toward them and calmed the sea. He asked them why their faith was so small, but the scary part was the explanation for intentionally putting them at risk in the path of a violent storm: *"their hearts were hardened"*.[8] Jesus set up the storm crisis because their hearts were hard. Every single disciple had intentionally refused to believe that Jesus was in control or could do miracles!

God always attacks pride: *"God opposes the proud but gives grace to the humble"*.[9] The Jewish prophet Jeremiah reported: *"The human heart is the most deceitful of all things, and desperately wicked. Who really knows how bad it is? But I, the Lord, search all hearts and examine secret motives. I give all people their due rewards, according to what their actions deserve".*[10]

Don't mislabel your circumstances.

That might mean more time in a fish belly.

What do you think? Better look inside.

Broken things get tossed. God only uses what's broken.

Billy Graham said, "We're suffering from only one disease in the world. Our basic problem is not a race problem. Our basic problem is not a poverty problem. Our basic problem is not a war problem. Our basic problem is a heart problem."[11]

God won't use you—actually He *can't* use you—until your heart is broken over the things that break His heart. God doesn't care about *what might happen* to your career or ministry but what is happening right now in your heart. If necessary, He will shut down your career or ministry just like He temporarily shut down Jonah's life with a storm and fish. God can restore success or influence anytime. But He won't tolerate a heartless leader.

You can't fake compassion. God knows your heart.

You can't "out-compassion" God. God judges your heart.

If you don't have compassion, maybe you don't have God.

Jonah is one of only two books in the Bible that end with a question*: "Then the Lord said, "You feel sorry about the plant, though you did nothing to put it there. It came quickly and died quickly. But Nineveh has more than 120,000 people living in spiritual darkness....Shouldn't I feel sorry for such a great city?"*[12]

That question still hovers like a spy drone: *Do you care enough about lost and dying people to do something?* The question proves that the biggest issue to God was Jonah's *unbroken heart.* Specifically, if Jonah didn't care that moms and dads and kids might go to hell, then nothing about Jonah's career or ministry impressed God or made him useful to God.

The reality check was that God knew exactly how many people in Nineveh were living in spiritual darkness and at risk of a coming judgment—120,000! And God knew Jonah could care less.

God hates sin...especially when it's in the heart of somebody who pretends to be doing things in His will.

Convictions and compassion can co-exist.

Rick Warren, author of the best-selling book, *The Purpose-Driven Life*, believes:

> *Our culture has accepted two huge lies. The first is that if you disagree with someone's lifestyle, you must fear or hate them. The second is that to love someone means you agree with everything they believe or*

do. Both are nonsense. You don't have to compromise convictions to be compassionate.[13]

Jonah substituted *convictions for compassion*. That's legalism. God targeted him for this "come to Jesus" moment because Jonah was typical of his generation's national pride. Israel believed in exceptionalism—they were exclusively loved, blessed, and protected by God.

Because Jonah disagreed with the lifestyle of the Assyrians, he used their evil as an excuse to exempt himself from rescuing them. In other words, because they really were evil, he didn't have to show compassion. Jonah could have gone to Nineveh and spoken the message without ever giving up his beliefs. The problem was not "those people". By God's judgment, Jonah's heart was more evil, because he knew what could rescue them and refused to do it!

Jonah's convictions were dysfunctional. His identity came from his race and his righteousness. Big problem. Pastor Tim Keller commented on identity confusion:

> *If we get our very identity, our sense of worth, from our political position, then politics is not really about [issues], it is about us. Through our cause we are getting a self, our worth. That means we MUST despise and demonize the opposition. If we get our identity from our ethnicity or socioeconomic status, then we HAVE to feel superior to those of other classes and races. If you are profoundly proud of being an open-minded, tolerant soul, you will be extremely indignant toward people you think are bigots. If you are a very moral person, you will feel superior to people you think are licentious. And so on.*[14]

What is it that breaks your heart? What upsets you?
That will determine if God pursues you or prospers you.
Other people are *not* your biggest problem.
Circumstances...storms, fish, and terrorists are not.
You are.

Trendy Belief No. 10:
You are free to do whatever you want.

The best way to teach your kids about taxes is by eating 30% of their ice cream.
—Bill Murray, Comedian

Be decisive. Right or wrong, make a decision. The road of life is paved with flat squirrels who couldn't make a decision.
—Anonymous

"Throw me into the sea," Jonah said, "and it will become calm again. I know that this terrible storm is all my fault"....Now the Lord had arranged for a great fish to swallow Jonah. And Jonah was inside the fish for three days and three nights.
—Jonah 1:12, 17, NLT

You just think you're free. Making choices without a gun pointing at you doesn't equal freedom. You make thousands of choices every day. Not all of them are smart. Most of them won't make you successful.

Comedian Jeff Foxworthy admitted, "I'm just two decisions away from putting up drywall for a living."

Jonah was two decisions away from getting swallowed—just two decisions between God calling Jonah and a huge fish choking him down. One was Jonah booking the cruise to escape God's presence. The other was Jonah hiding his sin during the storm from the panicked ship's crew.

Neither one was smart. Jonah really wasn't free.

You can choose a direction.

You can't choose the consequences.

There are no choices without consequences.

American pastor and Christian apologist, Tim Keller said, "The Bible teaches that God is completely in control of what happens in history and yet He exercises that control in such a way that human beings are responsible for their freely chosen actions and the results of those actions."[1]

Freedom is not living without *boundaries* but living for *blessings*. Not getting what you want, but wanting the best.

In a Q&A with Dennis Prager, Christian apologist Ravi Zacharias, recalled Tiger Woods' statement after his extreme lifestyle went public. When asked by the media how could he lie to so many for so long, Tiger confessed, "Because I first lied to myself." Zacharias explained,

> The real lie is that you can violate the sacred boundaries God has set and in doing that you find happiness. When you remove a fence, pause to ask why it was put there in the first place. G.K. Chesterson said, 'Meaninglessness doesn't come from being weary of pain, but meaninglessness comes from being weary of pleasure.' Pleasure without God and His boundaries will leave you emptier than before. The loneliest people in the world are the wealthiest and most successful who know no boundaries.[2]

People tend to talk about being free to do anything they want as though God didn't exist. Pretending God isn't *real,* or God isn't *ready* for your choices or God doesn't *react* to your choices...or God can't *rule* or *overrule* your choices proves the point. You aren't technically free to do whatever you want.

The late pastor, Adrian Rogers, taught: "Where God doesn't rule, He will overrule."

Freedom is an illusion. In the sense of doing whatever you want, it doesn't exist. Jesus said you already belong to whatever you value the most.[3] Actually, the Bible is graphic—you become a *slave* to whatever you follow.[4] You can make an idol...but then the idol remakes you! What you have already chosen is who you are.

Who you are today is the result of choices you made. No way to blame anybody or anything else. You choose how you will react to every situation, good or bad.

But you can't do anything you want because God is in control, moving your life toward His pre-planned purpose. God gives you *life...and love...and limits!*

There are built-in limits to what God will allow you to do.

Ultimately, if you spend the ridiculously short life God gave you living by your own rules, you will have punched a ticket for an eternity in hell, separated from God. Why? Because, there are no choices without consequences. God set up life to work like that.

Jonah just *thought* he was free to board any random ship heading away from Nineveh. God limited his escape plan to that specific ship so Jonah would be swallowed and spit out near Nineveh. Even the duration of his rebellion was controlled because the storm was sent by God at a specific time to shut down the cruise! And if you argue that God is unfair, think again. God was merciful. He limited Jonah's time in the fish belly to just three days and nights. To be blunt, God controlled everything from the ship to the storm to the spitting!

Life only has two lanes—going in two different directions—and we're already condemned by past choices until we decide to believe on Jesus.[5]

You are either doing what God wants with your life or doing what God will ultimately have to stop.

Follow God or fight God. Those are your only choices.

Jonah chose to fight. So did God.

Getting what you want doesn't mean God wants it.

You think you are *successful*.

You may actually be *stuck*. Even if you get everything you thought you wanted it won't fulfill. What looks like success might be slavery. Sometimes God will let you have what you want to make you realize it's not what you need. Your *freedom* may actually be a *fence* that will limit what you do from the moment you tried to leave God behind.

Jonah boarded the ship to *escape* God.

God used the ship to *enclose* Jonah.

Jonah thought God couldn't speak *if* he took the cruise.

God started speaking *because* Jonah took the cruise!

At any given moment, your choices are influenced by a secret desire or a superior devotion. What you love drives what you live. God wants you to love Him...more than the other stuff you think you have to have to be happy.

In FORBES, Maureen Henderson got it right: "Happiness is a moving target." Without Jesus in your life, the search for happiness is a wild adventure that always leaves you empty.[6]

When Jesus engaged the Samaritan woman at Jacob's well in conversation, He shocked her by asking her to go get her husband. She confessed that she was not married. Jesus confirmed she had told the truth but added He knew she had been married five times and was currently living with a man. Jesus also explained that the series of relationship failures proved she was searching for fulfillment in men when life could be found only in Him.[7]

The Samaritan woman got what she wanted.

It wasn't what God wanted. She knew it because no matter how good those five guys were, they didn't fill her soul-hunger.

Jonah's choices to board a ship to avoid God and try to ride out the storm God sent to shake him up, were motivated by anger at God that he might NOT get what he wanted!

Jonah got what he wanted...briefly.

But God didn't want that.

Nobody walks around with zero beliefs.

A crisis doesn't help you decide what to believe—it just exposes what you already believe. Threats may cause you to rethink what you believe about God...and people... and your own limits, but you go into a crisis convinced you've got everything worked out.

So did the crew of the ship...and Jonah.

But when Jonah's ship was ready to break apart in the storm, the crew members *"were afraid, and each cried out to his god"*.[8] Obviously the crew believed some powerful god had to be in control and prayer might work. They also believed in good and evil—as in, sin against a god could bring judgment: *"Tell us on whose account this evil has come upon us".*[9] Amazing what you really believe when you think you might die!

When you are under pressure, what comes out is what you really believe in your heart! You can't fake it.

Then Jonah reluctantly admits he knew exactly why they were in that crisis: *"Throw me into the sea," Jonah said, "and it will become calm again. I know that this terrible storm is all my fault".*[10] He knew God was in control...and he was going to pay for his rebellion.

Worst moment ever? When consequences finally hit!

Because nobody can ever successfully hide what's in their heart, it's easy to know Jonah's fixed beliefs:

- ✓ *You can choose when you want to obey God*
- ✓ *God wouldn't really hurt you if you disobeyed*
- ✓ *There's always a grace period you can stretch*

Turns out those beliefs had been there all along.

During your first marriage argument, it dawns on you that both partners came with pre-packaged, protected beliefs. On the first day of your new job, you realize the company already has a culture and you've got to bow or blend to survive. No coach opens the first practice confused about what she expects out of her players. Surgeons don't start operations without a pre-chosen protocol.

Everybody already has a set of beliefs they think are right.

God reserves the right to shake you up when you're wrong.

It's impossible to stay in the same place spiritually.

Nothing ever stays the same...and you're probably good with that! Just open your high school yearbook...and laugh. Passwords have a life span of hours now. My wife and I have moved over 20 times since we got married. Elections change the political landscape. Millions of students graduate each year. The iPhone 6 is outdated. Hurricanes change coastlines. McDonald's changes their menu...or do they?

Between temptations and trials, you will never stay the same spiritually. In fact, the Bible says at any given moment, you are either moving closer to God or farther away.[11] God never changes. You do. God wants a relationship. You mess it up.

When the hurricane-force storm tossed the ship, the crew cried out to their gods, cast lots to surface the sin, caved into fear, challenged Jonah to get right with God,[12] called upon Jehovah God for forgiveness and made some new commitments.[13]

The crew moved *forward* spiritually *during* the storm!

Jonah created distance between himself and God.

Jonah had a spiritual free fall from the moment God told him to go speak out against Nineveh and he ran. Worship disappeared. Commitment weakened. Anger escalated.

If runners take a break from workouts, aerobic fitness starts declining in 14 days or less. Regular exercisers feel a quick drop in fitness during the first 21 days after dropping workouts! The same principle applies to your spiritual life.

Every day, you are either improving how you *listen* to God or you're *losing* yardage spiritually. The storms and currents of temptation are powerful. If you don't *fight it,* you'll *flow with it* and drift backwards spiritually.

Even when you are running from God, you can only survive briefly off your ability.

The problem is never that *you can't find God.*

It's that you *can't get away from God*!

Being confident doesn't mean you are right.

Good leaders normally aren't afraid to make decisions.

Jonah made five in quick succession: he set a goal (*to avoid God*), traveled to Joppa, located a ship, bought a ticket, and boarded the ship.

Jonah made five *confident* decisions.

Every one of them was a *bad* decision.

Which means he was not innocent.

Nobody sins *accidentally*. Rebellion is an intentional choice. And it never happens suddenly or spontaneously. There's a sequence to temptation so if you don't exit early you get stuck on a ship that *will* hit a storm! In the Garden of Eden, Eve left herself alone, listened to Satan, lingered by the tree, lusted for the fruit, and lifted the fruit.[14] Adam and Eve hid from God. People have been hiding ever since.

Nobody gets swallowed *accidentally*. The storm that got Jonah thrown overboard and the huge fish that swallowed him were set up by God as interventions—saving grace, but scary. The storm *shut down* his decisions and the fish *shuttled* him to his destiny. God is big enough to overcome your worst decisions. Even the ones you knew were crazy but did it anyway.

Being confident doesn't mean you're doing the right thing.

That's how people get lost in the mountains.

Uncertainty can trigger bad decisions.

Uncertainty about direction can also lead to mistakes. You need to be confident you are operating in the will of God.

The best leaders can explain their call in a 30-second elevator pitch. They believe that whether anybody else cares or participates or follows or agrees or commits, leadership is moving with God. They get out front and risk something.

Leadership has been described as the ability to hide your fear from others. Uncertainty paralyzes.

Nobody volunteers for a campaign. They sign up for a cause.

Mostly because strong leaders can *define* a destination and *defend* it!

It was March 15, 1958. A rising 40-year-old political star in an impossible presidential campaign, then Sen. John F. Kennedy had been hammered by the media. Reporters accused his father of using the family fortune and influence to buy the election. Speaking at Washington D.C.'s Gridiron Club, Sen. Kennedy's opening line revealed a confident leader facing his critics with humor. Reaching into his pocket, he pulled out a telegram he claimed to have just received from his "generous daddy", and read it: "Don't buy a single vote more than is necessary–I'm not going to pay for a landslide." *

Out of respect, one gratuitous word in the line was omitted.

Jonah's mistake was not *buying in* to the unlimited grace of God. Jonah's uncertainty about God's fairness in forgiving the Assyrians he hated, prompted him to temporarily throw away his greatest opportunity to be used by God.

The apostle Paul wrote to Christians in Rome, "Whatever *is* not from faith is sin".[15] If you cannot move forward with a decision in full confidence that you are in the center of God's will—that He totally approves of what you plan—then it is a sin for you. God views any decision without His endorsement as a major spiritual mistake.

In his blog, *Coaching for Leaders*, Dave Stachowiak said, "On planes, nobody would care much about the management of turbulence, food service, or arrival time if they didn't know where the plane was going. The destination is the whole point of the trip. People don't fight to get an aisle seat on a plane bound for nowhere. In times of change, people need to know where they are going."[16]

To be uncertain is to be unprotected.

To be unprotected is to be unsuccessful.

To be unsuccessful is to be unusable.

Leaders don't crush hope, they create it!

A major league baseball star recently said, *"You are either a faucet or a drain."* A faucet contributes. A drain takes.

Committed people are like faucets, pouring their lives into what they are doing. Conflicted people are like drains, stealing energy from the situation.

When Jonah ran from God's call, he drained hope, starting with the ship crew fighting for their lives in the storm God sent to shut down Jonah's rebellion. Ultimately Jonah's stunt nearly deprived the Assyrians of an opportunity to be forgiven.

Leaders create hope by keeping commitments. They pour into a call and sellout to a cause. Even if you disagree, you know where they stand and what they believe. They inspire.

Leaders don't create more headaches.

They solve problems. They create hope.

A police officer's 5-year-old daughter was playing "Wedding." Her version of the wedding vows must have been based on what she heard daddy say: "You have the right to remain silent. Anything you say can and will be held against you. You have the right to have an attorney present. You may now kiss the bride!" Those vows might solve some problems!

Jonah had an opportunity to create hope.

He became the problem. He crushed hope.

Want to identify a good leader? Follow the hope.

Remove distractions and your purpose becomes clear.

Angela Duckworth chased her purpose. She left her high-profile role as management consultant for a global company to become a 7th grade math teacher in a New York City public school. The classroom confirmed to her that passion and effort, not income or intelligence, predicted success. With a best-seller, *GRIT: The Power of Passion and Perseverance*, a TED Talk with 14 million viewers in 49 languages and creating the Character Lab as a distinguished professor at the University of Pennsylvania, she proved talent is overrated. Angela said *grit* is "both perseverance and passion for long-term goals. Not just working hard but loving what you do....not the same thing as talent, which also helps you achieve great things in life but has logged a disproportionate share of the spotlight in American culture."[17] She claims that gritty people can state their purpose in 10 words or less! "Self-control...is that internal conflict between what you want to get done—a goal—and anything more fun or pleasing in the moment, like Snapchat, binge watching *Downton Abbey* or a doughnut. I'm sure we all know people who are gritty and self-controlled, but there are people who are one but not the other."[18]

Angela is right. Talent alone doesn't create success. It's refusing to quit and walk away from your purpose. For believers, it's more specific—sticking with God's purpose for your life.

I can state my purpose in two words: glorify Jesus! That's it. Anything that doesn't glorify Him doesn't belong in my life. Simple. Export anything that *distracts* from that purpose! Import everything that *develops* that purpose! If playing FortNite or a round of golf drains my energy for Jesus, then it has to go. If making $2M or going to an SEC football game causes me to lose focus then I should avoid that stuff. Same goes for drinking or going to Disney World.

If it distracts, it defeats!

Long-term view? Jesus-followers can't afford that.

Jonah moved toward the ship, not away.

The closer you get to a temptation the more confused you get about your purpose and the more conflicted you become.

Confused? Usually that's an indicator that you are trying to hang on to something God doesn't want in your heart. Confusion increases the closer you get to the edge of a bad decision!

Back off. Quit thinking about the escape the ship represents, your right to enjoy that ship, or good things you think you could do for God if you got on that ship and think about what God already told you to do.

Don't be fooled. Distractions are not always packaged as obvious wastes of your time. Some distractions come as bonuses...blondes...or buddies.

Remove the distractions or God will!

Most decisions are about purpose, not moral vs. immoral.

James Kouzes and Barry Posner, co-authors of *The Leadership Challenge*, nailed it: "There's nothing more demoralizing than a leader who can't clearly articulate why we're doing what we're doing."[20]

Leaders succeed by defining their purpose.

A mentor told me, if you can't write your purpose on the back of a business card, you don't know what it is...or maybe you need to write smaller? Not sure, but I think I get it.

Jonah knew what he was doing and why. He hated the Assyrians and made that clear to God two times...without apology![19]

So what was his purpose? To wipe Assyria off the map!

He made a strategic spiritual decision to do everything in his power to postpone or prevent forgiveness reaching Nineveh. His vision did not include turning the whole nation of Assyria to God.

Most choices are not between good and evil.

Your choices are frequently about purpose.

And that means choosing priorities with eternal impact.

Choices between right and wrong are easy...except for lying. Everybody lies. That's the truth! A UMass study found 60% of Americans can't go 10 minutes without lying.[21] Seriously, those choices are eternally black and white, Captain Obvious!

Successful leaders make decisions...normally the hard ones that nobody else wants to risk.

Choices about purpose—*why God put you here*—are hard.

They shape a destiny.

Jonah didn't deserve to be in charge of the Nineveh project. He didn't buy in to God's purpose.

81

Trendy Belief No. 11:
You can't please everybody.

Stop trying to make everybody happy. You aren't chocolate.
—Toby Mac, Christian Hip Hop Artist

Be who you are and say what you feel, because those who mind don't matter and those who matter don't mind.
—Dr. Seuss, Author

Care what other people think and you will be their prisoner.
—Lao Tzu, Chinese Philosopher

Your self-worth is determined by you. You don't have to depend on someone telling you who you are.
—Beyoncé, American Singer

Your time is limited, so don't waste it living someone else's life.
—Steve Jobs, Founder of Apple

Always go to other people's funerals, or they won't come to yours.
—Yogi Berra, 1972 Baseball Hall of Fame Inductee

Then they cried out to the Lord, Jonah's God. "O Lord," they pleaded, "don't make us die for this man's sin. And don't hold us responsible for his death. O Lord, you have sent this storm upon him for your own good reasons." Then the sailors picked Jonah up and threw him into the raging sea, and the storm stopped at once! The sailors were awestruck by the Lord's great power, and they offered him a sacrifice and vowed to serve him. Now the Lord had arranged for a great fish to swallow Jonah. And Jonah was inside the fish for three days and three nights.
—Jonah 1:14-17, NLT

Are you kidding? **Trying to please everybody has never been the issue.** Get real. Nobody is crazy enough to live that way...or thinks they could actually please their wife or boss or parents or coach 100% of the time! That's an excuse to cover disappointment with people. It kills your energy to succeed.

Toby came into the office an hour late for the third time in one week and found his boss, Mr. Epstein waiting for him. "What's the story this time, Toby?" Mr. Epstein asked sarcastically. "Let's hear a good excuse for a change." Toby sighed, "Everything went wrong this morning. My wife decided to drive me to the harbor. She got ready in ten minutes, but then the ferry didn't turn up. Rather than let you down, I swam across the river, ran over the mountain, borrowed a bicycle and cycled the 20 miles through the field to this office." "You'll have to do better than that, Toby," said Mr. Epstein, disappointed. "No woman can be ready in 10 minutes!"

Be honest. You focus every day on *your* happiness, not stressing out to make sure your buddy, boss, mate, kids, or neighbors are giving you 5-star reviews! If things get crazy with family, a friend or a follower, you'll react. Everybody wants to be accepted on some level and tries to please, but why? Normally most people get it that even the President only gets about 50% of the votes.

The real challenge is the search for your own peace.

Peace is only found in Jesus...not in relationships, revenge, retirement investments, or riches and entertainment: "I have said these things to you, that in me you may have peace. In the world you will have tribulation. But take heart; I have overcome the world".[1]

Hate to contradict Beyoncé, but self-worth is pre-determined by God. You have secure value because He created you and loves you! Please God and self-worth increases. Live for what you want and self-worth falls off a cliff.

SWALLOW ALERT: *Jonah's suicide threats started when he tried to push God out of his life because he couldn't get his way. (Jonah 4:1-3, ESV)*

Taking life is not the only way people commit suicide. Some plunge into reckless immorality, crazy spending, marital unfaithfulness, extreme partying, or even revenge.

If you got caught in a hurricane-force storm, thrown overboard from your ship...*by the crew*, swallowed by a huge fish and spent your 3-day getaway inside that fish, when you knew from the start you were messing up God's plan big time, you might be thinking God was not happy with you.

You already know you can't please everybody. Most of the time we don't even like ourselves! Happiness comes from knowing you are pleasing God with the right decisions. Until that is settled, you are miserable...missing something.

If you are not leading the way, you are in the way!

Jonah's defiance threatened to delay God's plan to save the Assyrian nation. He was in God's way.

When you *fight* instead of *follow*, **you** are the problem!

How inconsistent could Jonah be? He was a famous prophet of God in Israel but didn't have time to share hope with innocent families in terrorist-leaning Assyria?

SWALLOW ALERT: *If even one person on a leadership team or in a family is fighting God on an issue, it kills momentum. You may not like it, but God approved of the crew throwing Jonah overboard because he was in the wrong place. When a person is not where God wants them to be, it's miserable for everybody!*

Momentum-killers have to be confronted. Meetings can slow down momentum. Thomas Sowell nailed it: "People who enjoy meetings should not be in charge of anything."[2] Most meetings are substitutes for getting things done—a way to avoid making hard decisions...*except for this crew's meeting.*

Leaders are supposed to inspire others with their values—set the pace—by example and by expecting others to live up and keep up. Jonah messed up any opportunity to define a leader as someone passionate about doing God's will.

Another proof that Jonah was in God's way? When the pagan ship crew threw Jonah overboard and the storm immediately ended, they were so amazed that they converted to Jehovah God! No motivation for the crew to believe in God when the cruise began because, tragically, even though Jonah was a spiritual leader, he didn't board the ship to make believers. The storm changed their belief...not Jonah.

When you get a chance to lead...LEAD!

If your heart isn't in it, get it right or get out of the way!

Coach Lou Holtz believed, "Motivation is simple. You eliminate those that are not motivated!"

God's spin on that was to eliminate the options by allowing Jonah's *and* his excuses to get SWALLOWED!

When God gives revelation, He gives responsibility!

Whether you are President or the parent of five kids, you have responsibility for lives, not just making a living. Like Jonah you will be judged for what you speak into those lives.

Jesus said, "On the day of judgment people will give account for every careless word they speak" .3 Paul warned, "The day is coming when God, through Christ Jesus, will judge everyone's secret life".4

The only way God is fair is not to sentence people unless He's spoken to them. The Bible says God has made Himself known to every person on the planet in one of three ways: by intelligent design they see in His creation of nature; by awareness of the commandments given originally to the Jewish people; and, by a sense of right and wrong in their conscience.5 So nobody will be able to argue with God or make excuses for leaving Him out of their lives.6

Following surgery for a brain tumor, Amy was on life support—unresponsive. A friend contacted my church in Atlanta to pray. We begged God to save Amy. I raced to ICU. Doctors announced a 25% chance to survive and prepared to remove life support. I prayed for a miracle. By morning, Amy came to life! Later, I visited Amy and her live-in boyfriend, Jim, at home. Knowing God miraculously healed her, she wanted to get her life right. Jim grew up in gangs—a wild biker—no God and no fear! But he saw Amy's miracle and was shaken. When I asked if he would turn from his sin and accept the Jesus who healed her and died for him, he didn't hesitate! The change was radical— he told all his biker friends. I baptized them and they got married! Months later, Amy called, totally broken. Jim had just died in a freak biking accident. Bikers packed out his funeral. I opened the service: "Jim was a good guy." They acted like bikers—yelling and cheering! I continued, "And he's in heaven today!" They celebrated like NFL players in the endzone after a touchdown! But then it got real quiet when I said, "But he's not in heaven because he's good. It's because he turned from his sin and gave his life to Jesus!" I didn't know if I'd be attacked or adopted into a gang! After the graveside service, Jim's parents came over, "We want the Jesus that changed Jim."

God became real to Amy and Jim. They gladly became responsible for family and friends.

Nobody knew there was a deadline for Jim.

God gave Jonah the revelation for a city—the actual words that would save every family: "Go to Nineveh, that great city, and cry out against it; for their wickedness has come up before Me".7 Jonah became responsible.

What God plans for you to do, He prepares you to do.

God is not only faithful...He is fair.

Leaders don't run from fights.

Trusting God always comes at a cost. So does allowing resentment to take over. Resentment makes you run. There's risk in going forward with God but bigger risk in doing nothing.

Waiting on perfect conditions to obey? Won't happen.

Waiting to feel excited to move forward? Won't happen.

Waiting for someone to change? Won't happen.

Just follow-through with what God told you to do. He becomes responsible for the results. Why not trust God to protect you and prosper you?

Afraid? So is everybody. Go for it anyway.

Ambrose Redmoon said, "Courage is not the absence of fear, but rather the judgment that something else is more important than fear."

Jonah didn't want the fight. No desire to rescue the evil nation. Why take on more stress? Why sacrifice a career or die to debate a bunch of insane terrorists?

Turns out he was closer to dying in the sea than in Nineveh's suburbs.

Following God means *fighting for God*. A believer's life is total spiritual warfare. We exist to set people free with the truth which immediately puts us in tension with the culture. Challenging people with truth can be exhausting, uncomfortable and ugly. You have to love people as much as Jesus. Jonah didn't. It was too hard to love his enemies. Obeying what God has called you to do is hard...*but so was dying on a cross for Jesus.*

Jonah simply didn't want to be held accountable for what God expected him to do. People exit church for the same reason today. They want to feel something in worship and think they are part of something bigger. Which has nothing to do with following Jesus. But start talking commitment...and right and wrong...and the authority of God and His Word...AND you risk losing the crowd—just like Jonah. Jesus outed people who say they are committed but quit under pressure.[8] Fake commitment is still a trend.

If it was real, Jonah had to go public with his commitment to God and fight to save a city. Going to Nineveh meant Jonah could no longer be casual about the spiritual condition of people near him.

God set up the project to change Jonah, not just Nineveh.

To Jonah, the city wasn't worth saving.

Real leaders know what to fight for

Real leaders don't like losing. Injustice motivates them. Evil angers them. Unbelief challenges them. The status quo kills them.

People fight for what they value. Like the parents of a 5-year-old diagnosed with cancer who shut down their careers and go to St. Jude's to fight for their child's life.

Only dead fish float with the stream.

Leaders hunt elephants. They don't feed them!

Jonah's cruise was total denial.

He refused to deal with the biggest issue in his life.

Life is about your relationship with God. When that's not right, nothing is right. You know it. People around you sense it. The elephant is alive! Leaders don't *hint* about elephants in the room—they *hunt* elephants!

If a leader doesn't target the elephant, people fill in the blanks with their own beliefs and solutions—a sort of DIY *elephant removal* plan. That's what the crew did when the violent storm hit. Panicked by raw fear, the sailors started praying to their gods, threw the ship's cargo overboard to make the ship lighter, interrogated Jonah, prayed and offered a sacrifice to the Lord, made all kinds of promises, and kept rowing intensely.[9] Somewhere in that panic, Jonah was tossed overboard...and his still unresolved fight with God went with him.

When you haven't submitted to God on an issue, you are stuck until you get it right. It's humbling to admit there's an elephant in the room. It's hard to push them out. But it's really miserable if you choose to live with one. You can't really have a normal life while working around a noisy, messy, stinking elephant that drains your energy to care for and is exhausting to have to repeatedly explain.

Life's just easier when you deal with the big, gray thing that is really not invisible. Elephants are normally not low maintenance.

Success doesn't mean you are a good leader.

American church culture in my generation made growth an idol: *lots of followers equal success*. This golden calf is defended because, after all, aren't ministries supposed to reach as many people as possible? Once ministry leaders bow to the golden calf, it can create bondage to a new definition of success as: *more participants and a money pipeline*.

A new language emerged with exciting phrases like marketing, branding, social media presence, platforms, traffic, customer service, making connections, creating experiences, leveraging content, etc. In the new wave, to be successful with scaling the organization to the next level you had to copy corporate models, especially in defining leadership.

Microsoft founder and philanthropist, Bill Gates, said, "A leader is someone who empowers others." Leadership scholar Warren Bennis commented, "Leadership is the capacity to translate vision into reality." Author and motivational speaker John Maxwell gave a concise definition: "Leadership is influence."[10]

But biblically, there is no such thing as *secular* leadership and *spiritual* leadership. God doesn't separate your life into pieces like church, family, work, or recreation with different standards for each. There's just leadership, either done God's way or driven by culture and competition. We should be teaching biblical definitions of success and leadership.

Leadership is defined by influence and driven by integrity. A leader in ministry doesn't have to be constantly motivated. They pursue God because they want to see the gospel scaled, lives saved and God's name supreme.

A leader of spiritual integrity would have already been pleading with God to call and send someone to be a missionary to Assyria.

Jonah's resume wasn't worth the paper it was on.

Is yours?

Happiness is determined by what you love.

Your happiness in ministry is not about a better *location* or a better *life*. The flavor and fruitfulness of your ministry is determined by what you *love*.

People know if you love your wife and kids and work.

It's actually possible to love a lifestyle more than the Lord.

Love God and you won't be totally crushed when the stock market tanks, your friends are at Turks and Caicos Islands and you aren't, your buddy lands the big job or big church, or you and your wife can't have kids.

Happiness is not in stuff...it's in the Savior.

Love a Person and He's amazingly enough! Love possessions or perks and you'll never be happy. Because one day that season will be over—something big will swallow you and take it all.

What made you happy will swim away...

Jonah served God, but he didn't love God. Jesus said, "Those who accept my commandments and obey them are the ones who love me."[11] Whatever commitment Jonah had in Israel was not real. He was a drain on the spiritual energy of the people without knowing it, simply by pretending to be a leader...minus the commitment piece.

Just listen to what a leader talks about the most.

Or, think about what they aren't saying...

What you are in the secret things...is what you are.

Integrity is the currency of leadership.

Without it, you are bankrupt!

Your moral integrity determines your usefulness.

Jonah was called by God to speak out against the evil in the city of Nineveh.[12] There was zero interest on his part about standing against the evil. Jonah's heart was more corrupt that the Assyrians. Jonah's heart was filled with anger against God, he tried to deceive God, and wouldn't perform his job until all other options were off the table.

Your ability to lead is controlled by your character.

What you are in the small things is what you are.

What you are in the secret things is what you are.

The late pastor, Adrian Rogers, told the story of a rising young corporate manager who was being watched carefully by the leaders of the company. His promotion to vice-president was all but sealed until they saw him try to sneak an item through the company cafeteria line without paying for it. They knew if he would lie about something small, he would lie about other things. That decision was more than a weak moment. It revealed a character flaw that would eventually destroy his leadership and discredit the company.

Opportunity lost.

Jonah didn't deserve to lead God's Nineveh project because he lacked moral authority. No way can you call out someone else's sin if you are covering up your own! There is no credibility if you shout one value and live another.

Leadership means you do more, not less.

When God told Jonah to go to Nineveh, the bar was raised. God didn't give Jonah the option of cutting back. He demanded more of Jonah.

If you want to be successful, you have to take on *more risk, more responsibility*, and *more relationships*.

Leadership is discipleship. It's simply one function of discipleship. Discipleship equals living the life Jesus has mapped for you. It means choosing obedience but is always driven by the heart. In other words, you would do anything for the Savior you love. So when He asks you to be the first to speak up for what's right or get out front with the truth in a situation or challenge people in your community to do something they've never done, that's leadership.

Leadership is influence. It's your energy focused on influencing people to see and move with God's plan—to get them across their "Red Sea".

Leadership is accountability. It's taking on the God-task in front of you, stepping up and getting it done. In the process, others see you and the boldness of your commitment challenges them. They reason that if you got involved then it must be important. And people who follow-through on what God expects make a difference. God uses them.

Leadership is excellence. It's about giving your best even when asked by God to do something you don't like it or agree with.

Leadership is direction. It's a life-path that God designs. And He has already set the direction and rules.

Jonah was living off the *perks* in his role as prophet.

Should have been living *prepared*.

A leader's priority is not to cast vision, but define reality!

The biggest contribution a leader can make is not to cast a vision for people, but to capture reality...not your version, but the truth God shows you about your situation.

Once you define the reality of a situation as God sees it, then He reveals His plan. Vision comes together when God's perspective of the real need merges with God's plan to meet that need.

A lot of train wrecks in careers, especially ministry careers, have been caused by leaders defining vision as creating their plan and selling it to reach their goals. Willow Creek Global Leadership Summit founder and now disgraced accused former megachurch pastor, Bill Hybels, ironically once warned, "Vision leaks." He was right...and it ultimately came back to bite him as well.

Motivation dies.

People forget.

Mistakes happen.

Temptation swallows.

Distractions come.

Momentum stops...unless...you keep listening to God.

A call from God takes a lot of hits over time and has to be refreshed. Successful leaders are those who keep praying and keep listening to the voice of God.

That's why God called Jonah to intervene before Assyria launched the final wave of terrorism on Israel. The reality was that it was a terrorist nation gearing up to wipe Israel off the map. To be a successful leader in this moment of history, Jonah needed to act on that reality---to put the fear of God's judgment in their hearts. Evil was rising. That was reality.

Jonah would never have launched a vision to evangelize Assyria at that tense moment in his career, but God knew the potential tsunami of terrorism Assyria could unleash. Who knows? Jonah's vision might have been to start a fund-raising campaign to add another wing to the Temple while Assyria was planning a "9-11".

Jonah's vision for his ministry career was so self-centered he chose a cruise over moms and dads and children who were 40 days out from dying!

Jonah's vision was limited to his *preferences.*

God's reality was linked to a nation *perishing.*

Defining reality always has to precede casting vision. Jesus defined the reality of a wealthy young leader's spiritual emptiness when He asked the guy to do something hard. Jesus knew his wealth owned him, so he asked him to walk away from that lifestyle. Instead, that millennial with so much potential walked away from Jesus.[13]

Defining realty usually means facing yourself.

Defining reality usually means facing God.

Defining reality usually means facing change.

Defining reality usually means doing something hard.

Raising the bar separates the crowd.

You discover who really loves Jesus.

Maybe people and churches and organizations stop growing because we lower rather than raise the standards.

Most people don't want reality...they want reinforcement. They want somebody to tell them God is okay with their direction.

Sad truth? That may not be reality.

Integrity, not ability determines success.

Atlanta mega-church pastor, Andy Stanley, said, "God is not out looking for influential people he can make faithful. God is looking for faithful men and women whom he can elevate to positions of influence."[14]

Jonah was faking it. He was a famous prophet in Israel but didn't really believe the sacred scriptures. God's original covenant agreement with Israel's founding patriarch, Abraham, pivoted on their purpose to bless the nations.[15] Israel was miraculously birthed and mysteriously preserved through the millenniums—*neither Herod nor Hitler could eliminate them*—for a singular purpose—to make God's name known. Their existence and emergence in 1948 can only be explained by God's sovereign protection. Israel was always to be the nation that prophesied and produced the Messiah, and they will be prominent in the last days!

Calling the Assyrian nation to belief in Jehovah God was Jonah's big moment in that stream of salvation flowing from Israel. This was never about Jonah being chosen because he was the best communicator of his generation but because he was the most corrupt in his beliefs—and that trend had to be shut down! Jonah's hatred of the Assyrians meant he vetoed God's original purpose for Israel and the nations.

Jonah lived to save a career not fulfill a call.

Integrity is the sole key to success.

Integrity is more than the right standards or character. Integrity is keeping your life aligned with the purpose of God. Simply, it is staying faithful to God.

Huge talent, global fame, influential connections, or massive wealth does not equal success. Success is staying true to what God wants you to do—just uninterrupted faithfulness!

You are only as strong as the last time you worshiped.

Jonah was positioned wrong. Getting swallowed by the huge fish was totally predictable. You could see it coming.

Worship was shut down to walk away. Jonah didn't pray about whether God wanted him on that ship because he knew God didn't. He didn't praise God because He was protesting God by getting on that ship.

That's the way it always happens. When people stop praying it's because they have started partying. When they stop participating it's because they've started planning escape. When they stop displaying passion it's because they've started compromising purity.

You are only as strong as your last prayer or principled choice to resist sin. You stayed pure last week? Great. Outside of the fact that choosing right last week made you a little smarter and stronger spiritually...it was *last week*!

Now you've got to do it all over again or the world wins!

The battle never stops. The bruises always hurt.

Hate the things God hates. Love what God loves...or you will feel self-righteous and find an "Assyrian-free" ship!

God does judge lifestyles. Jonah was right. The Assyrians were evil: *"Get up and go to the great city of Nineveh. Announce my judgment against it because I have seen how wicked its people are"*.[16]

But God was judging *two* lifestyles—the Assyrians *and* Jonah! Calling out Nineveh *and* Jonah was proof that God's love has limits on the resistance He will tolerate. Judgment was only 40 days away unless the terrorists got the message to repent. But judgment on Jonah was only 1 day away—the time needed for a storm to form, and a fish to follow.

Because God is loving, His primary motive is to save us from choices that can destroy us. The longer you stay in a destructive lifestyle the more right it feels and the harder it is to break away. Minutes away from the total fiery annihilation of Sodom and Gomorrah, Lot was still hesitating to take his family and get out.[17] A lifestyle of unrestrained sex will result in God abandoning those persons to their death wish.[18]

Ultimately, God's judgment in the end times of being thrown into the Lake of Fire will fall upon eight specific lifestyles that include unbelief and liars![19]

Moral authority is the espresso in leadership.

Espresso is coffee brewed by *expressing* or forcing a small amount of nearly boiling water under pressure through finely ground coffee beans to create a bold but not bitter flavor with *crema* (creamy foam). It makes coffee bold!

Moral authority makes leaders bold! It validates your leadership but it also energizes your leadership. Compromise your values and you lose your ability to lead.

You can't lead from behind.

You can't lead where you aren't already willing to go.

You can't expect others to do what you avoid.

"Leadership is not, "Hey, you go do this thing for me,'" asserts Digital Press founder, Nicholas Cole. Aligning with my views on the power of integrity in leadership, he believes leaders specifically have to follow the rules, keep their word, admit when wrong, keep promises, stay out of the spotlight, take criticism, and stay open-minded.[20]

Having counseled thousands of family members during my ministry career, the number one reason for teenage rebellion coming out of those conversations is *anger*! It's real and the kids are right! Not just the leftover anger from divorce or debt, but daily *moral anger*. They wonder why they can't drink if dad drinks, why they can't have sex if dad watches porn, or why they have to go to school if dad lies to his boss about taking a sick day. Kids know their parents aren't perfect, they just want them to be honest, not hypocritical—consistent, not condemning. They know right from wrong, but desperately want the security of parents leading right. God's original answer to teenage anger targets dads not kids: *"Fathers, do not provoke your children to anger by the way you treat them. Rather, bring them up with the discipline and instruction that comes from the Lord".*[21] If dad starts living consistently, the kids will want to honor him and hang out with him!

Jonah was inconsistent. He had no moral authority.

Jonah chose to run, and risk being swallowed so he wouldn't have to tell others to obey he wasn't obeying.

You can't tell people to repent and hang on to your sin.

Where is the moral authority in our culture's leadership?

What do non-believers—like the crew on the ship with Jonah—believe about *your God* as a result of your decisions?

Quitting is normally not the result of career confusion.

Jonah didn't temporarily bail on God and the Nineveh project because he was doubting his call as a prophet or didn't feel like the role fit. Jonah knew his life and career belonged to God. Actually, that was the source of the tension. Jonah boarded the ship to escape God's legit purpose for his life at that critical crossroads of history.

People don't quit because the *role* doesn't fit.

They usually quit because the *responsibility* doesn't fit.

LifeWay reports trendy statistics that say 1,700 pastors per month are burned out, hurting, and quitting the ministry are "unsubstantiated and...exaggerated". Only about 1% quit.

Pastors aren't quitters. That's awesome! Ministry is tough: 84% feel on call 24/7, 80% expect conflict, 54% say the role is overwhelming, and 21% say churches have unrealistic expectations. But ministers are a tough tribe![22]

People do quit when they get angry or overwhelmed.

Jonah was a whiner. Pastors can be whiners.

At the risk of sounding like pastors are being targeted...welcome to the real world! Every day, people in the corporate world get fired, transferred, cheated, lied to, and told they are expected to perform better than yesterday. People in the military sacrifice in ways American pastors will never face.

Want to survive? Expect to sacrifice.

The real threat to your future is entitlement.

JoJo5000 posted, "I know someone who bought a condo without realizing that it was very near a train track. Entitled person was outraged and called a major rail freight company and asked them to stop running trains at night. **Spoiler: it didn't work."**

Eric Geiger blogged, "Leadership is most dangerous when it ceases to be humbling....So how can leaders recognize our drift from humility to pride? Look for entitlement. Entitlement always rises as pride rises. It is impossible to be filled with humility and a sense of entitlement at the same time. Whenever we feel we are owed something, it is because we have forgotten that God is the One who gives all good things. Leaders, especially in seasons of success, can develop a sense of entitlement."[23]

Entitlement is *pure* pride. Like 100% pure Vermont maple syrup.

Google "entitlement" and an image of Jonah pops up first in the search. Well, probably not, but he felt God owed him an exemption from the controversial Nineveh project with his *we-are-the-chosen-people* arrogance and the whole *prophets-are-special* attitude.

When you drift into pride, decisions are made on the basis of what's best to preserve your lifestyle. That entitlement mentality shifted Jonah away from compassion and toward condemnation. It was the original *identity politics*. Jonah saw winners and losers. Entitlement means you are no longer serving something bigger than yourself. Life shifts to getting what you think you deserve and giving people what you think they deserve.

Samson was given a gift of supernatural strength to defend his nation.[24] After years of legendary feats for God and country—*ripping apart a lion with your bare hands qualifies here*—he felt entitled to enjoy drinking parties and a prostitute, and give up God's secret to his strength.[25] He lost his ministry *and* his life.

After surviving death threats from King Saul, ascension to Israel's throne, and winning multiple military victories, King David felt entitled to commit adultery and simply took

Bathsheba, the wife of one of his nation's military heroes.[26] The consequences? The baby from that night of pleasure died despite David's 7 days of prayer, *plus* chaos, rape, murder and shame ruled his family from that moment forward.[27]

Entitlement always leads to ignoring God's boundaries.

Ignoring God's boundaries always leads to indulging in sin.

Indulging in sin always leads to getting **SWALLOWED**.

God doesn't want you to be comfortable with sin.

Living by convictions, not preferences, brings prosperity.

FOX News reported recently that 70% of American families are one paycheck away from crisis. Many families are also living one bad decision away from crisis.

What are your non-negotiable values? What beliefs are so important to you that you will not surrender them under any circumstances?

A preference is a *flexible* belief. Under pressure, you will give it up for something more important to you in the moment. It's more about convenience. With a preference, you *favor* a position, but you don't *fight* for it in every situation. I prefer pizza for every meal, but won't fight for that when my wife says, "Let's go to The Cheesecake Factory!" I'd rather be married than happy.

A conviction is a *fixed* belief. If President Trump offered you a cabinet position or Jimmy Fallon booked you for the *Tonight Show*, you would have no intention of changing what you believe or compromising because it's a core heart issue—it's who you are. It's more about commitment. You will *fight* over it.

Attorney David C. Gibbs, Jr. said, "Convictions will always show up in a person's lifestyle."[28]

If you live by preferences, you'll eventually do things you know are not right and thought you'd never do. If you live by convictions, you will follow-through with your beliefs. A lifestyle dependent on preferences may temporarily make you popular but will bring *regret*. A lifestyle driven by convictions may temporarily make you unpopular but will bring you *results*.

Daniel lived by convictions, not preferences, and got results! When Daniel was captive in Babylon, forced to serve the King, he drew a line when expected to compromise his Jewish religious beliefs: *"Daniel purposed in his heart that he would not defile himself with the portion of the king's delicacies, nor with the wine".*[29] God gave him favor with his immediate supervisor and the King changed his menu! So, no surprise when a law was passed by Daniel's enemies prohibiting prayer, Daniel continued praying 3x per day even though it got him tossed into the lion's den. Daniel survived the night with lions because he "believed God",[30] prompting King Darius to issue an executive order proclaiming to the nation that God ruled!

Jonah lived by preferences, not convictions. That's how he could be okay with boarding a ship to run from God and sleeping through a storm that threatened to kill the ship's crew. He preferred not to care about people different from him or get involved to save lives.

So much for preferences. Jonah got swallowed and spit out where he still had to do what God originally told him to do.

Daniel got results. Jonah got consequences.

Trendy Belief No. 12:
It takes a long time to get past failure.

If a book about failures doesn't sell, is it a success?
—Jerry Seinfeld, Comedian

It is the ability to...use failure that often leads to greater success.
**—J. K. Rowling, Author of the Harry Potter series whose 1st book
was rejected 12 times**

Successful people keep moving. They make mistakes, but they never quit.
—John Willard Marriott, Founder of Marriott Hotels

*Then the sailors picked Jonah up and threw him into the raging sea,
and the storm stopped at once! The sailors were awestruck by the Lord's
great power, and they offered Him a sacrifice and vowed to serve him. Now the
Lord had arranged for a great fish to swallow Jonah....Then Jonah prayed to the
Lord his God from inside the fish. He said, "I cried out to the Lord in my great
trouble, and he answered me. I called to you from the land of the dead,
and Lord, you heard me!*
—Jonah 1:15-2:2, NLT

Recovery is underrated. People spend more time *talking about failure* than *taking on recovery*. A *Pepsi* truck driver was called in to see the boss and got bad news: "You're fired, Bubba. You've tested positive for *Coke*!" Breaking the rules gets more media than keeping them.

Recovery is actually the point.

Realizing failure is easy. Moving past failure is trickier.

But bad stuff can turnaround faster than expected.

Bouncing back is God's specialty—it's what He does.

In his book, *Adapt: Why Success Always Starts With Failure*, economist Tim Harford says "Few of our own failures are fatal. Success comes through rapidly fixing our mistakes."[1]

Like Adam and Eve, people don't normally die immediately after a single sin. Nor does an NFL quarterback throwing an interception result in him being benched or traded to another team. Delayed consequences are probably the biggest reason people aren't scared to repeat a sin.

Failure creates a learning opportunity. It doesn't have to define your life from that point forward. Things can change. Question is, how do you change and how quick can it happen?

Bad choices can happen quickly. Bad consequences can unfold slowly. Voting against God is always wrong *and* risky—Jonah got swallowed and nearly died. You fail yourself, God, and others on some level all the time. What happens *after* you've run from God and been swallowed by the consequences is the bigger deal.

Hurricane Florence hit the beaches in my state of South Carolina on 9-14-18 with 100mph wind gusts, dropping up to 39" of rain in places, and creating a Cat 1 storm surge of 11' waves. Scary power. Millions evacuated from the coast. Lives disrupted, including me and my friends. Hundreds of millions in damage. The tropical storm hit land and moved through the state in 4 days!

Sins hits quickly with huge force and is over.

Recovery takes longer, *but*...you can put failure in the rearview mirror quicker than you think. Let's break it down.

God deals with the source, not the symptom.

First, review the bizarre sequence of events, because you're not tracking a storm, you're tracking God's methods:

- ✓ *God sends a violent storm against Jonah's ship (1:4)*
- ✓ *Fearing death, crew shouts to their gods (1:5)*
- ✓ *In desperation, crew throws cargo overboard (1:5)*
- ✓ *Jonah remains asleep below deck (1:5)*
- ✓ *Captain demands Jonah pray to his god (1:6)*
- ✓ *Crew casts lots and identify Jonah as cause of storm (1:7)*
- ✓ *Jonah admits to running from God (1:10)*
- ✓ *Jonah tells crew to throw him overboard (1:12)*
- ✓ *Crew decides to row harder to reach land (1:13)*
- ✓ *With sea too violent, they asked God to forgive (1:14)*
- ✓ *Crew throws Jonah overboard and storm stops (1:15)*
- ✓ *Crew amazed at God's power and worships (1:16)*

Jonah's anger at God was so extreme that God couldn't overlook it. But the anger was so well hidden in Jonah's heart that he wouldn't own it until he was out of options.

So God arranged the storm and the "shark" adventure. Nothing short of the craziest survival story in nautical history would expose Jonah's heart attitude.

Think about it. Worst storm ever hits! The crew thinks they'll die. They row like crazy and nothing changes! Actually, things did change—it got *worse*!

Author Seth Godin advised, "When a project appears to be in...a permanent holding pattern...where no one can figure out what to do...Cancel it. Cancel it with a week's notice. One of two things will happen: A. A surge of support and innovation will arrive, and it won't be stuck anymore. B. You'll follow through and cancel it, and you won't be stuck anymore. It costs focus and momentum to carry around the stalled. Let it go."[2]

Well, the crew cancelled that stalled cruise! They stopped fighting the symptom (storm), and found the source (Jonah), and *let him go*!

When your marriage is stalled...look for the source, not at your spouse. When your ministry feels like rowing in a storm...look for the source, not at your skill. When your momentum with the team is lost...look for the source, not at the score. When your motivation to love your teenager is low...look for the source, not at your son. When your mindset to pray has died because you have prayed and prayed and prayed...and your child hasn't been healed...look for the source, not at the sorrow.

Don't *fear* the storm. Don't *fight* the storm.

Don't keep trying to *fake* it in the storm, pretending you know what you're doing and have it all under control.

Follow the storm. God will expose the source.

The source was Jonah's hidden rebellion.

The source is *always* a heart at war with God.

Recovery isn't miraculous...it's predictable.

Just like the crew going after Jonah below deck, God drills deeper! To save Jonah, God set-up a predictable path to recovery. Think of it this way. Trendy belief says just *confess and change*. Simple. No, that's simplistic. Confession isn't the starting point and confession alone isn't enough to reverse failure. It's tempting to bypass some, but here's God's stages:

➢ **Before recovery, there must be repentance.**
God wants you to reject what you have done.
➢ **Before repentance, there must be confession.**
God wants you to be responsible for what you've done.
➢ **Before confession, there must be conviction.**
God wants you to regret what you've done.
➢ **Before conviction...there must be exposure!**
God wants you to realize what you've done.

Until a person, church, group, team, or business deals with the core dysfunctional attitude, you're going to be stuck rowing in the storm!

Exposure of sin is God's starting point. Not confession.

Or if you are in the corporate world...exposure of the *shortcut* in quality is the starting point.

Until Nathan the prophet publicly called out King David's well-kept secret of adultery with Bathsheba and murder of her husband, David was haunted 24/7 by guilt but hadn't confessed.[3] Exposure preceded his confession! Having sin uncovered or discovered doesn't guarantee conviction, confession, repentance, or recovery. But unless sin is made public, the rest *can't* happen!

Somebody at your company busted? A family member caught doing wrong? The teammate breaking rules? Don't panic. It's just God. God exposes sin to start the baby steps to recovery. The sin we *cover*, He *uncovers*. And the sin we *uncover* (confession), He *covers* (forgiveness).

God always targets the source, not the symptom. That meant using the storm to expose Jonah's rebellion to the crew. Jesus could have calmed the storm hours before He walked on the water to reach the panicked disciples on the Sea of Galilee. But He waited until they wanted Him in the boat before He ended the storm because they were holding back on belief.[4] God always targets the source—what's out of sync in the heart—things that you might not even realize.

Isn't it interesting that God used a secular method—casting lots to non-existent gods—by a pagan crew to surface and shame a believer to face God? God doesn't care if you get embarrassed or enraged, lose friends or finances, or suffer health or harassment issues if it ultimately turns you around. It took the storm *plus* the fish to save Jonah and Nineveh.

That's what motivates God—saving people! Want to understand what God is doing? Just look for whatever it takes to save people and you'll find Him driving it! Think a storm and swallowing is extreme? *There was . . .*

Something bigger at stake: *souls.*

Something worse than the crew finding out: *fighting God!*

Something worse than to get swallowed: *God leaving you!*

The speed of recovery is more important than sincerity.

Dan Duvall tweet: "My autobiography would just be a really long Taco Bell receipt." Rex Huppke tweet: "Nothing more American than getting on an airport's 'moving walkway' and standing still as it slowly carries you to a Cinnabon."

Activity doesn't equal change. *Sincerity* doesn't either!

Starting up new *commitments* after failure can be done quickly. But like rebuilding after a hurricane, working through the *consequences* of failure is slow.

Once you've tried to run from God, getting back to normal isn't a vacation. Rebuilding relationships takes time. Restoring trust is challenging. Rekindling passion for God requires tough choices. Restarting prayer and bible study demands daily energy and accountability.

But just because you've got a mess to clean up is not an excuse to slow down restoring your intimacy with God.

It's not just that you can work through failure fast and move on...*you have to!*

God's not impressed with sincerity if you are stalled! Movement toward the goal is a win. God wanted Jonah off the ship and in the city speaking in 3 days! The fastest way to make that happen with a compliant attitude was getting Jonah swallowed and spit out at the original destination.

Jonah's recovery was fast! Not perfect. Not pure. Just prompt. When seaweed wrapped around his head in the fish belly and he thought he was going to die, he started praying and making fresh commitments!

Confess and repent. That kicks off the recovery obstacle course. Recovery needs to start *asap*.

Making moving past failure complicated or equating being super cautious with being more spiritual are huge mistakes. 1 John 1:9 says if you confess your sins, forgiveness and cleansing is immediate. Call your specific sin what the bible labels it (e.g., porn is lust, not entertainment), admit that you have minimized the blood sacrifice of Jesus,[5] receive the forgiveness God promises...and move on!

There's nothing in scripture that says you have to agonize for months with conviction, confession, and repentance to come out of failure right. When God exposes your sin, repent quickly. Hesitating gets you stuck spiritually. The ship starts looking comfortable. The idol-worshipping crew becomes your buddies. And you think you can survive storms. The longer you live in Sodom, the harder it is to leave.[6]

Jesus started His ministry with one word, "Repent!".[7] Why not start whatever you lead with one word that sums up "turnaround"? And He expected immediate turnaround! Jesus also warned that if the Church at Ephesus did not repent quickly and recover their love for Him He would shut it down![8] Repentance is not complicated—tell God you're sorry and step away from the sin!

When you do that, you have technically and biblically "moved past the failure" quickly and have started the hard process of recovery—restoring an uninterrupted love for God.

How do you know you're recovering? Not when you think you don't sin anymore. That'll never happen. It's when God says, "Go to Nineveh" *(represents the hardest thing God could ever ask of you)* and you jump on the first ship...*for Nineveh!*

You can't exalt God and enjoy sin at the same time.

Jonah couldn't be on the ship and in Nineveh at the same time. You can't simultaneously be comfortable with sin and be connected to God's will. You can't simultaneously worship God and walk in sin: *"the flesh lusts against the Spirit, and the Spirit against the flesh"*.[9] Don't argue with God that you can participate in sin and be equally passionate about worship. Worship begins when sin ends.

When Jonah boarded the ship, he quit worshiping and didn't restart it until inside the fish belly! No matter how focused or spiritual you think you are, the heart only allows one passion at a time: *"friendship with the world makes you an enemy of God"*.[10] Even NFL QB Tom Brady can't play for two competing teams simultaneously!

Surrendering your life to Christ doesn't make you perfect. Jesus just starts the salvation process inside you by slowly changing your thinking, your character and your desires. You can...*and will*...still sin but you will never enjoy it again. The Holy Spirit in you will make you aware when you are about to do something wrong *and* make you miserable after you've done it. Nobody who belongs to Jesus can worship God and party at the same time.

God hates sin. He knows where it can take you.

He knows where it took Jesus...to the cross.

The goal is progress, not perfection!

JUST START! The secret of getting started is...*getting started*! The one thing Jonah did right in this whole crazy 4-day fight with God was to start praying again (Jonah 2:1). So what if it took a near-death experience? Better to come to God after big sin than to curse at God after a big sin.

Citizen Way sings:

> *These are the things that I need to pray*
> *Because I can't find peace any other way.*
> *I'm a mess underneath and*
> *I'm just too scared to show it.*
> *Everything's not fine, And I'm not okay*
> *But it's nice to know, I can come this way.*
> *When I'm with you*
> *I feel the real me finally breaking through*
> *It's all because of you, Jesus.*
> *Anytime, anywhere, any heartache*
> *I'm never too much for you to take.*
> *There's only love, There's only grace*
> *When I'm with you.*
> *Nobody knows me like you do.*
> *No need for walls, you see right through*
> *Every hurt, every scar, every secret you just love me.*

And where did the comeback start? In the fish belly!

The best time to pray and come back to God? When you are messed up, can't find peace, and in the wrong place! It's not like Jesus is going to be shocked by your sin! He already knows every sin, scar, and secret...and still loves you!

Big mistake to think you have to wait until you are in a better place, life is great, you've got things under control, or you *feel* like you can make it before you try to get you're your failure...*you'll stay swallowed!*

If you are not going after your God-given purpose now...then when?

By the time Jonah delivers God's judgment message in Nineveh and plops down on the mountainside with suicidal rants, it's obvious he still had mega unresolved anger. Not acceptable. That's why God kept the heat index up and kept mercilessly cross-examining Jonah with life and death questions.[11]

Jonah's bitterness against God was out of bounds. But so is postponing repentance. Getting past failure asap is not going to be as clean as a Chick-fil-A commercial or predictable as a Hallmark movie. If you wait until you feel good about yourself and God, or have all your attitudes and addictions worked out, nothing changes! Why? Because you don't clean up to come back to God. You can't do it by yourself. Come back and God will get you cleaned up! Working through anger is never fun but God is faithful to work through it with you.

Lots of people are drowning *spiritually* because they won't come to God *for* answers or *with* their anger!!! The fake trendy belief in our culture that kills momentum and success is that nothing can be started unless everything is perfect—you can't go forward if you're still upset about what's happening or still have big questions about God and life.

So Apple would never launch another iPhone?

So couples would never adopt?

What are you waiting on?

You'll either get stronger or swallowed.

Do something every day that scares you!

"It is impossible to please God without faith".[12]

It doesn't take a crisis to break a real leader's heart.

When Jonah thought he was going to die inside that huge fish's belly, he flipped. Suddenly, talking to God was a priority.[13] His worship moment was weird, shifting from blaming God for the whole incident to bragging that God saved him because he was special—*not* an idol-worshiper.[14] It was a *I-messed-up-but-I'm-still-better-than-those-sinners* kind of twisted confession. So, while Jonah was still wrapped in seaweed and floating in gastric juice, he agreed to go to Nineveh.[15] Who wouldn't?

Jonah finally followed-through on God's original project by promising to go to Nineveh, but only to get out of the fish belly. Ultimately, he admitted what God knew from the start—Jonah would rather die than forgive a terrorist.[16]

If it takes a crisis to force a leader to do what's right, then there's a hard heart. There's some anger issues that are still live. And that person is not prepared or qualified to be leading in a key role until they get it right.

When a leader's heart is right, he or she is proactive. Not even God has to motivate them to respond to needs. If 120,000 people are going to die without God[17] and it doesn't bother you—it doesn't take over your conversations and prayers and schedule, and in fact, you see them as an inconvenience—then you've got a bigger problem...God!

What did it take to get you moving the last time God spoke?

If God had to wreck your life or it took you more than a few seconds to decide to move...you may not be a leader.

You are a role model whether you like it or not.

Scores of students lined up on the basketball court at Bourbonnais Elementary School in Illinois to have their yearbooks signed by Mr. Steve...*the custodian!* Parents were moved to tears. He's their hero and a really good role model. You'll never know how many people watch your life.

There was a line for Jonah—the crew lined up to throw him overboard when they learned he was running from God.[19] The fact that Jonah could sleep below deck during a violent storm that threatened to bust the ship into pieces revealed he didn't care about his influence. Jonah had an opportunity to move the ship's crew toward belief in God, but he had already opted out of that pressure by hiding on this cruise.

The crew specifically called him out for "not praying",[20] so they knew he was totally not serious about whatever god he believed in. Jonah was a role model...a really bad one! You can't control who agrees with your beliefs, but you can control your example of believing.

Jonah was attacked by the crew for denying his beliefs![21] The crew knew he was fake! People may not agree with your beliefs, but they need to know you will die for your God before they will listen.

Faking being spiritual is exhausting. It never works. It's like trying to remember which lie you told to what person. Your life becomes a joke, not credible to believers or non-believers. Yet not even Jonah's sin could shut out God! The whole crew started believing when they quit looking at a backslidden leader and saw God's power shut down a storm!

You have an image...*and* you make an impression.

You are accountable for every life you influence!

Jonah really didn't care who believed. Running from an opportunity to save thousands of souls may be interpreted as not even believing there is a hell or believing some people don't deserve to go to heaven!

Christ-followers are expected to be intentional witnesses for Him.[22] But many have bought in to the fake trendy belief that believers are supposed to be tolerant and compassionate and non-threatening. Translation? Never offend anybody, wait until someone asks, and don't ever try to persuade! So when faith is discussed there's no sense of urgency or eternity at risk—if someone wants to believe, great! The Bible teaches believers to initiate conversations and persuade people.[23]

You don't have the option of saying, "It's my life and I can live it any way I want!" Your choices—including your sins, mistakes, and failures—influence lots of people. Nobody makes choices on an island. God created your life for a purpose. You can try to throw it away on a ship, but God knows where you are on the ship, why you're there, and whose lives are influenced by your choice to quit.

Believers will actually be held accountable at judgment for people they misled by their example and turned away from belief in Christ: *"We must all appear before the judgment seat of Christ, that each one may receive the things done in the body, according to what he has done, whether good or bad. Knowing, therefore, the terror of the Lord, we persuade men".*[24]

Jonah's life didn't belong to him. Neither does yours.

One person makes a difference!

London, 1938. A 29-year-old stockbroker, the son of German-Jewish immigrants, was enjoying the good life but war was on the horizon. Nicholas Winton was following the rise of Hitler and the Nazis. Hitler's troops had just marched into Czechoslovakia creating the war's first refugee crisis. A friend challenged Winton to cancel his ski trip vacation, join him in Prague, and see the refugee crisis in person. Deeply moved but without any political experience, Winton boldly set up an organization to transport children to England on trains. He recruited workers, met with desperate parents, and created lists of children. Back in London, he set up a fake organization, put his mother to work running a small office, and began negotiations with the British government for permission to bring unaccompanied minors into England. Meanwhile, he searched for families to take them in. He raised money, paid bribes, procured transit papers and, when necessary, forged documents. Winton was unapologetic, saying simply, "It worked." On March 14, 1939, the first train carrying 20 children left Prague. Neither the children nor their parents knew this was likely the last time they would ever see each other. Six more trains left between March and August 1939. An eighth train, carrying 250 children, was scheduled to leave on September 1, 1939, but that day Germany bombed Warsaw, beginning WWII. Borders were closed and transportation halted. Train No. 8 never left. No one knows for sure what happened to the 250 children who were already in their seats that day. They and their families are presumed to have died in the Holocaust. The war ended Winton's efforts to save children, but 669 children were saved![25]

Winton had only a few months to do something to save lives. He did everything he could, and generations of families are forever thankful.

The power of one life is amazing. One person's voice can start a movement. One person's love can start a ministry. *But...*one person's failure can stall momentum.

Jonah was unknown and insignificant to the ship's crew until the tropical storm hit and his failure went public. He put innocent lives at risk and nearly sunk not only the ship but the Nineveh mission.

Which ONE are you?

Worship can happen in any situation...even failure.

Comedian: *"I tried Weight Watchers one day. Ran out of points at 9am."*

Who can't relate to that failure? Started it. Sank with it. Jonah failed God at multiple points but when he looked like sushi with seaweed wrapped around his head and had the sensation of drowning in the fish's belly, worship returned! it was weak and shaky at points, but Jonah wrapped up his third night in the fish's belly with praise.

Right before getting spit out on the beach he seemed broken: *"Those who worship false gods turn their backs on all God's mercies. But I will offer sacrifices to you with songs of praise, and I will fulfill all my vows. For my salvation comes from the Lord alone".*[26] But he didn't mean it. As soon as Jonah saw the whole population of Nineveh repent and God cancel the judgment, his anger at God resurfaced.[27]

This side of heaven, we'll never get worship perfect. Why? Because, even when redeemed, our understanding is limited—unable to fully appreciate the mystery and majesty of the holy God. Under the consequences of sin, we tend to think life is unfair and God is unloving. So our worship is not all that pure on our best days. But God still wants our praise, even if it's sloppy and selfish and from a fish belly.

God expects worship. God kept Jonah *in the fish* until his prayer changed. Want to know why worship is boring or pronounced DOA in some churches on Sundays?

Because people are not yet tired of being in their fish belly experience. So they come to church with their sin—*unconfessed...intact...protected.* Worship will never block sin, but sin can block worship. Pastor Adrian Rogers taught, *"We don't come to church to worship. We bring our worship to church!"* If they ain't worshiping outside, they won't be worshiping inside.

Tired of being in a fish's belly? Want the discipline and trials to end? Repent and start worshiping again. You can be soaked in fish vomit and lying on a sandy beach, but that still isn't enough until you have spoken and served where God originally intended.

Then God will be awesome to you again.

Then you've moved past failure.

Where are you *right now*?

Are you on a boat...in a fish belly...on a beach...walking down Nineveh streets...or sitting on a desert mountainside?

LOCATION. LOCATION. LOCATION.

Trendy Belief No. 13:
Keep believing and the breakthrough will come!

Never give up. Miracles happen every day.
—**Zig Ziglar, Motivational Author**

If you need a miracle, be a miracle.
—**Dr. Phil, TV Psychologist**

No one has ever drowned in sweat.
—**Lou Holtz, Famous College Football Coach**

Progress is the key to happiness.
—**Tony Robbins, Life Coach**

Disappointment is inevitable. But to become discouraged...there's a choice I make. God would never discourage me. He would always point me...
to trust in Him.
—**Charles Stanley, Pastor and Author**

Then Jonah prayed to the Lord his God from the fish's belly...So the Lord spoke to the fish, and it vomited Jonah onto dry land.
—**Jonah 2:1, 10, NKJV**

You don't have a clue what you really need. The sooner you get your *real need*, the sooner things change. "Pastor, I need you to pray for my hearing," begged Bubba. The pastor put his hands over Bubba's ears and prayed for God to heal him. When he was done, he asked, "How's your hearing?" "I don't know," said Bubba. "It isn't until next Tuesday." Regardless of whether you're talking about a company...a church...a child...or a college, if the focus is totally on *gotta-have-a-breakthrough,* then you can miss what's most important AND the breakthrough!

A breakthrough means you have moved past a big challenge. It's a sudden, dramatic change in your situation—something that you've waited for and prayed to happen.

At some point, we all face something bigger than us—something we can't get out of or overcome on our own. Plans and perseverance get stretched to the breaking point and the doubts about surviving kick in. Everybody has trials and temptations, so don't give up!

Everybody needs hope.

Jonah got hope...but he didn't deserve it or appreciate it.

He got a breakthrough...but God got to pick it.

God deploys fish, so He gets to define "breakthrough"!

Jonah was in the fish's belly solely because God deployed the huge fish to swallow and ship him to Nineveh. Jonah was out of the will of God and got jerked back. Two definitions of "breakthrough" were competing here *(or "miracle" if you prefer that language)*.

All Jonah wanted was to *survive*.

All God wanted was to *save*.

For Jonah, the breakthrough was to survive the swallowing and do a career startover back home. God's definition of miracle breakthrough was Jonah with a broken heart for the people farthest from God. That didn't happen, but there was a breakthrough. After Jonah restarted worship in the fish belly, God relocated him to Nineveh.

Jonah lived. Nineveh lived.

And that's what made him so angry—*wrong miracle!*

When people are desperate, their definition of *miracle* gets sucked downstream and wrapped around their biggest dream or biggest fear in the moment—like being offered an amazing job, approved for financing the dream home, given a cancer-free report, picked for the team, or told you'll have twins.

All good stuff. God answers prayer.

Nothing wrong with believing real promises from Philippians 4:19 like *"God shall supply all your needs"* (NKJV). A God of grace wants to bless and prosper you.

But a miracle...*a breakthrough*...has to line up with God's purpose. Compared to a believer's life surviving persecution in the 10/40 window, some prayers for a breakthrough start to look selfish—*no eternal purpose.*

Like Jonah asking for a bailout...for him, not Nineveh.

Sunday afternoon in El-Arish (a small city on Egypt's Mediterranean coast). After worship, Baghat, a Christian veterinarian, goes to help a Muslim friend. According to his 17-yr-old son, Marqos, two young masked men enter the pharmacy, drag his father outside, tell him to kneel in the street, point two guns at his head, and demand he convert to Islam. But he shakes his head, refusing to deny Jesus. Then they shoot him. Marqos said, "I was proud of my father, for standing by his faith until the last moment. It made me curious. When my father was still alive, he woke up every morning at 5am to study the Bible and pray. Apparently, that helped him become a strong believer. My father's death for Christ has made me search for Jesus."[1]

Guess what kind of a breakthrough the first Christians prayed for under persecution by Jewish government in Jerusalem? Not for escape, but *boldness!* They became more *vocal*, not *victims*![2]

Your biggest need is not a breakthrough. It's brokenness.

Jonah was further from God than the terrorist Assyrians.

A storm...a swallowing...and a sermon didn't change him.

If you are in a fish belly with zero hope, nobody to blame but you and a crazy plan to run from God, and the worst-case scenario is unfolding—drowning—your *miracle* is getting out alive! Jonah thought he was dying—swallowed by a fish, pushed under by tons of water in huge rushing waves, weeds wrapping around his head, fighting to breathe, in the total darkness of a fish stomach, lungs collapsing as the fish plunges to radical depth. *And yet*...all he could think about was crying out to God to save him! Scared but not broken...

Contemporary Christian artist, Natalie Grant, describes brokenness in her song, "More Than Anything":

I know if You wanted to You could wave Your hand
Spare me this heartache and change Your plan
And I know when he said You could take my pain away...but even if You don't I pray
You know more than anyone that my flesh is weak
And You know I'd give anything for a remedy
And I'll ask a thousand more times to set me free today...but even if You don't I pray
Help me want the Healer more than the healing
Help me want the Savior more than the saving
Help me want the Giver more than the giving
Oh Help me want you Jesus more than anything
When I'm desperate and my heart's overcome
all that I need You've already done
Oh Jesus Help me want You more than anything

Brokenness means all the resistance and resentment is gone. You're done fighting God. And it goes a step further—releasing your trust to God's purpose in total abandonment.

Our culture abandons people when they become broken. God can't use you *until* you are broken. You're surrounded by people with broken lives from destructive choices. Brokenness is moving away from the disaster and moving toward God. Pride is crushed. You're wrecked over your sin against God: *"The sacrifices of God are a broken spirit...and contrite heart"*.[3]

You know you're broken when...

You want the Healer more than the healing.

Believing is good but doesn't guarantee a breakthrough.

A leading American pastor said, "It's our faith that activates the power of God."

Jesus was impressed by "great faith" only two times in His ministry—by a Roman centurion whose servant was dying and a by Gentile mother whose daughter was demon-possessed.[4] In both cases, it was not statistically or emotionally "more faith" than anybody else Jesus met, but *settled faith* as proved by their perseverance and confidence Jesus could heal from a distance.

Jesus actually called people out multiple times for "little faith"—when His disciples were caught in a storm, when Peter walked on water but began to sink, and when the disciples had to food to feed the crowd of thousands.[5] But the Greek word used is the equivalent of "no faith".[6]

Clearly, there are not degrees of faith.

There's just faith or unbelief.

In faith, Abraham believed God would give a son in his old age[7] and then offered his son Isaac as a sacrifice. Moses had faith to cross the Red Sea. Joshua showed faith that the city walls of Jericho would collapse. David threw the stone that killed Goliath by faith. Elijah prayed in faith that it would not rain in Israel for three years in order to bring down evil King Ahab. A woman suffering 12 years from internal bleeding was healed by her faith as she touched the hem of Jesus' garment.[8]

So believing, or having faith, isn't a secret formula that prompts God to act or releases His power for a breakthrough.

Jesus rebuked His disciples for zero belief when they failed to heal a demon-possessed boy having constant seizures[9]...and then healed the boy despite lack of faith! God's power was there. Faith was not! Faith is the single most important response to God. It is impossible to please or even approach God without faith.[10]

Faith is not something you keep confessing or repeating until you "have enough". Faith comes by hearing the Word of God[11]—simply believing revealed truth about God.

Faith is believing God for what He has already decided or promised to do—choosing to be in the center of His will—even if your breakthrough doesn't happen. And a whole lot of believers had faith but died without a breakthrough or a miracle deliverance![12] Biblical belief or faith is simply accepting what God and HIs Word has already promised. Belief is not a demand. You can't force God to do something outside of His will.

Jonah feared God would rescue the terrorist Assyrians and didn't want it to happen. God's power changed the hearts of Nineveh[13] independent of Jonah and his stinking attitude—*zero faith* from Jonah! Jonah wanted them dead.

Inside the fish's belly, Jonah showed more fear than faith.

As soon as Jonah started sliding past the fish's teeth and down the throat drowning and fighting for breath, he started pleading with God.[14] It was more *begging* than *believing*!

You can't do faith in steps...or pieces. Either you are trusting God or you're not. Either you believe or you doubt: *"Let him ask in faith, with no doubting, for the one who doubts is like a wave of the sea that is driven and tossed by the wind".*[15] No gray area.

Faith *opens* your heart. It doesn't *obligate* God to do anything. Faith is your *agreement with God's authority* in the situation. God decides, you depend. God works, you wait. Faith is simple trust in the character of God. Jesus even healed a paralyzed man, not because of that man's faith, but when He *saw* the faith of his four friends and wanted to prove to skeptical Jewish leaders that He had the authority to forgive sins as the Messiah.[16]

God doesn't need you...but He chooses you. Just because you believe doesn't mean God has to bless.

God isn't waiting to answer your prayers.

God waits for you to agree with His plan.

Inside the fish's belly is when you get real!

The Sperm Whale, growing to over 60' and 60 tons with the largest brain on earth and a lifespan of over 60 years, is the largest toothed whale and the only known whale big enough to swallow a human. The giant mammal has 4 stomach chambers full of digestive chemicals but no air. They dive more than 3,000 feet in search of squid to eat, while holding their breath for up to 90 minutes on such dives. Immortalized in Herman Melville's 1851 classic novel, Moby Dick, the sperm whale eats about 1 ton of fish and squid daily. Driven by their tale fluke, about16 feet from tip to tip, they can cruise the oceans at ~23 miles per hour. The species is protected by the International Whaling Commission but follows more than currents in their pods of 12-15[17]—God controls them![18] No problem believing God instructed the huge fish (maybe a sperm whale) to chase the rocking ship in the storm and swallow anything thrown overboard that looked like a Jewish prophet on the run!

It is possible for a whale to swallow a man. A sailor was swallowed by a sperm whale near the Falkland Islands in the early 1900s. The ship's log shows when the whale was captured by the crew and cut open, the missing sailor was found inside the whale's stomach, "doubled up and unconscious". Although he was revived with a salt water shower, he was delirious for nearly three weeks before recovering sanity.[19]

The first time Jonah showed sanity was inside the fish's belly! Jonah didn't pour out his heart *until* he was stuck inside a fish for 3 days and nights. Jonah only got vomited out *after* he prayed and repented.

Your situation doesn't change until you start doing things God's way. Men, honor your wife and your prayers are no longer hindered.[20] God may withhold an answer if you are out of His will: " *"no good thing will He withhold from those who walk uprightly"*.[21]

And compliance starts with worship.

You can't place conditions on worship.

God will not be held hostage. You can't tell God to crush your enemies or remove your suffering and then you'll worship. Worship precedes breakthroughs. Jesus went to a synagogue leader's home and raised his 12-year-old daughter from the dead because that father got on his knees and worshiped Jesus as Lord![22] Worship can happen in a boat or in a fish belly. But worship is neither natural nor spontaneous.

Here's my big-tent, big-package definition of worship, derived from merging a lot of scripture research: ***Worship is the intentional choice to honor God in all circumstances regardless of the cost.***

If you buy in to that biblically-driven statement, you get the universal nature of worship. That means worship is not weird or rare. It can be planned or spontaneous, passionate or structured, loud or quiet, expected or unexpected—but always tied to recognizing and reacting to the presence of a Holy God in your moment!

Authentic biblical worship will be as diverse as a New York City public school and as de-centralized as a Disney World crowd. For example, worship was the natural overflow...the irresistible impulse...the spontaneous reaction...the visceral emotion of a tear-covered prostitute who was forgiven by Jesus,[23] of the shocked parents of a 12-year-old girl who was raised from the dead by Jesus,[24] and of the innocent political prisoners who survived torture and an earthquake while they worshiped Jesus.[25] Worship isn't emotion but will always impact emotions.

But worship also emerged through the planned dedication of a national monument (2 Chronicles 6), in the aftermath of a near-death war experience,[26] and when a national leader was threatened by a terrorist nation and later learned he was dying.[27]

Because worship is specifically focused on pleasing God and fulfilling His purpose, nobody has exclusive rights on how to do it. Worship is a dynamic experience with God which cannot be limited, controlled, or defined by location, circumstances, liturgy or a set order, specific preferences in style, leaders, appearance, participation, or tradition.

Because worship is inseparably connected to the eternal God, it can evolve or explode anytime or anywhere because God has no limits. Jesus can be worshiped in the halls of the Capitol or during lunch in the school cafeteria...during chemotherapy at Children's Hospital or over coffee at Starbucks...in secret home gatherings in China and Egypt or in a prison cell in Iran...through a post-game interview with Tim Tebow or when a contestant falls off the stage at an American Idol audition.

Nobody can control it because you cannot control God. Worship is the deepest response to God. It's heart...soul...strength...and mind consumed with Him. Everything you are and have surrendered to all you know of Him.[28]

You can experience worship, but never really totally explain it because you cannot absolutely explain God and His ways.[29]

Prayer is the starting point for a breakthrough.

If good planning guaranteed victory, Hillary would be President and the New England Patriots would have been the 2018 Superbowl champions! Plans don't equal a win.

Jonah planned an escape from God on a cruise.
Got swallowed.

Jonah prayed for an escape from the fish's belly.

Got spit out.

Execution—*what you do with plans*—is the difference.

Pastor Adrian Rogers observed, "Our biggest problem is not unanswered prayer, but unoffered prayer." Breakthroughs happen when we quit fighting God and come into agreement with His plan. Prayer should cover a crisis, not be created by it. Jonah didn't start his journey or make his decisions with prayer. He was forced into it from inside the fish.

The origin of prayer is when you realize you can't make it without God. Again, the late Memphis pastor, Adrian Rogers taught, "You will never learn that God is all you need until He Is all you have."

God values prayer more than planning because there's nothing worse than a well-organized failure. Prayer is simply opening your heart to what God wants to do with you next!

In his book, *Talent is Overrated: What Really Separates World-Class Performers from Everybody Else,* author and *Fortune Magazine* Editor, Geoff Colvin, argues that getting knocked down twenty thousand times is where great performance comes from. Colvin thinks the world's top performers in music, sports and business, from the violin brilliance of Jascha Heifetz to the golf dominance of Tiger Wood, got there by "deliberate practice".[30]

Jonah's failure definitely forced him to get better at prayer.

We don't pray much when we're running—only when we're stuck. Without prayer, you are doing life on your own and might as well be wearing a t-shirt that says, "SWALLOW ME!" Prayer is what God wants to hear *now*—*not later*. You can pray when *desperate* but not when you're *defiant*. Even the pagan crew prayed![31]

After the prayer, *then* the Lord spoke to the fish to vomit Jonah onto dry land.

Prayer creates breakthrough if you align with God's will.

When there's no breakthrough, there's no brokenness.

There are always signs when a breakthrough is close.

English author and poet, G.K. Chesterton stated the obvious: "The most incredible thing about miracles is that they happen."

Miracles are real. Breakthroughs happen.

And there are signs.

Though Jonah failed to take advantage of the startover opportunity God gave him *after* getting vomited out, there were multiple signs that God was delivering a breakthrough.

God does give signs. Signs are experiences and circumstances God sets up intended to create belief and bring glory.[32] Building the ark was a sign by Noah that God would judge the world. Moses turned the Nile red with blood as a sign for Pharaoh to let the Israelite slaves go. Gideon's fleece was a sign confirming going to battle. The mark of the beast is a sign to identify the Antichrist in the end times. Jesus said Jonah's 3 days and nights in the fish were a sign predicting His death and resurrection three days later.[33]

Life-coach Tony Robbins says the first of five signs that you are approaching a breakthrough is when "You've had enough...of your financial problems...of your uninspiring career...of that extra 20 pounds you've been carrying around."[34]

Drowning inside the fish's belly was enough to make Jonah reach his limits! The first sign that Jonah would get a breakthrough second chance was surviving a storm and swallowing back-to-back. Getting vomited out on dry land was the second sign. God repeating the message for Nineveh was the third sign.[35] Walking through the terrorist capital city yelling judgment and not getting killed was actually sign four!

Ancient cave drawings from Jonah's time show Ninevite fishermen lived on the shores of the Mediterranean Sea. The Ninevites worshipped the goddess Ashtoreth, and feared the god Dagon, who had the upper body of a man and a fish tail. Researchers say Jonah would have been bleached completely white by the gastric acids in the belly of the fish. He might have looked like a ghost emerging from the waves, convincing the fisherman that he was Dagon's messenger, and scared them so bad they fell on the ground in worship![36] That theory could explain how Jonah could walk through Nineveh intimidating people with his message of coming judgment!

Witnessing the miraculous repentance of the King and entire population of Nineveh was sign number five that God was handing an undeserved, breakthrough second chance to Jonah.

What signs has God given you?

What kind of a sign is it going to take for you to believe?

Trendy Belief No. 14:
There's always a second chance

Sometimes giving a second chance is like giving someone another bullet for their gun because they missed you the first time.
—**Anonymous**

I believe in second chances. I just don't think everyone deserves them.
—**Anonymous**

It was my duty to shoot the enemy, and I don't regret it. My regrets are for the people I couldn't save: Marines, soldiers, buddies. I'm not naive, and I don't romanticize war. The worst moments of my life have come as a SEAL. But I can stand before God with a clear conscience about doing my job.
—**Chris Kyle, Navy SEAL and American War Hero (Murdered in 2013)**

We all make mistakes, have struggles, and even regret things in our past. But you are not your mistakes, you are not your struggles, and you are here NOW with the power to shape your day and your future.
—**Steve Maraboli, Author of *Unapologetically You***

Making a big life change is scary. Know what's even scarier? Regret.
—**Lou Holtz, Former Notre Dame Championship Coach**

Then the Lord spoke to Jonah a second time: "Get up and go to the great city of Nineveh, and deliver the message I have given you." This time Jonah obeyed the Lord's command and went to Nineveh, a city so large that it took three days to see it all. On the day Jonah entered the city, he shouted to the crowds: "Forty days from now Nineveh will be destroyed!"
—**Jonah 3:1-4, NLT**

Nobody knows how many chances you get. You don't get another life to live. This is it. And yet people make choices like there are no consequences, no God, no referees, no principals, no bosses, no divorces, no security systems, no eternity...and expect a free do-over...as though nothing changed.

It's like playing the lottery. One guy joked, *"What's the difference between a man arguing with his wife and a man with a lottery ticket? The man with a lottery ticket actually has a chance to win!"* No guaranteed second chances either.

Second chances are normally controversial. If you get one, you're excited. If you don't get another opportunity, you're crushed. If somebody gets one that doesn't deserve it, you're angry.

Jonah got a second chance. But he didn't want the terrorist Assyrians to get one. What's crazy is that the very words that God told Jonah to speak gave Nineveh a second chance... *but put an expiration date on it of 40 days!*

Whether it's missing the cut for an NFL team or missing the concert by your daughter, there is not always a second chance for what you missed the first time.

And there's no guarantee of other opportunities. I passed on the opportunity to buy Apple stock for $7. Doubt that price will be back any time soon.

Rejecting God's plan has a greater opportunity cost.

God is in control of second chances.

God opens and closes doors: *"If He opens something, no one else can shut it, and if He closes something, no one else can open it"*.[1] That means God is in control of every opportunity that comes your way *and* the ones that will *never* happen.

God protects you even when you can't see it or get upset about closed doors. The ministry of Paul and Silas in Philippi was falsely attacked and shut down. They were beaten and thrown into prison for the sole purpose of leading the jailer to faith in Christ during an unexpected earthquake! Author Max Lucado: "When God locks a door, it needs to be locked. When he blocks a path, it needs to be blocked."[2]

A guy was building crates at his church to ship clothes to an orphanage in China. Later, his glasses were missing. After a search, he realized the glasses had fallen into a crate headed for China! In hard times financially, he complained to God that it wasn't fair. Months later, on a tour of U.S. partner churches, the director of the Chinese orphanage visited the guy's church in Chicago. He reported that Communist soldiers had targeted the orphanage and destroyed everything, including his glasses. He couldn't function. Then the crates arrived and a pair of glasses that fit his prescription was lying on top![3]

There's always a reason when doors close.

First chances are *appointed* by God[4] *and* second chances have to be *approved* by God. Everything has a season.[5] Seasons end. You can't relive college or parenting or your last job.

But getting shut down doesn't mean God is done with you.

Daniel was so predictably spiritual that even his enemies knew when to catch him violating a new law in Babylon prohibiting prayer. God allowed Daniel to be jerked from his home *during* prayer[6] so when he survived a night in the lion's den, the King would become a believer, the critics would burn, and Daniel would become a national leader!

Not exactly a predictable career or ministry path.

And the promotion happened *after* Daniel's closed door!

Trendy belief says it's crazy not to move on after a closed door. But that's not's true. Some believe that once an opportunity is lost it can't be recovered or that you can never be used by God again. If you believe that, then getting fired ends your career, getting divorced means you'll never be successful at marriage, and a leadership mistake means your ministry will never be elevated.

God's grace prompts lots of second chances.

But a second chance is pure *grace*, not a *guarantee*.

God controls second chances.

A closed door doesn't mean the opportunity is lost.

Billionaire Kevin O'Leary is sarcastically called *Mr. Wonderful* on SHARK TANK. When an entrepreneur refuses his offer to invest, he puts a time limit on it and tells them not to listen to the competing offers from other investors ("sharks"). If they hesitate, he announces: "You are dead to me!" The opportunity to work with him is forever lost!

A door isn't closed until God says it is. And God never says that until you refuse multiple, repeated offers of grace. A closed door does *not* mean opportunity is gone. There may be a *delay* or a new *direction*. Being in a fish's belly for 3D/3N looked like a closed door on a second chance, but God spoke to Jonah again...*post-vomit.*

Pastor Adrian Rogers taught, "God doesn't flunk His children. He re-enrolls them." We tend to think that our rebellion, sin, lack of preparation or prayer, weakness, or lack of ability is what closes doors, and our goodness as what opens them. NO!!! There has to be a reason—call it election, predestination, sovereignty, grace or desperation—but a city of 250K was still open to the gospel! The people of Nineveh believed immediately and ended their evil.[7]

Never doubt God.

Second chances are all about God's purpose, not you.

Giving Jonah chance number two meant God intended to save Nineveh, not just Jonah. What God is doing is always bigger than you.

The terrorist nation was actually afraid of God. Their hearts feared the very death and destruction they had inflicted on others: "*Who can tell? Perhaps even yet God will change his mind and hold back his fierce anger from destroying us*".[8] When people admit they already know the consequences of their sin will one day catch up, they are finally starting to get real with God. Jonah wasn't.

Basically, it's not over until God says it is—until He's done everything He wants to do in a situation to show how great He is. Despite Jairus' servant and friends telling him to give up because his 12-year-old daughter had just died, Jesus told him to *keep believing*...and then raised her to life![9] Jesus purposely delayed travel for two days when Lazarus was critically ill,[10] so He could raise him from the dead! A woman caught in adultery was spared from stoning by Jesus and given a second chance.[11] The Samaritan woman Jesus met at the well had been given five chances at marriage before Jesus forgave her.[12]

God pre-selected the exact day on which Jesus would be crucified[13] and Jesus chose the moment He would die,[14] so our sin-debt would be correctly paid.

If you get a second chance...take it.

God is about to do something!

Second chances are about opportunity, not just obeying.

Built in 1961 to prevent East Berliners from escaping communism to the free world, the 12' high Berlin Wall was 87 miles long. About 5,000 attempted to escape over the wall, past no-man's land, minefields, guard towers, border guards, and a river that separated east and west Berlin. Children drowned in the river because rescuers were not allowed to save them. My aunt was one of only a few to escape East Germany by climbing the wall and swimming across a river. She soon met and married my uncle, a U.S. Army sergeant stationed in Germany, and became a voice for freedom. The wall was torn down in 1989. My aunt was always grateful for that one opportunity for her life to be forever changed.

Her second chance became her greatest opportunity.

Jonah was vomited out on dry land only to hear God repeating the original command—get up, go to Nineveh and speak up. God expected Jonah to follow-through. The original Nineveh project had not been cancelled simply because Jonah protested. Obeying God the first time is really important—you probably won't become fish bait.

But second chances aren't just about forgiveness and a startover for the one who failed. They are also about opportunity...***unused opportunity***. Grace is getting something you don't deserve. Jonah didn't deserve a second chance for the same opportunity but got it. And the opportunity to see an entire terrorist capital city turn to God was a rare moment in history.

Of all the Jewish preachers, God had chosen only one—Jonah—to be the voice, lead the way, start a movement and experience a miracle. It was his privilege to see Israel's enemies collapse in fear and repentance over their evil.

God's call was not to punish Jonah but promote him.

God's choice to send Jonah to Nineveh was actually a gift.

The legendary story, *Acres of Diamonds*, begins with Al Hafed, a wealthy man who owned a large farm in south central India. He was content until he became obsessed with the idea of becoming wealthy by finding diamonds. After selling his farm, he travelled the world to search for diamonds until he had spent all his fortune. Depressed, he took his life. The new owner of Hafed's property discovered a brightly colored rock near a stream and learned it was a large diamond in the rough. That discovery became the diamond mine of Golconda, producing the largest and finest diamonds in the world for years. Hafed was unaware of his opportunity.[15]

Can you see the opportunity in front of you?

God has deadlines. They don't change.

Want to limit your ministry or career? Delete purpose...the *chasing-something-bigger-than-you* kind of purpose...the God-piece. Don't act like God exists. Run from everything spiritual. Avoid probing questions about what life is all about anyway. Keep distance between you and believers. Change the conversations when it gets too emotional or personal. Go back to your military unit or oncology unit or research unit and double-down on the next decision.

But here's reality. Your life circumstances can't be explained without factoring in God and some special purpose He chose for you and nobody else. There's a reason why you're still alive after the college parties and cancer treatments and car crashes and company mergers.

Between mistakes, messing around, and misfortune, you will wake up one day and realize you don't always have time to settle the God-stuff later.

Jonah was tasked with telling Nineveh they had 40 days.

40 days. Not 41 or 47 or 50. 40 days and grace gone!

No negotiating. No changes because of politics or weather or family situations or previous commitments. The countdown started with the first warning near the city limits.

Every purpose has a deadline. Every life has a deadline.

God has pre-set deadlines. They are irrevocable. Nothing you can do or say changes them. You don't have to believe in them. Deadlines survive. You don't.

There's not always a second chance.

Without a spiritual turnaround, Nineveh would be leveled in 40 days. Because the entire city humbled themselves before God in repentance, we'll never know if the total destruction was set up to happen through an enemy invasion, earthquake, tsunami, hurricane, or fire from heaven.

Doesn't matter. In a rare move, God told them the exact time left on the clock—when the second chance disappeared. That is the exception. For the return of Jesus, He has just said "Be ready," and listed signs that will indicate He is coming soon![16]

It's not true that if you make a mistake, God is done with you. It's not *one and done!* But neither is it true that there's *always* a second chance. There are limits to the opportunities to repent of sin, rebuild a family, restart a business, restore your credit, revive a relationship, or recover a ministry.

My uncle was diagnosed with cancer, but the best doctors couldn't predict to the day how long he would live. My mother-in-law walked to the mailbox and dropped dead there instantly. No way anybody saw that loss coming.

God shut the door on the ARK. Sodom and Gomorrah were actually fried. Pharaoh and the Egyptian army drowned. Moses got angry once too often and never entered the promised land. Samson lost his eyes. Saul had his kingship removed. Jesus pointed to a rich man who died and couldn't get out of hell. Judas committed suicide.

Second chances expire. Sometimes you end them.

Every deadline as a purpose.

The *40 days or else* message was not a marketing campaign or scare tactic. It was God saying ENOUGH! There are times when a culture or country *knows* they've sinned.

The terrorism of the Assyrians had crossed a line. Slicing open pregnant women to grab their unborn babies and bash them to death was typical for this nation. Not just tolerated but a chosen tactic. That's evil.

Today's culture can't even agree that some things are evil. There are so few rules, consequences, crimes without justice, and deadlines without any penalty that we can't get our minds around a God who isn't bothered by screaming from hell.[17]

If God didn't set deadlines, we wouldn't fear Him or hell!

There is a purpose for every deadline.

Deadlines scream urgency. Deadlines demand change.

Without a challenge, people don't change.

RISE AGAINST HUNGER has deadline of ending hunger by 2030. What if hunger was 97% ended by then? Worth the concern? Absolutely. No goal, no change.

Schools schedule graduation, doctors schedule surgery, and couples schedule weddings. Nothing happens without a deadline.

God told Jonah to go speak to some people who were going to die if they kept living the way they were living. Even though they were totally evil there was still a chance for them to be saved. Their history didn't have to be their destiny.

God hates sin on any level—individual or national. Jonah was sent to call out an entire culture that had become evil. Sin is never excused or tolerated by a holy God. Otherwise, the cross was a mistake and Jesus' death was a good life wasted. To be fair, God has to judge sin. We struggle because we expect God to intervene and stop evil and abuse and terrorism and corruption and violence yesterday...and it doesn't happen. A final judgment is coming as promised.[18] But until then, we only get samples.

Some opportunities expire.

Grace has limits. Forgiveness ends.

Trendy Belief No. 15
Some situations are impossible to turnaround.

Near-death experiences can help one see more clearly sometimes.
—Steve Jobs, Trying to turn Apple around in the '90s

I've learned life is a lot like surfing. When you get caught in the impact zone, you need to get right back up, because you never know what's over the next wave...And if you have faith, anything is possible.
—Bethany Hamilton, Surfer who lost arm in shark attack

The people of Nineveh believed God. They called for a fast and put on sackcloth, from the greatest of them to the least of them....When God saw what they did, how they turned from their evil way, God relented of the disaster that he had said he would do to them, and he did not do it.
—Jonah 3:5, 10, ESV

When God is involved, anything is possible. Most people believe that you can't recover from really bad decisions. That either God can't forgive or if He does forgive, your life is forever scarred and it could never be great again. Like the person who's lived through a divorce, had an abortion, failed a course, buried their family in debt, lost a farm or business, coached a losing team, or led a church that's declined. On the flip side, some believe a person who has made evil, crazy, or destructive choices either can't change or won't ever want to change.

And when unthinkable tragedy strikes, many believe even strong faith can't guarantee healing and recovery. That somehow life can never go forward from that crazy loss. If God was ever there, He inexplicably allowed lives to be damaged forever. Like the combat vet who lost her legs, the parents of a girl tragically murdered, a drunk driver killing your family, a false accusation that ruined a career, or cancer taking a child.

Either way, you've labeled it impossible.

Nothing is going to change.

Big things couldn't happen in your situation.

Hope and healing from what happened is a big joke.

No chance for some quick miraculous turnaround.

...And that's exactly the huge mistake Jonah almost made...at least, until God did an intervention.

God doesn't allow sin to win. Tragedy will not go unanswered. Hope will always surface in the least expected places and darkest moments.

You are God's next choice for a turnaround.

You *can* get through this!!!

Comebacks are powerful . . . and pricey!

A DUI arrest. Four back surgeries. That's just some of the unexpected stuff that's happened since Tiger Woods won his last golf tournament in 2013. 1,876 days since the last win. Scandal and surgery set up the perfect story for the fan favorite to turnaround his career...and life. Barely able to walk after back fusion surgery last year, playing with his kids became a priority. Now thousands mobbed Tiger, in his signature red shirt, as he approached the 18th green at the 2018 Tour Championship in Atlanta to wrap up one of the biggest comebacks in sports history. Winning his 80th golf tournament and almost capturing the $10 million FedExCup title for a third time, Tiger tweeted: "I just can't believe I pulled it off." While the encircling crowd chanted "Tiger! Tiger! Tiger!", he uncharacteristically lowered his cap to cover his emotion.

Tiger came back. The moment was powerful!

Nobody thought it could happen. Tiger did it.

Jonah came back. The moment was powerful!

God knew it would happen. God did it.

Jonah's comeback chances were even more remote. Who survives getting lost overboard in a violent ocean storm and being swallowed by a huge fish? For that matter, who survives a war with God or a walk through a terrorist capital city?

Jonah messed up the mission. God had to fix it.

God's grace gave Jonah a *"get-out-of-jail"* card but it wasn't *FREE!* From that point forward, Jonah was labeled—got him a whole book in the Bible so nobody would ever again think you can fight God and hate people...*and win.*

An awesome survival story tagged with scandal.

Bouncing back from suffering and scandal is not *pretty...or painless...or popular.* There's a price to be paid for getting things back to normal. Make the wrong choices and you lose, even with a comeback. You'll get a history...a past...a story. There's no "do-over" for some things. You can rebuild after a hurricane, but you can't remove a cruise or redo words spoken.

Comebacks are unbelievable...*and ugly.*

Comebacks are what God does. From the prodigal son who returned home to the paralyzed man Jesus healed, our God heals, forgives, and restores. There's forgiveness and new opportunity but you don't get to pretend it didn't happen.

History's greatest comeback event is the resurrection.

But before the resurrection was the cross.

Sin had to be exposed in all it's horror and shame...*and then crushed.* Only God can do that.

Comebacks are exciting...and exclusive.

Not everybody wants one...or gets one.

There are no comeback stories without sin being crushed.

What happens in your situation starts with you.

Life changed in seconds for a top amateur surfer, 13-yr-old Bethany Hamilton, when she was attacked by a 14-foot tiger shark just offshore in Kauai, Hawaii. Her friend's dad grabbed a t-shirt and surfboard leash to stop the bleeding. Bethany lost 60 percent of her blood from the shark attack and her left arm to the shoulder but miraculously survived! Only one month later, she was back in the water...surfing! Her amazing comeback story was detailed in a book and movie, "Soul Surfer." Limited in paddling and balance with just one arm, nobody expected her to become a world class surfer, but in the 2016 Women's Pro she beat Tyler Wright of Australia, the world's No. 1 surfer.[1]

> *I have this thought every second of my life—Why me? Not negatively, like 'Why did this terrible thing happen to me'? But more like 'Why did God choose me and what does He have in mind for me?' God is able to use my story to help others....A girl told me that she had cancer. When she learned my story it made her realize that she didn't need to give up. When people ask me what my faith in Christ means to me, I usually answer in just one word—everything! This was true before and after the shark attack.[2]*

No matter how impossible it feels at the moment, God can give you a comeback story! Like Bethany, it starts with your faith—believing God has a *big purpose* and *chose you*!

With God, nothing is impossible.[3]

With faith, you just started your comeback!

Yet turnarounds don't start until you focus on *God's agenda* instead of the *shark attack!* When you're tired of your life the way it is, you know you can't live that way anymore, and you don't want the rest of your life to be defined by *being swallowed*, then things start moving.

God wasn't waiting on the ship's crew to write a new worship song. God knew the huge fish was following His instructions. God didn't expect the people of Nineveh to start asking for a satellite worship campus from Jerusalem.

God's target was Jonah. The turnaround was on him.

You can't wait on a mate, boss, kids, or school to change.

Jonah had to decide he would change...*while he was still inside the fish's belly.* He did. Nineveh was next.

Running from God makes you think God left you!

Jonah's turnaround didn't start with the huge fish getting harpooned and killed by a random passing whaling ship. The comeback wasn't launched because Jonah got word Nineveh was begging for a prophet and he could be a hero. Jonah thought he was drowning and screamed for God like a 6th-grade girl dropping in the Tower of Terror at Disney World.

The bizarre sequence of events started with the storm nearly shattering their ship, Jonah being tossed overboard by a panicked crew, and getting sucked into the ocean depths, down the throat of a giant fish. Wrapped like sushi in seaweed, fighting not to drown, Jonah suddenly wanted God!

Why? Because he thought God was done with him...totally left him!

> *You threw me into the ocean depths,*
> *and I sank down to the heart of the sea.*
> *The mighty waters engulfed me;*
> *I was buried beneath your wild and stormy waves.*
> *Then I said, 'O Lord,*
> **You have driven me from your presence.**
> **But you, O Lord my God, snatched me from the jaws of death!**
> *As my life was slipping away, I remembered the Lord.*
> (Jonah 2:3-4, 6-7, NLT)

Just the opposite. Jonah couldn't get away from God! Being in crisis doesn't make you more spiritual or even guarantee you want God. It reveals whether you want God or not. Yes, you have to get things right with God before you start to feel or see your circumstances change.

Ready for this?

If you think God left you...you're probably running.

When you stop running...God is *already there.*

A turnaround doesn't mean things change quickly.

A middle school teacher saw a new substitute teacher standing outside his classroom with his forehead against a locker. She heard him mutter, "How did you get yourself into this?" Knowing he was assigned to a difficult class, she tried to offer support: "Are you okay? Can I help?" He lifted his head, "I'll be okay as soon as I get this kid out of his locker!"

Getting out of stuff normally doesn't happen quickly!

Put a Google map pin at the intersection of brokenness over your past and belief in God's faithfulness. That's the location of a turnaround.

Brokenness without belief results in *despair.*

Belief without brokenness results in *disaster.*

Brokenness with belief results in *deliverance.*

A turnaround is a moment when direction is reversed—your confidence returns. Even if your circumstances don't immediately change...you know you're not stuck anymore. There's a *surge of hope*—stronger than a 16oz Monster energy drink, creating fresh energy to *try again.* There's *separation from hurt*—you're not going to be defined by regret or disappointment or fear another minute but choose to *believe again!*

Whether it's you or your family, a church or company, team or group, things are now moving in a new direction. There's been a breakthrough—police have arrested a suspect, your dream bakery was opened, your church gets new leadership, your husband moved back in, your brother is coming home from Afghanistan, your daughter got that first job, a marriage is staring over, there's a new medical procedure, unexpected funding to keep the orphanage afloat just came through...

And you just know *somehow* God is behind this.

Mostly because...

...nothing was happening until God was invited to come.

It's really all God because you know you couldn't do it.

But it's only a *start.*

Jonah's turnaround only started in the fish's belly.

Turnarounds equal a breakthrough...a startover...a new opportunity...NOT *lottery won—all problems solved!*

Jonah's circumstances didn't change for 3D/3N—choking for every breath, swallowing saltwater and fish chum while getting tossed against giant ribs by pounding waves.

C'mon man! This guy was vomited out on a beach, not elevated to *Disney Cruises Castaway Club* Platinum level. With *zero* recovery time for Jonah, God forced him to:

- ➢ *take a position on an issue he hated.*
- ➢ *risk his life in a terrorist capital city.*
- ➢ *participate in a different culture.*
- ➢ *watch people he hated be saved.*
- ➢ *endure being stuck in a city he hated.*

Had a turnaround? Congratulations! *You're just starting.*

Turnarounds should start immediately...where you are.

Jonah's story didn't end on the beach. The remotely-controlled fish vomited him on the beach...alive.

When he got *miserable in the belly*, he got *moved to the beach.* When he feared being swallowed *more than* he hated serving God in Nineveh, the comeback started!

God doesn't want you to wait until it's more convenient, you've tried to change, or you can spin the story to avoid shame and embarrassment.

And you don't have to have it all figured out. That'll never happen anyway.

START . . . *now!*

Turnarounds get started when you're in a *weird*—okay, *bad* place. God is good with that. Why? Because repentance just means you've changed your mind about sin and God and want out of the mess you've made. The prodigal son's comeback started *after* he spent all his inheritance and *when* he was still living with pigs![4] Jesus forgave a woman *when* she was caught in adultery.[5]

The turnaround was started in total isolation. Most breakthroughs start in private... in pain...when you want forgiveness more than freedom. Getting vomited out of a fish proved God accepted Jonah's best effort at confession.

It's like a dad looking at his 3-yr-old's drawing: "Great giraffe!" "It's a dog, dad!" Encouragement is tricky.

Just because you get right doesn't mean God will immediately remove the challenges. Jonah wasn't immediately delivered from the fish just because he prayed.

God kept him in the fish's belly for 3D/3N.

And never shredded the Nineveh ticket.

God works through, not around, personalities.

Remodeling is crazy. Mostly because of Chip Gaines, Joanna's goofball husband on HGTV's mega-hit series, *Fixer Upper*. Chip painted on a green mustache, ate a cockroach, fell asleep on cactus, jumped through a wall, dressed up as Santa with reindeer and lost his pants, ate all their cupcakes, interviewed their pigs, mastered the #HammerFlipChallenge, played drums on a hill, camped out at Target for the launch of Hearth and Hand with Magnolia, cut his hair to raise $230K for kids at St. Jude's, and more. And yet, somehow, every week, their fixer-upper homes in Waco got done!

Pray for Joanna?

Projects would be great if it wasn't for all the personalities involved. Nothing surprised God. God knew Nineveh's evil and had compassion anyway! He knew Jonah's prejudice and temper...and chose him anyway! In fact, God called Jonah because he would get the Nineveh mission done even though Jonah would create multiple crises.

Leaders know big, impossible projects are tough and even committed people bring their issues to the adventure.

Leading people without losing momentum is the challenge.

Believing God can turn around people is a good start...

Turnarounds are messy.

About 75% of the NFL labeled him as a failure. He was fired from the NFL's Baltimore Ravens staff and had four losing seasons as head coach of the Cleveland Browns. Ian O'Connor, author of the new sports insider book, *Belichick*, said "his public personality was challenging." Now he's been to the SuperBowl 8 times—won 5. Labeled as polarizing and mysterious, New England Patriots head coach Bill Belichick took the biggest risk of his career. His big moment came disguised in tragedy. When Patriots quarterback, Drew Bledsoe, was injured, Belichick took a chance on a guy that was pick no. 199 in the 6th round of the 2000 NFL draft—backup Tom Brady. The rest is history. O'Connor said every great coach needs a great player to lead his program.[6]

But their relationship got rocky. "It's remarkable that it took 17, 18 years for any fracture to come into public view...being coached in an unforgiving way by Belichick wore Brady down....If you're married 18 years to a grouchy person who gets under your skin and never compliments you, after a while you want to divorce him....Tom knows Bill is the best coach in the league, but he's had enough of him. If Tom could, I think he would divorce him."[7]

Turnarounds are messy. Why? Because there's always a lot of toxic attitude to clean up. There's no straight line from collapse to comeback...*and no fast lane.*

There are stages—no TSA pre-check privileges or Disney FastPass to avoid screening or waiting. God screens you every moment and slows you down to deal with restarting the right way.

Stage 1: the *breakthrough* moment.

Stage 2: the *breakdown* moment—all the stuff you set up to run from God has to be put on display and broken down! It' clean up time!

Jonah started his *turnaround* but kept his *temper.*

A turnaround doesn't make you perfect. You're not suddenly strong or spiritual just because you owned your mess! God forgives you and chooses to recycle you back into doing His will like Jonah, but you've still got serious changing to do.

The test is always whether you'll go to "your Nineveh".

Turnarounds are not going to be pretty. When you startover with God you have to face the deception and defiance that got you swallowed in the first place. One day you make legit progress and the next day you give in to the worst. Turnarounds are real war...against yourself!

Jonah suspected that if God was sending him to Nineveh, it signaled the Assyrians were getting a second chance—God had already put forgiveness on deposit for them. When the people of Nineveh believed God and turned from their evil lifestyles, Jonah exploded!

> *This change of plans greatly upset Jonah, and he became very angry. So he complained to the Lord about it: "Didn't I say before I left home that you would do this, Lord? That is why I ran away to Tarshish! I knew that you are a merciful and compassionate God, slow to get angry and filled with unfailing love. You are eager to turn back from destroying people. Just kill me now, Lord! I'd rather be dead than alive if what I predicted will not happen."* (Jonah 4:1-2, NLT)

Even though Jonah sounded super spiritual when he thought he was dying inside the fish's belly, he slipped backwards spiritually as soon as God cancelled the Nineveh judgment.

Jonah's attitude was the same *before and after* being swallowed!

When her child's towel was stolen during a school swimming trip, an angry parent confronted the teacher, "What kind of criminals are in class with my child?!" The teacher calmly replied: "I'm sure it was taken accidentally. What does it look like?" Mom: "It's white and says *Holiday Inn* on it."

Getting swallowed doesn't make you spiritual.

It only makes you stink.

Turnarounds are not your call. They are God's story.

God scheduled the storm and the huge fish. Technically, God set-up the conditions for Jonah's turnaround.

God could have drowned Jonah but really wanted to detox him. None of us are created to hate. What's the benefit if God has to keep putting His players on the bench? Coaches would rather have their best players competing even while complaining!

Jonah wasn't thinking turnaround when he was boarding the ship or bunked up during the storm. He didn't have a clue about what was coming or when he would be thrown overboard. And Jonah definitely wouldn't have chosen to be saved by a huge fish anyway.

Nobody gets to decide how far they will go in sin, how long they'll stay or when they'll come back.

God makes the call. He chooses when to shake your life.

He knows His love and your limits!

Only God can offer a way back...*His way.*

It will always be on God's terms. Noah's ark was open until one pre-scheduled day when God Himself "closed the door".[8] Saul was delivering arrest warrants to Damascus, Syria for Christians to be put to death when Jesus appeared and blinded him to turn him around.[9]

Turnarounds are always a gift of God's grace. God owes you absolutely nothing! Nothing you've ever done or could do impresses Him or obligates Him. The only thing that ever impressed God was Jesus giving His life on a cross to pay for your sins and mine.[10]

And God's turnaround track is different for everyone.

It took Jonah **getting swallowed in the ocean** to change.

It took Louie Zamperini **swallowing the ocean** to change:

> *You'd think a man who survived two plane crashes, a Japanese POW camp and 47 days adrift in the ocean could conquer anything. But*

WWII veteran and Olympic athlete Louie Zamperini couldn't win his battle with alcohol and depression.

The world-famous Olympic runner was serving in WWII when his plane crashed into the south Pacific. Only Zamperini and two others survived. "I...popped to the surface swallowing fuel and blood." While clinging to a life raft, Zamperini prayed for one of the first times in his life: "God, if I survive this ordeal and get back to America alive, I'll seek You and serve You." Zamperini did make it home, but only after being picked up by a Japanese boat and suffering through two years of torture in POW camps. As Zamperini nearly starved, a Japanese officer known as "The Bird" made it his personal mission to break him. "His belt was about five inches wide, half-inch thick with a big steel buckle. He took that off and hit me across the temple, knocked me to the floor. Blood spurted out of my head. I was constantly being tormented by the guy. And you talk about hate. I wanted to kill him."

Nightmares began in prison camp and plagued Zamperini long after he returned home to California. "The nightmares were every night. I couldn't get rid of it." One night Zamperini dreamed he was strangling The Bird. Instead, he woke up strangling his wife. Scared and desperate, he started getting drunk to forget about the horrors that plagued him. With her husband out drinking every night, Zamperini's wife Cynthia filed for divorce. After surviving so much, Zamperini was about to lose everything.

That's when a concerned neighbor invited Cynthia to the Billy Graham Crusade taking place in a Los Angeles tent dubbed the Canvas Cathedral [1949]. She accepted the invitation and then accepted Christ. Her husband wanted no part of Christianity, but his heart softened when Cynthia said she no longer wanted a divorce. After storming out of the tent the first night, Zamperini amazingly returned for one more evening. That time, the Bible verses Billy Graham quoted went straight to Zamperini's heart. "Of all my near-death experiences my life never passed before my eyes, but when Billy Graham quoted Scripture my life did pass before my eyes." For the first time in years, Zamperini remembered the promise he made to God when he was floating in the south Pacific. "My life passed before my eyes, and I saw an ugly life. Yes, I had a lot of great times, a lot of great experiences, and a lot of escapes from death, but I still didn't like my life after the war. It was terrible." That night in L.A., Zamperini...accepted Christ, and the biggest miracle of his life was set in motion. "I knew I was through getting drunk," Zamperini said. "I knew I was through smoking, and I knew I'd forgiven all of my guards including The Bird. Never dawned on me again that I hated the guy. That was the first night in all those years I'd never had a nightmare, and I haven't had one since."

Zamperini's transformation was so all-encompassing, he returned to Japan to share the Gospel with hundreds of Japanese troops he once hated. This time, they were the ones behind bars, imprisoned for war crimes. Zamperini watched as many of them accepted Christ. He went on to share his faith around the world, speaking at several Billy Graham Crusades and cultivating a friendship with Billy Graham that lasted until Zamperini's death on July 2, 2014. "The way it spread out. I'm one guy that got saved, and I've spoken to hundreds of thousands and had my testimony in papers where millions read it. One person! Think of the spider-web effect all over the world."[11]

Originally his unbelievable story was told in the 2014 movie *UNBROKEN*, directed by Angelina Jolie. Now the turnaround part of his life is told in the 2018 movie, *UNBROKEN: Path to Redemption*.

God does turnarounds—Louie, Jonah, Nineveh—to display His love and grace to people dying in unbelief.

God can't ignore sin and you can't ignore God.

Turnarounds are all about God and His holiness. They're more than emotional stories. God demands exclusive, energetic worship and respect for His holy character—the whole point of the first four of the Ten Commandments.

The whole storm and swallowing and spitting and saving episode started because God drew a red-line with the evil in a terrorist nation. God does judge nations and leaders when their evil reaches a tipping point. In fact, God giving Israel the Promised Land was not because they were special but because the nations occupying that area weren't redeemable: *"Do not say in your heart, after the Lord your God has thrust them out before you, 'It is because of my righteousness that the Lord has brought me in to possess this land,' whereas it is because of the wickedness of these nations that the Lord is driving them out before you".[12]*

God is never random. There's always a reason for His judgment to fall on a person or nation...and it's always deserved. No innocents. God chose Israel to conquer the Promise Land because of the history in those nations of specific, sequenced sins: adultery, child sacrifice (abortion), homosexuality, and bestiality.[13]

Pastor Adrian Rogers said, "Satan isn't interested in telling lies about little things. He wants you to believe lies about the biggest subject—God. If Satan can get your mind

twisted about who God is and the trustworthiness of His character, then he has you....
With his *'you shall not surely die'* response, Satan wanted Eve to believe God would not
really hold Eve's sin against her. Some today think, "God is too good to punish sin." He's
too good *not* to punish sin. He is holy and righteous.[14]

Nineveh was saved because God can't ignore sin.

Jonah got swallowed because God can't ignore sin.

Jonah turned around because you can't ignore God.

You can't explain evil, forgiveness, or God.

Evil has to be endured.

Forgiveness has to be sacrificial.

God has to be sovereign.

One mile from the White House. A former Civil War refugee camp for freed slaves.
Flipped into a trendy historic district. Recently the scene of what police call a random
and unprovoked attack. Now the site of unexplained forgiveness. Wendy Martinez, 35,
a tech company employee who just 7 days before posted her engagement photo, was jog-
ging in Logan Circle when brutally stabbed to death. Thankfully the killer was arrested
24 hours later with awesome police work and street camera video. In a calm and soft
voice, her grieving mother Cora shared a perspective that could only come from a seasoned believer: *"My heart has been broken into 1,000 pieces, but I forgive that man. I feel
relieved, in peace. I have forgiven him completely. My heart has no room for hate, resent-
fulness....We believe in the greatest judge, the ultimate person that is going to give what is
deserved. So, I am asking my family to do the same. Just let it go. Wendy is happy, she is in
peace."* Wendy and her mom had already found a wedding dress: *"Wendy lived the happiest seven days of her life. She was in the happiest moment. When I saw her in that dress
I never figured...that was the dress for her burial."*[15]

God showed up at the center of total evil.

Most of us can't wrap our minds around that.

Yet that is exactly what happened at the cross.

Jonah's story is controversial because it surfaces and gives answers for the two biggest life questions everybody struggles with: *Why does God allow evil and suffering?
How can you forgive?*

The answers are simple but never comfortable. Nobody wants sound-bite explanations. I wrote most of a book on it (*What's In Your Backpack?*, Amazon, 2012) but
here's my sound-bite answer: the CROSS!

Every question about sin and suffering is answered in Jesus' death on the cross. The
cross is the intersection of God's sovereign purpose and Jesus' sacrificial death to pro-
vide forgiveness. Because God is holy, He had to judge sin. God loves you. Jesus died
to conquer death, sin, and evil. Forgiveness starts and ends with Jesus. You can't do it.
No suffering can touch your life unless it has passed through the hands of God. Jesus'

death on the cross proves there is no such thing as meaningless suffering or evil winning or people beyond the reach of God's forgiveness. Done!

God can't be explained. He can only be experienced.

You don't live by explanations...only by hope.

So the bigger question is not "Why was Nineveh spared?"

It's "Why was Jonah spared?"

There's no turnaround without truth.

Arguing that your greatest battle is not doubt about God but desire to escape, Pastor Adrian Rogers said,

> *One of the most terrifying verses in the Bible is: "they believed not the truth, but had pleasure in unrighteousness" (2 Thessalonians 2:10b-12). They had the truth; they wouldn't believe the truth....Did they have intellectual problems? No. They believed not the truth because they had pleasure in unrighteousness. The opposite of truth is not error. The opposite of truth is sin....they wanted their sin more than they wanted the truth.*[16]

Turnarounds start with the truth. Marriages, ministries, or municipalities don't improve without dealing in reality.

Steve Belichick, father of the New England Patriots coach Bill Belichick, served in the then-segregated Navy during World War II. While on the island of Okinawa, Steve was the only white man to not walk out of an officer's club when Samuel Barnes (a black *officer*), walked in. A turnaround started...because of a commitment to truth.[17]

Fast forward a few years. Barnes became a NCAA executive.

Jonah knew the truth...about God, Nineveh, and himself.

The problem is never your *circumstances*.

The problem is always your *commitment*. Have you totally surrendered to the truth or are you still hanging on to things that pull you down?

Yes, you can fake it...*but only until you get swallowed.*

Trendy Belief No. 16:
Your potential is unlimited.

Potential is that moment when you walk into a spider web and suddenly become a Tae Kwon Do black belt.
—Anonymous

Right before I die, I'm going to swallow a bag of popcorn kernels to make the cremation more exciting.
—Anonymous

This change of plans greatly upset Jonah, and he became very angry. So he complained to the Lord about it: "Didn't I say before I left home that you would do this, Lord? That is why I ran away to Tarshish! I knew that you are a merciful and compassionate God, slow to get angry and filled with unfailing love. You are eager to turn back from destroying people.
—Jonah 4:1-2, NLT

God doesn't exist to help you reach your potential. Redneck comedian Jeff Foxworthy confessed, "My grandma's the most careful, safe driver in the world. But you put her in a rental car, and she's doing doughnuts in the K-Mart parking lot!" Foxworthy's grandma has potential...as a stunt driver!

It's maybe the biggest lie of our generation that life is all about reaching your potential—that God's main focus is helping you *"become all you were meant to be"!* Whatever that means...

The whole "potential" thing smacks of entitlement—a really selfish view of life—because you don't own your life. Life is a gift from God. The adventure starts, lives, and ends inside His map. Your potential **IS** unlimited...if you swap your life for God's purpose: *"Only those who throw away their lives for My sake and the sake of the good news will ever know what it means to really live".*[2]

You weren't put here just to open a fireworks stand.

God has a bigger purpose for your life.

Even if you are nonreligious, at some point you'll try to make sense of why you're on the planet and craft a purpose that works for you...*because you want more.*

But how do you ever know if it's enough?

Life is about discovering your God-given purpose. Apart from committing to that purpose, you'll never be fulfilled. It's not that your life will be empty. Even non-believers are already actively engaged in worshiping something—*football tailgating, entertainment, careers, all-inclusive island vacations, socialism, blogging, parenting, credit, iPhones*—whatever drowns out God's voice for the moment.

Jonah was given a purpose by God—to take the biggest risk of his life on a "Mission Impossible" to save a terrorist city. Thousands of families were days away from destruction. This was bigger than Jonah and any "reaching your potential" experience.

God controls nations. God calls out evil.

God called Jonah. Jonah challenged God.

God changed Jonah. So much for unrealized potential!

God defines potential.

Potential is defined by culture as the maximum you could achieve or the best you could become.

God has already defined potential—*His life goal for you*—specifically as becoming more like Christ: *"to be conformed to the image of His Son"*.[3] And God has already detailed His process: *"God makes all things work together for the good of those who love Him and are chosen to be a part of His plan"*.[4]

God isn't reckless or reactionary. God has never said, "That surprises me!" Everything that happens to you is part of His bigger plan. There are no random or meaningless circumstances. Nothing is ever an *accident*. Whatever touches your life is *arranged*. In the most ordinary and smallest details of your daily life, God is attempting to stretch and shape you to become more like Jesus.

Here's the tension. You don' know your limits and you don't know what God can do! Normally, you'll underestimate God and overestimate the challenges.

Two limits are important. First, God knows when you face a *temptation* that will take you down, so He creates an escape route.[5] Second, God knows when you face a trial that catches you unprepared—lacking faith—and He comes to encourage you.[6]

God knows your *circumstances* and your *capacity*. With His strength you can achieve more than you ever imagined.

When God called Gideon to defend Israel against their Midianite enemies, Gideon made the excuse that he was not capable of leading the battle. God responded that He would make him strong enough to do it![7]

Jonah's anger at God cancelling the judgment on Nineveh was intense...and he didn't internalize it! Jonah screamed *unfair*—complaining God should never have put him through all this if Nineveh's judgment was going to be cancelled.

God had defined Jonah's potential as becoming an emerging bold prophet to the nations.[8] The Nineveh project was the experience to launch that process.

Just because you disagree with what God wants to do with your life doesn't mean God has to change. You do. And it doesn't mean God has to dial back His expectations for what you *can* do.

God is never worried about challenging you beyond your expectations. Jesus told Peter he could walk on water and he did it![9] How's that for enlarging potential?

Jonah didn't want a *ministry to terrorists.*

Nineveh also trashed their God-given potential.

God judges *wicked people.*

God also judges *wasted potential.*

Your potential is limited by your faith, not your failures.

When you run from God, you always know why.[10] Even if you are sold out you'll still sin.[11] Jonah wasted 3D/3N trying to prevent God from forgiving the terrorist Assyrians. Jonah preached but fought with God all the way!

After Peter denied knowing Jesus three times prior to Jesus' trial and torture, he wept bitterly and never got over it. Even after Jesus was resurrected, Peter believed he had disqualified himself, so he quit the ministry—took six disciples and restarted his original fishing career. So Jesus showed up on the beach for a one-on-one talk to restore Peter. Three times Jesus asked Peter if he loved Him, always followed by a command to fulfill his potential as a leader in ministry.

Peter allowed his failures to limit his potential.

Failures don't limit what God can do with your life.

Sin never stops God's plans or caps your potential. Goliath, the Philistine giant, cursed God and threatened to wipe Israel off the map. A 17-year-old David picked up five stones and said, *"You come to me with a sword, with a spear, and with a javelin. But I come to you in the name of the Lord of hosts, the God of the armies of Israel, whom you have defied. This day the Lord will deliver you into my hand"* (1 Samuel 17:45-46, NKJV). Minutes later, Goliath is dead.

Refusing to believe God...*that gets you stuck.*

God is creating your story right now.

Reaching your potential depends on your participation—how quickly and seriously you look for God's purpose in every situation. The sooner you surrender to what God expects of you, the more confidence you gain in where God is taking you.

Jonah's potential was linked to following through on what God had told him to do. Speak in Nineveh and his heart for the nations gets bigger—compassion for people edges closer to the way Jesus viewed a hurting world. That was potential.

You were created for an amazing purpose. Waiting ahead is more joy and fulfillment that you could ever imagine. But how much you experience depends on how you react to the story God is creating right now.

Everybody is moving inside a bigger story right now that can take you closer to reaching your God-assigned potential.

As a freshman on the University of Michigan's soccer team, Nicky Waldeck couldn't find purpose: "Faith wasn't part of my life. I was just going with the flow, drinking, rolling with the crowd." In her sophomore year, teammates invited her to be a part of *Athletes in Action* (a Campus Crusade for Christ outreach to college and pro athletes), where she opened her heart to Jesus. As a junior, Nicky became an AIA leader but struggled: "I felt guilty because I was not making much of an impact." Nicky told her friend Sarah that she was concerned about her roommate, Whitney, following the same path as Nicky her freshman year. Sarah and Nicky prayed for Whitney. Two hours later, Nicky and Whitney were together in the car when Whitney suddenly turned off the music and said, "We need to talk. I mean we really need to talk. Can we go to a coffee shop?" Nicky listened to Whitney tell her story, then shared how Jesus had changed her life and how Whitney could know God personally. Nicky explained that she and Sarah had just prayed for her. Whitney started crying. When Nicky got back to her room that night, she got a text from Whitney: "Please come downstairs." They talked, and Whitney prayed to receive Christ. Nicky said they prayed and "hugged it out". Nicky admitted she didn't have all the answers: "I didn't do the best job sharing (the gospel)." But she was willing to take the risk to share herself, her story and the gospel. She chose to jump into a bigger story.[12]

Your level of participation makes the difference.

Potential is always time-sensitive.

In Tom Cruise's 2018 franchise movie, *MISSION: Impossible—Fallout*, Ethan Hunt and the IMF team fight a group of terrorists known as the Apostles, plotting a simultaneous nuclear attack on the Vatican, Jerusalem and Mecca, Saudi Arabia using 3 plutonium cores. When the weapons disappear, Ethan and team are desperately racing against time to keep them from falling into the wrong hands and save millions of people.

Like that plot, the city of Nineveh was on a countdown to destruction. This nation was going down. God had already scheduled judgment on *wide-open-anything-goes* immorality to ripping babies out of pregnant women. Nineveh had crossed a red-line on evil. There's nothing more evil than a generation raised to believe they don't need God.

It's not like Jonah had unlimited time to speak to Nineveh.

There was a 40-day window to complete God's project.

Opportunities to reach your potential with God are limited.

In his book *Visioneering*, Andy Stanley said, "We don't need to pray for more miracles, we just need to be more sensitive to the opportunities that God brings our way."[13]

Without forgiveness, you're stuck.

Apologetic husband: "I'm so sorry I get angry at you. How do you stay so calm?" Wife: "I always clean the toilet when that happens." Husband: "That helps?" Wife: "Yes, because I'm using your toothbrush."

Unbelief is a sin and belief is required for God to work in your life or answer prayer.[14]

But reaching your potential is linked to forgiveness.

You are never more like Jesus than when you forgive.

Jonah didn't want to forgive his enemies. But he knew God would and that meant Jonah had an issue with the love of God. According to *Jonah's gospel*: God only loves *his* kind of people and God shouldn't love or forgive evil people—especially those who have hurt you. Jonah was running from the responsibility of forgiveness.

If you can't forgive, you can't fight. No wins. Conquering a city is easier than controlling your heart.[15]

The biggest battle you face personally and professionally is with anger. When you get into conversations with people whose lives and careers appear to be stuck, start by asking "What are you mad about?"

Bitterness means you put a limit on what you will do for others when you've been hurt or rejected. That automatically caps your upward potential.

Forgiveness is your biggest challenge. Unforgiveness limits what God can do with your life.

Unforgiveness kills faith.

Resentment steals vision.

Bitterness poisons relationships.

Anger shuts God out.[16]

Jesus forgave the woman caught in adultery within minutes after her sin.[17] Getting caught and being publicly exposed was not God's punishment. It was God's mercy dragging her from a lifestyle that was killing her. Getting swallowed was Jonah's bailout.

She didn't deserve it. At least two families got messed up.

Yet, Jesus set her free...even though He had to pay for that later...at the cross!'

Jonah didn't think he had a problem with forgiveness until he was challenged to do it! Pastor Adrian Rogers said, "God would much rather forgive than judge. We would rather judge than forgive."

The biggest mistake is not talking about mistakes.

Come back to God after your mistakes. Do whatever it takes to get right with God, no matter how humbling.

Customer Tweet: *I ordered a pizza and it came with no toppings on it or anything. It's just bread.*
Domino's Pizza Tweet: *We're sorry to hear about this!*
Customer Tweet (minutes later): *Never mind, I opened the pizza box upside down.*

When Jonah shouted God's judgment, Nineveh's entire population repented. Their evil stopped immediately. It was real. Signs that it was radical included: the king stepping down from his throne, removing royal robes, covering up with burlap, sitting in ashes, and then issuing a decree telling the people to earnestly pray to God![18]

When's the last time the leader of any nation told people to repent and pray to God for mercy? The closest the American people get to hearing anything spiritual from national leaders is at the end of a political speech: *"God bless you and God bless the United States of America."*

Here's truth. God will never bless sin. He judges sin. Protecting children is the minimum moral threshold in a culture...and now maybe the final cry of a dying national conscience. Here's an example of the moral red-line America has crossed on the issue of killing unborn children.

Abortion activist Senator Elizabeth Warren quoted the Bible[19] in a hateful attack against President Trump's Supreme Court nominee, Brett Kavanaugh. Talking about fighting corporations, Sen. Warren said, "We are on the moral side of history." So morality is only invoked to slam evil corporations and it's immoral to protect unborn children? She led the fight against banning abortions after 20 weeks of pregnancy.[20]

Ashley McGuire, a Senior Fellow with The Catholic Association, shared as a mother: "When you're seeing a baby sucking its thumb at 18 weeks, smiling, clapping [it becomes] harder to square the idea that that 20-week-old, that unborn baby or fetus, is discardable."[21]

Warren wants the law to allow killing babies even *when* they are born arguing it's about safety, societal approval, and suffering: "Abortions are safer than getting your tonsils out....70 percent of Americans agree: Roe v. Wade is worth supporting....[banning abortions after 20 weeks] would force women to carry an unviable fetus to term."[22]

Jonah might as well have marched through Washington, D.C. declaring "40 days and you'll be destroyed". If God would judge Nineveh for the same thing, America is on life support.

That's why America is being judged right now. God is slowly and strategically removing the restraining influence of the Spirit and uncontrolled voices of evil and hatred are steadily filling in the gap.[23] These are signs of the last days before Jesus returns to remove believers from the massive, global judgment called the Tribulation.

Nineveh confessed and repented...and meant it.

Jonah's biggest mistake was not confessing his hatred...at least until he saw Nineveh repent. Then it exploded like the Mount Kilauea volcano on Hawaii's Big Island in 2018.

That hate got him swallowed and he still had to preach!

And God still forced him to defend his hatred.[24]

It took a storm, getting swallowed, and being forced to speak God's word to finally squeeze Jonah hard enough to confess what God already knew was in his heart.

Hiding your mistakes limits your potential.

If your career isn't moving...it's actually stuck.

Author of *Purple Cow*, the best-selling book of the decade, and owner of the most popular marketing blog in the world, Seth Godin, observed: "We've constructed a life where we rarely leap...and most of the time, we coast or fade or increment our way forward. It might be worth investing the effort into turning some of your decisions back into leaps."[25]

Without some big leaps, your career or ministry is stuck.

Most people think God will never bless them with success: *"It will never happen for me"* or *"I'll never be good enough."* Usually that's an excuse for not taking big risks or making big changes in your life when God has spoken.

From barefoot in small-town Brazil to one of the highest-paid international supermodels, to motherhood and marriage to NFL quarterback Tom Brady, Gisele Bundchen had everything. With all her wealth and success, in her newly released autobiography, *Lessons: My Path to a Meaningful Life*, Gisele blows up this image of the perfect life and admits she wanted to die: "I actually had the feeling of, 'If I just jump off my balcony, this is going to end, and I never have to worry about this feeling of my world closing in."[26]

Jonah shouted two times that he wanted God to just take his life![27] Many people have experienced suicidal thoughts, but this was an angry and *empty* threat or Jonah would have just swallowed the salt water when he was inside the fish's belly. Jonah claimed he had a *right* to be angry, and wasn't going to change, even if it killed him![28]

Jonah was telling God he didn't want to risk his ministry on an insane mission to a bunch of terrorists that he would always hate. When you're done taking risks... you're done! Ministry **IS** risk. To forward the gospel, leaders have to create conversations; challenge crazy beliefs, destructive lifestyles, and suffocating tradition; penetrate communities; speak out on issues; mobilize compassion; embrace cultures; and bring diverse groups together.

And...leaders have to eat change for breakfast.

If you don't want to be in ministry...leave! Don't mess up other lives or interfere with what God is doing.

If you don't want to be a leader...step down! Don't discourage other people with your attitude.

If you don't want to go forward...get out of the way! Don't cheat other people out of their opportunities to succeed.

...Or, you could just listen to God and...*change.*

No change means no growth. You have failed.

Faith means you take risks and make changes.

Try taking a big risk. Go with God like a bungee jumper over the Zambezi River. Do something good that scares you so bad you want to revise your will and confess something to your mom that you did in high school. Get out of your comfort zone long enough to get a new perspective and change—mentor a child, work with refugees, immerse yourself in another culture, volunteer for hospice, or remember a widow's birthday. But getting a double shot of espresso at Starbucks is not "stepping out in faith". Write down a monster goal and tweet it so you can't back out. Forgive an enemy and tell him that. Pray for what you know will never happen. Give a huge gift to a great cause and never tell anybody. Share your faith story with a total stranger.

And when you do...expect to get the weird mix of a rush *and* rejection. But do it...or God will force you to do it. Worse—God will leave you alone...for a long time.

When your life or your church or your company is stuck, review your calendar... and see if you canceled a project God asked you to do a while back.

Jonah was the perfect choice for this mission because it would be the mission that changed him or crushed him...which is what normally happens.

If you are willing to change...you'll be amazed at how much more potential you have!

Quitting derails potential.

Well, Captain Obvious, quitting means *you* decide all on your own to shut down your potential.

The Assyrians didn't crush Jonah's ministry. Their repentance was proof that God was still intimidating, and they wanted to change. Nobody else, not even the ship's crew or a rogue killer whale could be blamed for creating Jonah's anger.

If you're stuck, maybe based on some opposition or opinion you assumed you knew more than God and decided you couldn't or wouldn't do more. Either there was nothing left for you to give or something you refused to give up for God, but you drew a line with God and didn't change.

For Jonah, he didn't want to give any more. The limit he set on his potential had the image of a Nineveh map on it. If possible, Jonah intended to keep his anger and his career.

But...that wasn't possible. God doesn't allow that. College Hall of Fame Coach, Lou Holtz, said, "There will be one thing that will dominate your life. I strongly suggest it be something you can be proud of."

In the Harvard Business Review, Robert Steven Kaplan, now CEO of the Federal Reserve Bank of Dallas, said that during his career with Goldman Sachs, coaching managers at Harvard Business School, and teaching MBA students, he was surprised to find many successful executives were deeply frustrated with their careers: "They looked back and felt that they should have achieved more or even wished that they had chosen a different career altogether." One analyst with a large security firm confessed: "After 10 years, he was tired of his job, disliked his boss, and felt he had no potential for further upward mobility" and wondered if he'd been so busy checking off career goals and trying to "impress other people that he'd lost sight of what he really enjoyed doing."[29]

Life after limiting your potential is not fun.

Ask Jonah. He'll tell you what it felt like inside the fish.

God let Jonah mess up his life, but not end it.

You can ruin your career or ministry...but you can't forgive yourself. God has to do that.

He alone gets you unstuck. And sometimes it's no fun.

When your 4 Wheeler is stuck in the mud, everything will be covered in mud when you get unstuck.

Trendy Belief No. 17:
Serving others is the best way to live your life.

The joke was that President Bush only declared war when Starbucks was hit. You can mess with the U.N. all you want, but when you start interfering with the right to get caffeinated, someone has to pay."
—**Chris Kyle, Author of** *American Sniper: The Autobiography of the Most Lethal Sniper in U.S. Military History*

Honestly, Officer, I wouldn't have pulled over had I known you were just going to criticize me.
—**Bridger Winegar Tweet**

"Just kill me now, Lord! I'd rather be dead than alive if what I predicted will not happen." The Lord replied, "Is it right for you to be angry about this?"
—**Jonah 4:3-4, NLT**

Serving God first is the only way to save your life. Chasing God's purpose can be confusing. A Casting Crowns song, *Just Be Held*, says, "Your world is not falling apart. It's falling into place." What feels like disaster, is in reality, direction.

Definitely not what Jonah believed after the huge fish vomited him out on a beach and Nineveh repented and shut down their terrorist operations. Jonah thought God skipped a step. Maybe there was a box that didn't get checked. Don't people have to pay some consequences even if they repent?

Jonah defined justice as—*enemies removed, worship restored*. How are you defining justice for your situation?

To Jonah, the Assyrians were a *hindrance*. To God, the Assyrians were the *hope* for a seismic shift in history. If they had spiritual turnaround, Israel was saved from their future terrorist attacks! Besides, God's original purpose was for Israel to be a light to the nations.

God is on His throne. He sees every fish and every fit. The famous Israeli prophet, Jonah, was targeted to change a rogue nation…and in the process his own resentful heart.

Real change normally starts with one person plus some pressure. Until you get sick of living under attack and being stuck in fear, nothing changes.

In her book, *Red Glove*, author Holly Black said, "Change is what people do when they have no options left."[1]

Scientist, MIT professor, and author Peter Senge said, "People don't resist change. They resist being changed!"[2]

Jonah preferred to die rather than deal with his hatred and change his attitude. When he saw an entire terrorist city be protected by God it was more than he could take. Latest survey results? You can't rescue people if you're dead.

Serving God in Nineveh was the only way to save his life.

The window of opportunity for ministry is limited.

The gospel is either urgent or unnecessary. It can't be both! God's 40-day deadline for Nineveh to repent was a window of opportunity. Getting the message to them when they would be receptive was life and death for thousands of families.

There are reasons for urgency. Life is short and unpredictable. People harden their hearts on all kinds of stuff, including wanting a divorce.[3] Openness to Jesus is limited because the decision is so easily postponed. When Paul explained the coming judgment to Governor Felix, the politician said he would consider it at a more "convenient" time.[4]

Nobody knows their *last* opportunity to come to Christ.

Except...during the 7-year Tribulation after Jesus has removed believers. Those who refuse worship the Antichrist and take the Mark of the Beast (a number allowing you to buy and sell) will be immediately executed.[5] This is eerily similar to WWII Nazi Germany and the 2015 beheading of 21 Egyptian Christian men by ISIS.

So there is an urgency driving the gospel.

And it can get more complicated because believers can become resentful or indifferent. Jonah was supposed to speak to Nineveh, but he fought God on it—thought it was unnecessary or wasted on people who weren't worth saving.

The gospel is not just "Jesus loves you" or "Jesus forgives". What God made Jonah preach was judgment—the real outcome of unbelief. Part of the gospel is explaining to people that there are eternal consequences for rejecting Jesus as Lord and Savior—separation from God...*in hell...forever.*

Biblically, ministry is communicating the gospel to persuade people to turn to God before it's too late: "*For all of us must appear before Christ, to be judged by him....We know what it means to fear the Lord, and so we try to persuade others*".[6]

Believers should not be casual or neutral. Lives are at stake. You present the gospel to *persuade* people. Pray, urge, explain, argue, plead...or explain to Jesus why that person He told you to talk to was not worth serious effort.[7]

And sometimes there are only days to get your life right...sometimes nobody knows how much time is left.

Ministry is sharing the gospel. Serving is a method.

It's the *gospel* that changes a heart, not *groceries*.

Believe the cool, trendy idea that ministry is just building low-income homes or feeding the homeless and we'll lose the gospel mandate in one generation.

Serving is what Jesus came to do and the most visible and dramatic act of serving was to die on a cross for our sins: *"the Son of Man did not come to be served, but to serve, and to give his life as a ransom for many"*.[8] He healed, fed, and forgave people—serving to create a platform to save. Signs were intended to create belief.[9]

Jesus' ministry was always about His message.

You don't have to make a choice. Serve...*and* save! Volunteer for Habitat for Humanity. Take your family to serve in the boy and girls clubs. Just don't leave the gospel at home.

Trying to low-key the gospel behind serving is wrong. Put it out front. Be who you are. Be Jesus to that hurting person. That's why God put you there. Not to feed the multitudes with your five loaves and two fish, pray for them and then pack up and go home. Preach and heal and love and forgive in the name of Jesus *as you serve*.

God didn't send Jonah to Nineveh to feed homeless terrorists or mentor young terrorists in His love.

Nineveh needed to be saved.

If spiritual needs get ignored, *it's not ministry.*

In 2012, the international, non-denominational relief ministry, Samaritan's Purse (SP), led by Franklin Graham, plunged into the human tragedy of Sudan's civil war. Refugees in South Sudan suffered—victims of an unjust war, bombings and unimaginable horror. Over 90,000 quickly flooded into two refugee camps served by SP.

Families walked for days through the bush to get across the border to safety in the camps. With thousands pouring in weekly, SP was trying to meet basic needs of healthcare, water, and food as they restored an abandoned hospital and brought in 40 medical staff and a surgeon.

But that's not their ministry. Samaritan's Purse intentionally links their relief work with sharing the gospel, the good news of eternal life through Jesus Christ: *"For we do not preach ourselves, but Jesus Christ as Lord, and ourselves as your servants for Jesus' sake"*.[10]

The atrocities were real. That was the moment to save. Countless lives would have been lost without somebody risking serving...and sharing the gospel.

Ministry has a target audience—sinners.

Some time ago, I met with the pastor and executive staff of a large church, discussing the merits of a church adopting the corporate marketing strategy of having a specific demographic profile target. The argument was that if you target young families in your ministries, you will grow the church big time. Everything from convenient parking, signage, trendy music, video promotions, coffee bars, staffing with younger leaders, apps, visible security, iPad check-in, texting during sermons and 1-hour worship to baby changing stations in restrooms would appeal to and capture the generation.

Jesus laid out His target—it was simpler: *"The Son of Man came to look for and to save people who are lost"*.[11] The profile was non-believers. No age, race, religion, lifestyle, income, or background exclusions. Just sinners.

Many churches are tweaking the perks and updating approaches. Crowds are coming. The gospel is minimized.

When I arrived at my first church in Atlanta, they had just been bailed out of bankruptcy, the building needed repair, their reputation in the community was bad, and the few members that remained were divided. On the first Sunday, I explained our one and only reason to exist was to share the gospel—that the only thing that impressed God was His Son, Jesus, not us. The second Sunday I told the people that I would set the example and pulled a piece of paper out of my pocket: "Just want you to know that I have listed the names of 21 people that I had conversations about Jesus with last week." Then I read the names, told a couple of stories, and challenged them to do the same. God always honors those who pursue what Jesus came to do. In the next 5 years, over 4,000 people became a part of that fellowship.

Ministry is *driven by serving* but is *designed for sinners*. You can show the love of God, capture attention, or start a conversation around meeting a need, but a believer's priority is meeting their deepest need by explaining the gospel.

Everybody is right now running from God on some level. Some have permanently rejected God's voice. Others are avoiding something difficult God has asked them to do. People who are running know exactly what their sin is, what they deserve, and what should be done about it (Jonah 1:12).

Ministry is explaining the gospel to people are running from God, in order to bridge them to God—helping sinners be reconciled to Christ: *"All this is from God, who reconciled us to himself through Christ and gave us the ministry of reconciliation".*[12]

There are no "good" people.

Nobody understands, searches for, or fears God.[13]

Nineveh was evil. So was Jonah.

Jonah's anger proved he was as far from God as them.

Why would God want to send Jonah anywhere else? The Assyrians were evil, and judgment was imminent. The 40-day countdown to judgment was the radical love of God. Nobody ever deserves forgiveness or even a warning.

Jonah and Nineveh were really no different. If ministry leaders could just come to grips with the fact that people love themselves more than God, love sin and linger in sin until forced to deal with it—you'd be less vulnerable to discouragement in ministry.

The target is sinners. I'm really glad a couple of my buddies in college targeted me with the gospel. I didn't fit the church culture. God told them to come after me anyway.

Happiness depends on where you get your identity.

Jonah's story is about identity.

Jonah didn't want to be who God called him to be. He found his identity in his career, not in his call—serving wherever and whenever God wanted. So when God called him to Nineveh and it didn't fit the lifestyle and outcome he wanted for his career—he loses it!

If your identity is linked to your career, that's where you seek approval to feel good about yourself. When your career is threatened, your world is shaken. If you define your worth in anything besides serving God, you'll be crushed.

Your career is what you do, not who you are—even church careers can't be your life. Identity is found in Christ. Your career is the source of your provision and generosity. It's the impact you make on people by serving that they remember, not what you do for a living.

Serving others requires that you first sell-out to God's purpose: *"My servant Caleb has a different spirit and follows me wholeheartedly".*[14] *"Offer yourselves as a living sacrifice to God dedicated to His service and pleasing to Him".*[15]

Pastor Tim Keller said, "If we get our very identity, our sense of worth, from our political position, then politics is not really about politics, it is about us. Through our cause we are getting a self, our worth. That means we MUST despise and demonize the opposition. If we get our identity from our ethnicity or socioeconomic status, then we HAVE to feel superior to those of other classes and races. If you are profoundly proud of being an open-minded, tolerant soul, you will be extremely indignant toward people you think are bigots. If you are a very moral person, you will feel superior to people you think are licentious. And so on."[16]

Jonah got his identity from his career—a traditional Jewish prophet with huge pride and superiority. When God chose the terrorist Assyrians over Jonah's protest, he wanted to die.

Be careful what you live for. It might kill you.

God's miracles are for people who want Him.

My wife is a speech therapist for about 60 children and can relate to this mom and speech therapist. Pamela Spinney said her five-year-old, Matt, worked with a speech therapist on the *ch* sound, which came out *k*. The therapist asked him to say *chicken*. He responded with *kitchen*. They tried again and again, but it always came out *kitchen*. Undeterred, she pushed him for one more try. Matt sighed and said, "Why don't we just call it a *duck*?"[17]

When you're tired of trying to change, progress stops.

One big reason churches start dying is they don't want things to change. There's zero desire for a fresh work of God to do the hard work of rescuing people.

Churches don't trend into decline because of changing demographics, lack of member commitment, downturns in giving, outdated facilities, underperforming leadership, or websites that haven't been updated. Those are all symptoms of hearts that shut God out on some issue—quit just like Jonah.

External circumstances are never an excuse. Peter and the apostles were arrested, threatened two times not to preach Jesus, and flogged by Jewish authorities.[18] The church grew stronger after that! If any church had reason to quit, it was those guys and they kept preaching!

God deals exclusively with the heart. When your heart cannot be broken with the things that break the heart of God...you're done. Everything you do from that point forward in any organization is just faking it—going through the motions, trying to pump up passion, living off faded images of past success. It's not that dying churches simply lack passion. No, passion fades after purpose is lost.

When Jonah went ballistic with his anger over God saving Nineveh, it just proved he didn't want God. Anger is the big push back. Anger signals you don't want that person interfering in your life.

God did the miracle for Nineveh...not for Jonah.

God saved Nineveh. God crushed Jonah.

Courage in serving is doing whatever it takes.

His story was a runaway #1 *New York Times* bestselling memoir. U.S. Navy Seal Chris Kyle's military career was also the story for Clint Eastwood's blockbuster movie, *American Sniper*, nominated for six academy awards, including best picture.

Kyle was sent to Iraq with one mission: protect his brothers-in-arms. From 1999 to 2009, Kyle recorded the most career sniper kills in U.S. military history. His fellow American warriors, whom he protected with deadly precision from rooftops and stealth positions during the Iraq War, called him "The Legend". The enemy feared him so much they named him *al-Shaitan* ("the devil") and placed a price on his head, making him a big target for insurgents. Kyle, tragically murdered in 2013, faced the worst pain of war—the deaths of two close SEAL teammates and the battle to be a good husband and father from halfway around the world. Coming home after 4 tours of duty in Iraq, Chris struggled to leave the war behind. His wife, Taya, keeps his memory alive.

Kyle said, "The thing we all had in common wasn't muscle; it was the will to do whatever it takes." His courage to serve was obvious: "I am a strong Christian. Not a perfect one—not close. But I strongly believe in God, Jesus, and the Bible. When I die, God is going to hold me accountable for everything I've done on earth....I believe the fact that I've accepted Jesus as my Savior will be my salvation. But...when God confronts me with my sins, I do not believe any of the kills I had during the war will be among them. Everyone I shot was evil. I had good cause on every shot. They all deserved to die."[19]

Kyle risked his life for 4 tours to protect our freedom.

Nineveh turning to God was comparable to Iraq repenting.

It would have seemed impossible...and unfair.

Unlike Kyle, Jonah had to be forced to finish his mission.

Facing long held prejudice and hatred was harder for Jonah than a tour of duty in Iraq.

Courage is whatever it takes to finish the mission.

Jonah was stuck in Nineveh until God was finished crushing him. He goes out to the east side of the city, builds a shelter, and waits, hoping that God will change

His mind and wipe out the city anyway. So God decided to drive home a lesson. God arranged for a worm to kill the huge plant Jonah loved that was shading him from the blistering sun. Under intense heat from a scorching east wind God sent, Jonah wanted to die for the second time. So God launched the cross-examination: "Is it right for you to be angry because the plant died?" Jonah defended his right to be angry or die—basically saying he was right to want Nineveh to be wiped off the map.

Then God nailed him: "You feel sorry about the plant, though you did nothing to put it there. It came quickly and died quickly....Nineveh has more than 120,000 people living in spiritual darkness....Shouldn't I feel sorry for such a great city?".[20]

Jonah was more upset over being inconvenienced than thousands of families dying!

Bigger picture? Jonah was angry because God held him accountable to forgive his worst enemy.

Jonah didn't have the courage to finish that mission.

Weak people get revenge. Strong people forgive.

The first to apologize is the bravest.

The first to forgive is the strongest.

The first to forget is the happiest.

Serving adds value to your life.

In a national magazine, Nancy Clark joked, "I've given up social media for the New Year and am trying to make friends outside Facebook while applying the same principles. Every day, I walk down the street and tell passersby what I've eaten, how I feel, what I did the night before, and what I will do tomorrow. Then I give them pictures of my family, my dog, and me gardening. I also listen to their conversations and tell them I love them. And it works. I already have three people following me—two police officers and a psychiatrist."[21]

It's embarrassing to realize Facebook is sharing personal info publicly with people who don't care about your dessert, dog, or daffodils.

Unlike Facebook, serving people in Jesus' name is noticed and rewarded by God. Jesus said, *"My Father will honor anyone who serves Me"*.[22] Being faithful in this life pays blessings forward.

In my most recent church, we averaged 10 community service projects each year, as diverse as: Miracle League (baseball for children with mental and physical disabilities), meals for police departments, feeding the homeless, adopting every child for Christmas in the foster care system of a local agency, and mentoring elementary children, to serving a local women's shelter.

Serving to meet real needs in the name of Jesus should be our lifestyle. But our ministry is to introduce people to Jesus.

Serving adds value because God gives opportunity to make people aware that Jesus changes lives: *"Keep busy in your work for the Lord, since you know that nothing you do in the Lord's service is ever without value"*.[23]

Pastor Rick Warren said, "To be a servant you must think like a servant.... Servanthood requires a mental shift, a change in your attitudes. God is always more interested in why we do something than in what we do."[24]

Speaking the truth is the right way to serve others.

To save Nineveh, Jonah had to speak truth.

Destruction was coming. No details on God's method of judgment were given, which would have made it even more scary. Like in a horror movie, when a girl just keeps walking through a dark house. You hold your breath because you know what's coming...you just don't know when.

Speaking the truth is hard...but it can save a life.

Believing in your message helps.

Two Blind Brothers. That's not just their business name. It's who they are. At a young age, Bradford and Bryan Manning were both diagnosed with Stargardt's, a type of macular degeneration causing vision loss in the center of the retina and blindness over time. This condition has inspired a passion for details that carries over into their clothing line—graphic Tees, hoodies, three-button Henleys—made in part from bamboo fibers at the Dallas Lighthouse for the Blind. Their garment company has grown so big so fast that Bradford, 32, and Bryan, 27, both University of Virginia grads, left their full-time jobs in investment banking and big-data sales to focus on their brand. They've appeared on *Ellen* and have done a *TED Talk*. Bradford advises, "Believe in what you're talking about! You can always hear it in someone's voice when they believe in their message. Remember that what you have to say is worth listening to."[25]

The Manning brothers speak the truth about their condition and challenges wherever they go. Embracing their blindness makes them believable.

Jonah shouted truth for three days in the streets of Nineveh, but it wasn't believable. Hoping Nineveh would ignore it and be wiped out by God, Jonah exploded with anger when they repented.

Nobody changes without hearing truth.

Nineveh needed to hear it. Jonah needed to hear it.

You need to hear it. It makes you better at serving.

Trendy Belief No. 18:
You can't know God's will with 100% certainty.

The most terrifying thing any woman can say to me is,
"Notice anything different?"
—Mike Vanatta, Comedian

I just asked my husband if he remembers what today is...Scaring men is easy.
—Anonymous

"Nineveh has more than 120,000 people living in spiritual darkness, not to
mention all the animals. Shouldn't I feel sorry for such a great city?"
—Jonah 4:11, NLT

It's impossible to miss the will of God.

Q: How do you know if someone has an iPhone?
A: They tell you.

If Apple can get the word out so good that they've sold over 1 billion iPhones in just 10 years, then agree with me that the Creator of the universe can get a message to you.

You can *reject* God's plan for your life, temporarily *run* from it—you can never permanently hide or escape—or *rant* against it, but you *recognize* it!!!

If you actually buy in to the crazy trendy belief that nobody can guess God's will, good luck making any decision with confidence or certainty. You'll be the guy stuck in the Taco Bell drive-thru lane staring at the menu board.

If it were possible for you miss it, then you would always have to guess it. When God speaks you'll know it. There's zero doubt or confusion.

Nothing happens with God's will until you "leave".
My favorite tv program is ESPN Game Day. Can't beat the college campus craziness; surprise proposals in the student crowd; ridiculous signs; football talk and picks with Rece Davis, Lee Corso, Kirk Herbstreit, Desmond Howard, and David Pollack;

funny commercials; Corso putting on the mascot heads, local food served up to the crew; and, powerful insider interviews.

A 9-29-18 backstory video was about Texas A&M offensive lineman Koda Martin, who married Jazzmin Babers, who happens to be the daughter of Syracuse Orange football head coach Dino Babers. Koda transferred to Syracuse and the couple lives in her parent's basement. Jazzmin said she enjoys the free food and no cooking for this phase of their life. Koda said Coach Babers doesn't give him a single break in practice but thinks that's right and fair.

When Koda left College Station, he posted an emotional farewell on social media, mentioning the 12th Man, memories of teammates and coaches and the Aggie ring, But this caught my attention: "I know without a doubt that God brought me to College Station, Texas on purpose and for a purpose. I'm so grateful for the memories....I receive my degree in May, and this chapter of my life is coming to a close. After much thought and prayer, I made the decision to continue my education at Syracuse University for my final season of college football."

Jazzmin's dad, Coach Babers, said, "I like my daughter being around. It's good to really get to know Koda. But I raised them so they would leave! I didn't raise them so they would stay!"[1]

Two big takeaways. First, Koda had no doubt it was God's will for him to specifically do college and football at College Station, Texas. So, more proof people really do hear God and know with 100% certainty they are in His will. He had to *leave* home, *leave* his parents to marry Jazzmin, and later he had to *leave* the life he built at Texas A&M to follow the next step in God's plan. Second, like Coach Babers, God raises His kids to *leave* also!

It was God's will for Jonah to leave and go to a specific city at a set time for a special reason.

Nothing happens until you leave.

A lot happens when you follow-through.

The last time you left will not be the last time you leave.

So many lives yet to impact.

Will you "leave" or stay in the basement?

God doesn't have a communication problem.

A guy joked, "My girlfriend was complaining last night that I never listen to her... Or something like that..."

God doesn't have to listen to you. You need to listen.

You know when God is speaking and know what He is saying. You can never say you don't know His will. The perennial problem is listening and following through.

Jonah ran because he heard God clearly—not because he was confused about what God expected from him.

After the storm...after being swallowed...after being spit-out on the beach...after speaking through the streets of Nineveh...after the sackcloth and ashes of Nineveh's repentance...after the sun stroke when the worm killed the plant...God speaks directly to Jonah...again.

What happened was rare. God explained *why* he put Jonah through all this: *"Nineveh has more than 120,000 people living in spiritual darkness"*.[2]

Most of the time you are conflicted with doubts about whether God led you to do something or it was your idea. Almost never does God allow you to learn reasons *why* things happen like they do when you are still in the situation.

God spoke directly to Jonah. *He still does that for you.*

God gave Jonah *four* specific pieces of info *upfront!*

God answered Jonah's new prayer immediately.

God explained *why* He sent Jonah to Nineveh.

God communicates really well!

If you could totally miss God's will it would mean God struggles to get us to listen or explain things to us. That implies God could never get your attention long enough for you to know it was Him. Or penetrate your distractions well enough to adequately tell you the next step. Or clarify the big steps like career, marriage, dating, kids, investments, season tickets, home loans, ministry, or iPhone vs. Android.

American Episcopal priest, professor, author and theologian, Barbara Brown Taylor wrote: "Visions from God are not the exception, but the norm."[3] Visions were *not* the norm in scripture.

God speaks in diverse ways[4] but before you chase visions, read your Bible, man! God starts with scripture—that's His will for you. And seasoned believers will tell you it's almost never complicated. If you want direction, God will give it. Most of the time it is black and white clear...and common-sense simple.

Plus...He prompts thoughts when you pray, sets up circumstances to get your attention, sends people to advise you, squeezes your conscience in the right direction, loads you up with necessary gifts and resources and contacts, exposes you to multiple experiences, and either gives you a surge of peace or withdraws your contentment to re-direct you to the right decision.

God has plenty of options to get you to the right decision.

And He uses them...in a way you can't ignore.

If God wanted His name and fame to spread, why wouldn't He make the guidelines, rules, boundaries, principles, and precepts easy to get?

He gives signs.

He creates opportunities.

He opens doors. He closes doors.

He whispers to your heart.

He sends big fish to swallow you...

An open door may not be God's will.

Not every opportunity is from God. Jonah made the choice to run from God by buying a ticket and boarding the ship. The trip and the ship were available and accessible.

Just because you can do something doesn't mean it's God's will. An open door is not final proof that God is leading you through it.

Every opportunity has to be screened. Your security layers should include making sure the opportunity: aligns with scripture, is consistent with how God has been leading you in recent circumstances, meets the long-term goals you think God has for you, confirms what you have prayed, fits with counsel from mature, godly people in your network, and doesn't pull you in to any temptation.

Getting on that ship, Jonah violated everything on that list.

So Jonah interfered with God's plan and hung on to his incredibly dangerous anger a few days longer.

Opportunity does not equal permission.

It may not even equal smart decision.

Classic stories in scripture warn against those first open doors popping up—like Eve and the fruit.

What's your filter?

You don't know God's will until you commit to it.

2008. Tim Tebow had just won the Heisman Trophy. Florida Gators Coach Urban Meyer had built a monster football team with a roster that included Tebow and 29 other future NFL players. Everybody expected them to go undefeated—roll over opponents. But in the opening game of the season against unranked Ole Miss, Tebow failed to convert a final 4th and 1 play and the Rebels upset Florida 31-30. Fighting back tears at the post game media conference, in classic Tebow mode, he spoke from the heart:

> *To the fans and everybody in Gator Nation, I'm sorry. I'm extremely sorry. We were hoping for an undefeated season. That was my goal, something Florida has never done here. I promise you one thing, a lot of good will come out of this. You will never see any player in the entire country play as hard as I will play the rest of the season. You will never see someone push the rest of the team as hard as I will push everybody the rest of the season. You will never see a team play harder than we will the rest of the season. God Bless.[5]*

One of Tebow's teammates said that speech turned the team around. The Gators responded by winning the rest of their games and beating Oklahoma 24-14 to win Florida's 2nd national title in just three years.

Coach Meyer quickly had the speech engraved on a plaque labeled "The Promise" and placed outside the stadium. It sill inspires 10 years later. Without that intense commitment, there would not have another championship.

Most people don't know the biblical sequence for knowing God's will.

Commitment first. Details later.

God expects you make the commitment first and He fills in the details. Just say "YES" to God and let Him take it from there. The tendency is to ask God to explain what He has planned for you and then you decide if you can commit to it. That's backwards. Why?

Because surrender to God...not service...is His will.

Your relationship to Him...your worship of Him...is first.

God has a specific will for everything.

120,000. God knew the exact number of people in Nineveh living in spiritual darkness. That city and every family in it were valuable to Him. If statistics are needed to motivate you or educate you, God will overwhelm you with facts and stories.

Not only did God have compassion for all those families, but He refused to allow Jonah to change or remove that compassion. The result was an entire metro area coming to faith in God. An entire culture was quickly changed.

Isn't it amazing that God always emphasized the people factor in projects? Whatever He calls you to do will be about specific people...a specific location...a specific time... with a specific message. Originally, God not only directly told Jonah the specific city for his project and God's view of their current spiritual condition and degree of openness, but gave him the timing and specific words he was supposed to speak.

Some think it doesn't make any difference to God what career you choose—just pick something to make you happy and more money will make you happier.

Or who you marry, just as long as you choose somebody compatible that you can trust, believing that any relationship can work out. How ridiculous to assume that the same God who created the precision of the ocean tides and planetary rotations doesn't have a specific will about a life-time mate—a pre-determined plan that He wants you to follow to give you an amazing life and ministry together.

God isn't random. The biological mom and name for His Son were pre-chosen. God selected ahead of time the nation, country, city, town, village, mountains, desert, or jungle where every person would originate or migrate; your family, physical body and appearance, race, language, experiences and culture He wanted to shape your life, including your birth date:

> "God, who made the world and everything in it, since He is Lord of heaven and earth, does not dwell in temples made with hands. Nor is He worshiped with men's hands, as though He needed anything, since He gives to all life, breath, and all things. And He has made from one

*blood every nation of men to dwell on all the face of the earth, and **has determined their pre-appointed times and the boundaries of their dwellings** [emphasis mine], so that they should seek the Lord, in the hope that they might grope for Him and find Him, though He is not far from each one of us; for in Him we live and move and have our being..."*[6]

All of scripture portrays the sovereign God as having a specific plan for everything. For example, in the 60-plus Old Testament prophecies, with more than 300 references about the coming Messiah covering details from His birth city to His crucifixion that could only have been fulfilled in Jesus,[7] every event was planned and perfectly timed for an eternal purpose.

No coincidences. No accidents.

Nor does God adjust His plans "in flight", moment-by-moment, based on your whims, choices, failures, flings, or surprises. Proactive, not reactive. Author and bible teacher, John MacArthur, spoke about God's will for singles seeking dates and mates: "You don't go to an airport and take the first flight anywhere. You have a destination in mind."

God's into *control*...not *commentary*.

God wants you to succeed, despite your pride.

God is good. His will is good.

And set up to be perfect for *you*.[8]

From the launch of this project, God wanted Jonah to be successful. Think about it. God was setting in motion an opportunity for Jonah to see an entire city and culture reject evil and immoral lifestyles and turn to God.

Unprecedented. Jonah was chosen to play *the* key role in a miracle for thousands of families. The choice was undeserved and unexpected.

God has planned for your success...in His will.

Everything God does in your life is driven by love: *"For I know the thoughts that I think toward you, says the Lord, thoughts of peace and not of evil, to give you a future and a hope".*[9]

Thinking God might deliberately withhold information that could make you successful or mislead you so that you make the wrong decision is just...**wrong!**

God sent a storm and set up a swallowing to save Jonah's life, even though Jonah had run from God. Jonah's life was spared for 3D/3N *and* for three more days walking through Nineveh shouting a message that risked his life as a Jew and a prophet. When Jonah asked God twice to die, it was ignored. At every step and in every detail—including Jonah's rebellion—God was making sure Jonah would succeed, even if he hated what he was doing.

His father was a poor preacher who bounced from one small congregation to another, eventually landing at a church of just 35 people in Altus, Oklahoma, a small town surrounded by cattle ranches and cotton fields. The family of six children survived with hand-me-down clothes and food donations from their church. David Green's mother still gave generously to others, saying, "We don't give out of our need, we give out of our surplus."[10]

That legacy of faith motivated David and his wife, Barbara, to borrow $600 and start making miniature picture frames at his family's kitchen table with their two young sons, whose allowance was 7 cents. David opened a 300 square-foot craft-supply store in 1972 in Oklahoma City, and God began to prosper him.

David Green had founded Hobby Lobby.

Fast forward to 1986. His arts and crafts retail chain was in danger of foreclosure. Hobby Lobby founder, David Green, had made a near-fatal decision to over-leverage the company and expand too fast. Coupled with the collapse of the oil industry in Oklahoma that had already driven other businesses into bankruptcy, it threatened to take the company under.

Although the foreclosure of the business was the worst thing they could imagine, they came to see it as a defining moment in their business and spiritual lives. "I know I prayed prior to that time," David Green says, "but that's when I got really serious about it."[11]

The space underneath his desk became a private prayer closet. Crawling under his desk, he would cry out to God. Green described his leadership style: "It was a pride problem, and I had to get rid of it. It's sort of like God says to me, because I was arrogant, 'I'm going to let you have it by yourself.'"[12]

Green simply prayed, "God, this is your company; I give it to you. If you want it to survive, it's up to you."[12]

God did want Hobby Lobby *and* David Green to survive...and succeed.

Hobby Lobby is now a $3 billion arts and crafts chain—a retail monster that boasts 22,000 employees, and 680 superstores in 42 states. Worth about $5 billion personally, Green is the largest donor to evangelical causes in America and unashamedly shares:

> We're Christians, and we run our business on Christian principles. If you have anything or if I have anything, it's because it's been given to us by our Creator. So I have learned to say, 'Look, this is yours, God. It's all yours. I'm going to give it to you.' I don't care if you're in business or out of business, God owns it. How do I separate it? Well, it's God's in church and it's mine here? I have purpose in church, but I don't have purpose over here? You can't have a belief system on Sunday and not live it the other six days.

> Woolworth's is gone. Sears is almost gone. TG&Y is gone. So what? This is worth billions of dollars. So what? Is that the end of life, making more money and building something? For me, I want to

know that I have affected people for eternity. I believe I am. I believe once someone knows Christ as their personal savior, I've affected eternity. I matter 10 billion years from now. I matter. Someone that does all this doesn't matter. I'm sorry, it's gone.[13]

Our problem is never that we miss or even misunderstand what God expects in any decision. Our tension is with obedience. You can *reject* God's will or *resist* God's will or *run* from God's will, but you cannot say it was never *revealed* to you.

Truthfully, the more questions you ask, the more you debate a decision, the more tense or hyper you get over what to do...normally means that you don't want to obey what you already know God is telling you to do!

David Green has donated multi-million dollar facilities to Liberty University and a 170-acre ranch retreat to Rick Warren's Saddleback Church. He has restarted Oral Roberts University and sponsors the YouVersion Bible app for mobile phones, equipped to offer almost 300 different versions of Scripture in 144 languages--all available at the tap of your finger and downloaded more than 50 million times. Just three blocks from the U.S. Capitol in Washington, D.C. is the new $500 million Museum of the Bible that the Green family has largely funded for the purpose of inviting people to engage with the Bible.

And...for the sake of disclosure, David Green has blessed my life personally. A few years ago, I became pastor of a small church in a resort community in the Midwest that was struggling to survive. That is, until Hobby Lobby anonymously purchased a $3 million former show theater on 55 acres and donated it to save the church. People traveling from all over the world worshiped at our church in Branson, Missouri.

It's not amazing that God wanted David Green to succeed.

It's not amazing that David's pride was broken, and a miracle started during the *1986-under-the-desk prayer.*

It's not amazing that Jonah's pride was broken, and a miracle started during his *inside-the-fish-belly prayer.*

It's not amazing that David has become the largest giver.

It's not amazing that the entire city of Nineveh repented.

What's amazing is that Jonah never really did!

When an entire city starts worshiping God, that's success!

When one person refuses to worship God...that's crazy.

Tension is the result of following your own plans.

The only time believers have tension in their life is when they substitute their choice for God's will. Tension comes from refusing to do something God has already asked you to do. Fear comes from believing that God is not with you or will mislead you.

Lead Pastor of Forefront Church, New York City and Chairman of the Board for the African Dream Initiative, Brian Moll blogged about a weird call from a good friend who had moved to the West Coast. His friend explained that his marriage was falling apart, and God was telling him to "move on" because his wife was train-wrecking his life. He wanted Brian to agree with his decision as "God's best" for them both. So Brian asked some questions:

> "Has your wife ever cheated on you? Ever abused you, mentally or physically? Is she oppressive or has she been unfaithful in any way?"

> His friend, Will answered, "No. Never. Why?"

> "....it sounds like you're just really annoyed with your wife, and that's no reason to split up. Listen...I know marriage can be tough. I've been married to five different women in 14 years, all of them to a woman named Allison. In the past 14 years my wife has changed, and so have I. At times we've both wanted to throw in the towel, and at times we've both wondered (and asked God) if we married the wrong person, but had we given up we wouldn't be together today, and we would've missed out on the adventure we're currently engrossed in. Perhaps what you need to do is simply love your wife, best as you can, for the next six months. No complaining, no lists about what she's doing wrong. Just love and serve her, and see what happens. I'll even pay for counseling if that helps. But don't give up." Two weeks later he posted pictures on social media of him with another woman. I guess "God" led him to someone better for him, after all.[14]

God's will is in His Word. Jonah got God's word directly.
Jonah knew God's will with 100% certainty.
He was angry because he disagreed with it.
It's just easier to quit when you feel the tension between what God is telling you and what you want to do.

God doesn't have a compassion deficiency.

A Christian leader blogged this story about God's love:

> *Bonnie's daughter had lost her wallet, which contained her driver's license, social security card, debit card, their family's credit card, and several gift cards. They thought she might have dropped it at a certain gas station, so they drove back there, searched everywhere, and spoke to the attendant about it. But the wallet couldn't be found. However, Bonnie encouraged her daughter to pray over the situation. Her daughter reminded herself that God loved her and cared for her. Three days after the wallet was*

lost, they found it in their mailbox—with everything intact! "Not one penny, gift card, or any other item had been taken from it," Bonnie wrote, rejoicing.[15]

God loves all people. Jonah was more selective.

Jonah was being instructed like a Navy SEAL. God was hammering Jonah over his total blindness to the spiritual destiny of 120,000 people in the metro capital city.

No way Jonah could get his mind around God's limitless compassion. How insane for Jonah to try to block God's compassion for anybody!

Jonah likely had legitimate reasons to hate Assyrians for the terrorism and fear they had unleashed on Israel and the nations. Maybe his family or friends had been victims of their atrocities.

They really were evil. But that's not the point. God is good.

God doesn't love sinners too much. He just loves them too much to leave them alone. God's love has never ignored sin. It's prompted Him to invite all sinners to be forgiven. Loving sinners cost God the life of His Son, Jesus, on the cross. His death paid for the sins of the whole world. Simply by turning from your sins and asking Jesus to come into your life as Lord and Savior, you can have eternal life.

That's compassion...when anybody, including Nineveh and me, can be forgiven!

God's will is focused on the next generation.

The jokes say the 20-somethings millennials: spend too much money on avocado toast and pumpkin spice lattes to buy homes, think 2012 had the best music ever, that if all millennials died the headline the next day would say millennials are driving up funeral costs, swear constantly, file lawsuits about microaggressions, live in their parent's basements to pay off never-ending student loans, and that in the millennial version of Monopoly you move around the board renting property.

For teens, the label Generation Z is most frequently used, but they are also referred to as the "Selfie Generation," "iGen," "Post-Millennials," the "App Generation," "TransGeneration," and more. Dr. Sean McDowell has found 9 insights for Gen Z:

1. ***Digital Natives:*** *While Millennials grew up in a technologically savvy and connected world, younger members of Generation Z cannot remember a world without the Internet. They grew up swiping an iPad before they learned how to talk and are the first generation to be raised in the era of smartphones. Teenage members of Gen Z are connected nearly every waking hour of the day.*
2. ***Entrepreneurial:*** *Gen Z'ers have been raised with businesses such as Uber and Airbnb, seeing how easy and simple it is to use your own time and resources to make money. 72% of older members of Gen Z want to start their own business.*
3. ***Diverse:*** *This is the last generation that will be majority white (52%). Between 2000-2010, the country's Hispanic population grew at four times the rate of the total*

population. The idea of a black president is not exceptional to them—its normal. Gen Z'ers have grown up experiencing diversity, and they feel overwhelmingly positive about it.

4. ***Less Religious Identification:*** *In 1966, 6.6% of incoming freshman reported being unaffiliated with any religion. In 2015, nearly one-third (29.6%) of all incoming college students reported not identifying with any particular religion. The question is whether young people today are truly moving away from religion or just defining themselves differently than previous generations.*

5. ***Blurry:*** *Formerly distinct lines are now considered "blurry." Technology has blurred the lines between home and work, study and entertainment, and public and private. Gen Z'ers have a different experience of family—same-sex households, working moms, stay-at-home dads, three-parent families, and couples choosing not to have kids. The nuclear family will make up less than a third of all families by 2026. And, of course, gender and romantic identities have become blurry as well.*

6. ***Overwhelmed:*** *In her interviews with teens for her article in Time magazine, Susanna Schrobsdorff says that "there was a pervasive sense that being a teenager today is a draining full-time job that includes doing schoolwork, managing a social media identity and fretting about career, climate change, sexism, racism—you name it." 68% feel overwhelmed by everything they need to do each week.*

7. ***Lonely:*** *3 million adolescents 12-17 have had a "major depressive episode" in the past year. There has been in increase in anxiety and depression among high school students since 2012. And this upsurge cuts across virtually all demographics—suburban, urban, and rural.*

8. ***Progressive:*** *Most Gen Z'ers plan to get married, have children, and buy a home— although probably later than previous generations. And they are less likely to drink, smoke, and take drugs. Yet they hold more progressive views on issues like the legality of marijuana and the morality of same-sex marriage.*

9. ***Individualistic:*** *Anne Fisher captures the forces that have helped create an individualistic emphasis among this generation: "Gen Z is used to having everything personalized just for them, from playlists to newsfeeds to products features of all kinds. They've grown up expecting that."*[16]

This next generation needs God. God knows them just as he knew the young generation of Nineveh. The spiritual need will never change. The will of God is to get the gospel to the next generation regardless of their history, habits, or hatred.

Because God forced Jonah to warn Nineveh of a 40-day window of grace before coming judgment, the terrorist capital city ended their evil lifestyles and turned to God. Because of that radical change, when God prompted Assyria in 740 BC and 722 BC to conquer Israel as judgment upon Israel's idolatry and child sacrifice,[17] they were merciful, and did not annihilate Israel.

Everything about Jonah's call was targeted for Nineveh's Generation Next!

Jonah wrote off the next generation in Nineveh.

He didn't think they were worth saving.

Jonah's sin of pride had shifted his vision—downsized it to only love, lead, and lift up his group!

We are one generation away from judgment.

If you're not good under pressure, don't fight God.

A comedian joked, "I asked my North Korean friend how it was there. He said he couldn't complain."

No way we can understand life in the secretive nation. Under threat of death, over 28,000 North Korean (DPRK) refugees have made it to South Korea to tell their stories. Food and electricity are scarce and living conditions brutal. Lasting years longer than Soviet Gulags and Nazi concentration camps, the six known DPRK prison camps detain people for "political crimes" like listening to a South Korean pop song, attempting to make a phone call outside of the country, creasing the picture of a North Korean leader or otherwise doing anything to insult the authority of the leadership. North Korea punishes the "criminal" and up to three generations of that person's family by forced labor, life imprisonment, execution, rape, forced abortion, or torture. An estimated 80,000 to 120,000 people are currently being detained in North Korea's political prison camps.[18]

None of that compares to the brutality of the Assyrians in Jonah's generation. They were the original terrorists, boasting of skinning people alive and hanging their skins upon the walls. Enemies were beheaded, and their heads stacked in columns to create fear. Pregnant women had their babies ripped from their bodies. All of that and the history of threat to Israel was deeply embedded in Jonah.

Hating Assyrians was normal and justifiable...except when God decided to rescue them—to offer the nation, starting with the capital city of Nineveh—an opportunity to escape judgment. So risky was the mission that God called just one man and gave him one line: "Forty days from now, Nineveh will be destroyed!"

When God cancelled the destruction, who could blame Jonah for his anger against God? Just the thought of that evil being permanently ended—the threat gone in his lifetime with no more fear and military buildups and lives lost—was a huge hope. Then the miracle! But not in the way Jonah wanted.

Jonah refused his call—rejected not just the mission, but God's mercy, from the start.

And the pressure was on!

Pressure in North Korea is unbelievable.

Pressure from rejecting God is worse.

Fight His plan and you'll be judged...

Complacency is a sin.

Don't know if you care, but one of the worst sins is complacency.

Jonah's feelings of anger against God, the mission, and Nineveh has been identified as pride...sometimes as prejudice...or even deeper seated as personal bitterness. Regardless of source, the resulting attitude of complacency is definitely a sin.

Jesus hates it and gave an ominous warning to a 1st century church in Laodicea (modern Turkey): *"I know all the things you do, that you are neither hot nor cold. I wish that you were one or the other! But since you are like lukewarm water, neither hot nor cold, I will spit you out of my mouth!"*[19]

It was Jonah's sin. He didn't care if Nineveh perished.

God forced him to face what he hated.

Don't avoid God. Don't argue with God. Don't get angry with God.

You'll get SWALLOWED!

ABOUT THE AUTHOR

N ow a speaker and consultant, **Russ Shinpoch** has been a pastor and mentor for over three decades. Known as a bible teacher, he has led churches of thousands of members. His passion is mentoring leaders in churches, education, business, and sports. Russ and his wife, Carol, are blessed with three children and nine grandchildren. They live in the Greenville, South Carolina area.

Get to know Russ better @ redsharkadventures.com

Endnotes

Chapter 1

1. Jonah 1:17.
2. Jonah 1:12, NLT.
3. Jonah 1:14.
4. John 3:18.
5. 1 Peter 5:5.
6. Numbers 14:40ff, Romans 14:23; John 16:9.
7. Numbers 14:9-1.
8. Daniel 3:17-18.
9. Matthew 26:69-75; John 21; Acts 2:14.
10. Tim Keller, Christian Quotes, © 2018 Telling Ministries LLC. https://www.christian-quotes.info/quotes-by-author/tim-keller-quotes/#ixzz5Q9GCXN24
11. 2 Timothy 1:7.
12. Joyce Meyer, "Do It Afraid", Joyce Meyer Ministries, © 2018 Joyce Meyer Ministries. https://joycemeyer.org/everydayanswers/ea-teachings/do-it-afraid
13. Debbie McDaniel, "40 Inspiring Quotes from Elisabeth Elliot", Crosswalk.com, 6-17-15, © 2018 Crosswalk.com. https://www.crosswalk.com/faith/spiritual-life/inspiring-quotes/40-inspiring-quotes-from-elisabeth- elliot.html
14. Ephesians 6:10-18; 2 Corinthians 10:3-5.

Chapter 2

1. Matthew 4:19.
2. J. Maureen Henderson, "Why 'Do What Makes You Happy' Is The Dumbest Advice You Can Give Someone", FORBES, 2-29-16, © 2018 Forbes Media LLC. https://www.forbes.com/sites/jmaureenhenderson/2016/02/29/why-do-what-makes-you-happy-is-the-dumbest-advice-you-can-give-someone/#4d1f0cfc1501
3. Sarah O'Brien, "Consumers cough up $5,400 a year on impulse purchases", CNBC, 2-23-18, © 2018 CNBC LLC, A Division of NBCUniversal. https://www.cnbc.com/2018/02/23/consumers-cough-up-5400-a-year-on-impulse-purchases.html
4. Kahlid Saleh, "The State of Impulse Buying Persona – Statistics and Trends", Invesp, © 2006-2017 Invesp. https://www.invespcro.com/blog/impulse-buying/
5. Romans 12:2b.
6. Romans 8:28-29.
7. Matthew 16:24-26; 1 Peter 4:12-19.
8. Colossians 3:1-5; Philippians 3:12-14, 20.
9. Steve Irwin, Brainy Quote, https://www.brainyquote.com/authors/steve_irwin

[10] John McMullen, "Foles Reflects on a Crazy Journey", © 2018, 97.3 ESPN, Townsquare Media. http://973espn.com/foles-reflects-on-a-crazy-journey/

[11] Philippians 2:13.

[12] Matthew 13:20-21.

[13] Genesis 18:22-33.

[14] Exodus 32:7-14.

[15] 1 Samuel 17:45-50.

[16] Luke 19:41-44; 23:34.

[17] Neil T. Anderson, Liberating Prayer, (Eugene, OR: Harvest House Publishers, © 2012), Ch. 2.

[18] Matthew 26:39.

[19] Romans 12:2.

[20] Tricia Goyer, "Align Your Heart with God's Will", From *Mornings with Jesus*, Posted 3-10-17, © Guideposts, 2018. https://www.guideposts.org/faith-and-prayer/daily-devotions/devotions-for-women/align-your-heart-with-gods-will

[21] Genesis 3:6; 2 Timothy 4:10.

[22] Genesis 16:1-6.

[23] Isaiah 43:7; 1 Corinthians 10:31.

[24] Daniel 10:12-14.

[25] Genesis 37-39.

[26] Greg Evans, "The View's Joy Behar Apologizes for Mike Pence Mental Illness Remark", DEADLINE, 3-13-18, © 2018 Penske Business Media, LLC. http://deadline.com/2018/03/joy-behar-apology-mike-pence-the-view-mentally-ill-1202337398/

[27] Revelation 2:5.

[28] Mark 9:7.

[29] Luke 17:27.

[30] Genesis 39:7-10.

[31] Exodus 3:11.

[32] 1 Samuel 17:45.

Chapter 3

[1] Kelly Phillips Erb, "The Real Cost of Summer Vacation: Don't Get Buried in Taxes", *FORBES* Magazine, July 7, 2014. https://www.forbes.com/sites/kellyphillipserb/2014/07/07/the-real-cost-of-summer-vacation-dont-get-buried-in-taxes/#4fc8bdb6597a

[2] From Dave Ramsey's Blog, *When Good Vacations Go Bad: Hilarious Nightmare Stories* https://www.daveramsey.com/blog/vacation-budgeting-nightmares

[3] Matthew 6:24.

[4] John 21:15-17.

[5] Romans 1:24-25.

[6] 1 Corinthians 10:13.

[7] 1 Corinthians 6:12, 10:23.

[8] 2 Peter 2:19; Romans 6:12-13; Mt. 5:28.

[9] 2 Peter 2:19, NLT.

Chapter 4

[1] Oswald Chambers, "Is This True of Me?", *My Utmost For His Highest*, March 4, © 2018. https://utmost.org/is-this-true-of-me/

[2] From an Interview, "Clayton Kershaw: Living with Purpose", Beliefnet, © Beliefnet, Inc. http://www.beliefnet.com/entertainment/sports/clayton-kershaw-living-with-purpose.aspx

[3] 1 Peter 4:10-11.

[4] Acts 16:10.

[5] 1 Corinthians 6:19-20.

[6] Romans 11:29, NCV.

[7] Jeremiah 1:5, NCV.

[8] Philippians 3:7-12.

[9] Philippians 3:13-14.

[10] 1 Peter 3:15.

[11] 1 John 2:17.

[12] Galatians 1:4.

[13] Megyn Kelly, Interview with Jimmy Buffet, NBC Today Megyn Kelly Show, 3-2-18.

[14] Fr. Randy Sly, "Rejecting Christian Atheism", Catholic Online Article, 9-29-13. http://www.catholic.org/homily/yearoffaith/story.php?id=52526

[15] Matthew 6:21.

[16] Luke 12:16-21.

[17] https://www.brainyquote.com/quotes/tommy_lasorda_139458

[18] Ben Gilbert, "25 of the Biggest Failed Products from the World's Biggest Companies", Business Insider, 7-16-18, © 2018 Insider Inc. https://www.businessinsider.com/biggest-product-flops-in-history-2016-12#2016-samsungs-galaxy-note-7-25

[19] Jonah 1:2.

[20] Jonah 4:11.

Chapter 5

[1] 1 John 2:16.

[2] 1 Peter 5:8.

[3] 1 Peter 2:11.

[4] Luke 11:23.

[5] Peter Hasson, The Daily Signal, "Facebook, Amazon, Google, and Twitter All Work With Left-Wing SPLC", June 09, 2018, © 2018, The Heritage Foundation. https://www.dailysignal.com/2018/06/09/exclusive-facebook-amazon-google-and-twitter-all-work-with-left-wing-splc/?utm_source=TDS_Email&utm_medium=email&utm_campaign=MorningBell"&mkt_tok=eyJpIjoiTjJZNU56Z3lNVEpr-TUdFNCIsInQiOiJ1cDdsMlM4Mld0USs0anlvT1dlM1lcLzd3WGlWVGs4cVJ4b-1c1YkZoYjlzSnRFYzJ5TitBWEhydjc3VXpvRXBHVjUxUkNsNDFsXC9zNHFFK09jXC9DMGtad0IyNkVsNRd6dVFzdEJMcE1VcVdBd0x5XC9YNlp5eVwvRVgrVVJGGVStlZmlRIn0%3D

[6] Mark 10:21-22.

7   Wilkinson & Finkbeiner, "Everything You Need To Know About Divorce—Facts, Statistics, and Rates", (San Diego: © 2017 Wilkinson & Finkbeiner, LLP, Family Law Attorneys).
     http://www.wf-lawyers.com/divorce-statistics-and-facts/

8   David McCullough Jr., "You're Not Special", Wellesley High School Graduation Speech, TIME Staff, Nov. 17, 2015 (© 2017 TIME, Inc.).
     http://time.com/4116019/david-mccullough-jr-graduation-speech-wellesley-high/
     David McCullough Jr. is an English teacher at Wellesley High School and the author of You Are Not Special: ...And Other Encouragements.

9   Sam Eaton, "9 Reasons Why Following Jesus Can Be So Hard", Recklessly Alive Blog, April 11, 2017, © 2018, Sam Eaton LLC.
     http://www.recklesslyalive.com/9-reasons-why-following-jesus-can-be-so-damn-hard/

10   Tim Keller, Christian Quotes, © 2018 Telling Ministries LLC.
     https://www.christianquotes.info/quotes-by-author/
     tim-keller-quotes/#ixzz5Q9FyWaWr

11   Hebrews 11:6.

12   Ibid., Sam Eaton.

13   Brian Tracy, *Eat That Frog!: 21 Great Ways to Stop Procrastinating and Get More Done in Less Time*, (Oakland, CA: Berrett-Koehler Publishers, Inc., © 2017), Introduction.

14   Matthew 16:26.

15   Katie J. Davis, Kisses from Katie: A Story of Relentless Love and Redemption, (New York: Howard Books, © 2011).

16   Alex Daniel, How 50 Top Ballers Define Success, BEST LIFE, (New York: © 2018 Galvanized Media, 6-12-17).
     https://bestlifeonline.com/how-50-ballers-define-success/

17   Ibid.

18   Ibid.

19   Ibid.

20   Ibid.

21   Ibid.

22   Ibid.

23   Romans 4:20-22, The God's Word Translation.

24   Ibid., Alex Daniel.

Chapter 6

1   Drew Wood, "12 Jim Gaffigan Quotes & Jokes: Everything You Need To Know About Family & Parenting", Fatherly, 6-29-15, © 2018 Fatherly.
     https://www.fatherly.com/love-money/relationships/
     everything-you-need-to-know-about-parenting-in-12-jim-gaffigan-quotes/

2   Julie Huynh, "Study Finds No Difference in the Amount Men and Women Talk", Arizona UBRP Gazette, 6-19-14, © 2018 Undergraduate Biology Research Program.
     https://ubrp.arizona.edu/
     study-finds-no-difference-in-the-amount-men-and-women-talk/

3 Hacker Noon, "How Much Time Do People Spend on Their Mobile Phones in 2017?", https://hackernoon.com/how-much-time-do-people-spend-on-their-mobile-phones-in-2017-e5f90a0b10a6

4 Matthew 12:34; 23:1-7.

5 1 Thessalonians 1:8-9.

6 Liisa Jaaskelainen, Statista, "Eating out behavior in the U.S.—Statistics & Facts". https://www.statista.com/topics/1957/eating-out-behavior-in-the-us/

7 R.C. Sproul, "Objection: All Religions Are Good. It Doesn't Matter What You Believe", Excerpt from *Reason to Believe: A Response to Common Objections to Christianity* by R. C. Sproul, [Grand Rapids, MI: Zondervan © 1978], © 2017 Monergism by CPR Foundation. https://www.monergism.com/objection-all-religions-are-good-it-doesn%E2%80%99t-matter-what-you-believe-dr-rc-sproul

8 Life's Hard Questions Blog @ WordPress, "It Doesn't Matter What You Believe – As Long as You're Sincere", 5-11-11. https://fulfill.wordpress.com/2011/05/11/it-doesnt-matter-what-you-believe-%E2%80%93-as-long-as-youre-sincere/

9 Cory Warren, "How Common Is Identity Theft? (Updated 2018) The Latest Stats", LifeLock, 4-13-18, © 2018 Symantec Corp. https://www.lifelock.com/education/how-common-is-identity-theft/

10 "Wonder of the Day #1800: How Far Can a Sneeze Travel?", Wonderopolis, 2014–2018 © National Center for Families Learning. https://wonderopolis.org/wonder/how-far-can-a-sneeze-travel

11 Sam Blum, "Airport Security Trays Have More Germs Than A Toilet Seat", Thrillist, 9-5-18, © 2018 Group Nine Media Inc. https://www.thrillist.com/news/nation/airport-security-trays-more-germs-than-toilets-study

12 Rod Dreher, "God Bless Ted Turner", National Review online, 2-11-03. https://www.nationalreview.com/2003/02/god-bless-ted-turner-rod-dreher/

13 Bob Woods, "Navy SEAL Chad Williams Shares the Encounter That Changed His Life," Good News Media Group, 10-02-15, © 2018 The Good News. https://www.goodnewsfl.org/navy-seal-chad-williams-shares-the-encounter-that-changed-his-life/

14 Howard R. Gold, "Price Tag for the American Dream", USA Today, 7-4-14, © 2018 USA Today. https://www.usatoday.com/story/money/personalfinance/2014/07/04/american-dream/11122015/

15 Jonah 1:7-12 .

16 Jonah 1:14.

17 Debra Fileta, "We All Come with a Price Tag", TrueLoveDates.com, 9-29-14, © Debra K. Fileta M.A., LPC. https://truelovedates.com/we-all-come-with-a-price-tag/

18 Dave Ramsey, "The Cure for Excessive Spending", Dave Ramsey Blog, © 2018 Lampo Licensing, LLC. https://www.daveramsey.com/blog/the-cure-for-excessive-spending

19 Ecclesiastes 8:11.

20 2 Peter 3:9.

21   From a Blog: "Myths About Living Together", First Things First, 8-15-17, © 2018 First Things First, Chattanooga, TN. https://firstthings.org/myths-about-living-together

22   Barbara Ray, "Cohabitation's Effect on Kids", 3-19-13, Psychology Today © 2018 Sussex Publishers, LLC. https://www.psychologytoday.com/us/blog/adulthood-whats-the-rush/201303/cohabitations-effect-kids

23   Matthew 25:41; Luke 16:24-26; 2 Thessalonians 1:9; Revelation 20:11-15.

24   Isaiah 30:18; 2 Timothy 4:8.

25   Romans 2:11; 1 Corinthians 4:5; Jeremiah 17:10.

26   Revelation 20:12-13.

27   Matthew 25:41.

28   Romans 5:8, 6:23; John 3:16.

29   Caryle Murphy, "Most Americans believe in heaven ... and hell", Pew Research Center FACTTank, © 2018 Pew Research Center, 11-10-15. http://www.pewresearch.org/fact-tank/2015/11/10/most-americans-believe-in-heaven-and-hell/

30   Craig Harper, "Do You Determine your Beliefs, or Do Your Beliefs Determine You?", Lifehack, https://www.lifehack.org/articles/lifestyle/do-you-determine-your-beliefs-or-do-your-beliefs-determine-you-part-one.html

31   Lee Woofenden, "Did Jesus ever actually say, "If you don't believe in me you will go to hell?", *Spiritual Insights for Everyday Life*, 1-31-17, © 2018 Spiritual Insights for Everyday Life. https://leewoof.org/2017/01/31/did-jesus-ever-actually-say-if-you-dont-believe-in-me-you-will-go-to-hell/

32   Jordan Peterson, *Dangerous People are Teaching our Kids*, PragerU video, 6-11-18, © 2018 Prager University. https://www.prageru.com/videos/dangerous-people-are-teaching-your-kids

33   Matthew 6:21.

34   2 Kings 14:25.

35   "Jeroboam II", Wikipedia, Wikipedia Foundation, 6-13-18, https://en.wikipedia.org/wiki/Jeroboam_II

36   1 Kings 12:28-33.

37   Amos 6:1-8.

38   Joshua 3:14-17.

Chapter 7

1   "Hillary Scott Opens Up About Miscarriage", PEOPLE Magazine, 6-20-16, (New York: © 2016 Time Inc.). http://celebritybabies.people.com/2016/06/20/hillary-scott-miscarriage-thy-will-meaning-new-single/

2   Hebrews 4:16.

3   Romans 8:28.

4   Exodus 7-12.

5   Acts 16:20-34.

6   Jonah 1:15.

7   Geoff Colvin as quoted on Goodreads, Goodreads Quotes, © 2018 Goodreads Inc.
     https://www.goodreads.com/author/quotes/988764.Geoff_Colvin

8   James 1:2-4; 1 Thessalonians 5:18.

9   Mark 6:52.

10   John 9:1-3.

11   Romans 8:28.

12   Brad Schmitt, "MercyMe's Bart Millard Thought His Father was Going to Kill Him",
     Nashville Tennessean, 6-16-18, © 2018 www.tennessean.com.
     https://www.tennessean.com/story/entertainment/music/2018/02/13/
     bart-millard-mercyme-can-only-imagine-movie-book-father-abuse/320728002/

13   Jonah 1:6.

14   Jonah 1:14.

15   Jonah 1:12.

16   "Tullian Tchividjian Confesses Second Affair Concealed by Two Coral Ridge Elders",
     Christianity Today, 3-21-16, © 2018 Christianity Today.
     https://www.christianitytoday.com/news/2016/march/tullian-tchividjian-confess-
     es-second-affair-coral-ridge.html

17   Mark Martin, "Billy Graham's Grandson Fired: 'I Take Full Responsibility'", CBN News,
     3-18-16, © 2018 CBN.
     http://www1.cbn.com/cbnnews/us/2016/March/
     Billy-Grahams-Grandson-Fired-I-Take-Full-Responsibilty

18   Andy Andrews, "The 3 Undeniable Benefits of Adversity", Blogpost, 8-22-13, © 2008 -
     2018 Andy Andrews.
     https://www.andyandrews.com/benefits-of-adversity/

19   Tim Keller, Christian Quotes, © 2018 Telling Ministries LLC.
     https://www.christianquotes.info/quotes-by-author/
     tim-keller-quotes/#ixzz5Q9WQ2yoZ

20   1 Peter 5:5.

21   Jonah 1:5.

22   Max Lucado, In the Eye of the Storm, [Nashville, Thomas Nelson, Inc., © 1991, pp. 125,
     186-187]

23   John 3:16.

24   Jonah 2:2.

25   Dennis Prager, "I'm Back. Here's Where I've Been", The Dennis Prager Show online,
     01-09-18, © 2018 DennisPrager.com & Salem National.
     http://www.dennisprager.com/im-back-heres-where-ive-been/

26   Donald S. Whitney, Ten Questions to Diagnose Your Spiritual Health, [Colorado Springs,
     CO: © 2001, NavPress] as quoted in CROSSWALK.COM Blog, 2-22-02.

Chapter 8

1   Susan M. Heathfield. "Leadership Vision", The Balance Careers, Updated February
     28, 2018
     https://www.thebalancecareers.com/leadership-vision-1918616

2   John Ryan, "Leadership Success Always Starts With Vision". Forbes, 7-29-09, © 2018 Forbes Media LLC.
    https://www.forbes.com/2009/07/29/personal-success-vision-leadership-managing-ccl.html#731fcbf66349

3   Cyrus, "Top 15 Inspiring Steven Spielberg Quotes", *Goalcast*, 5-23-16, © Goalcast 2016.
    https://www.goalcast.com/2016/05/23/top-15-inspiring-steven-spielberg-quotes/

4   Acts 10.

5   Matthew 1:20.

6   Matthew 2:13.

7   Exodus 2:11-12.

8   Exodus 3-4.

9   Jeremiah 23:16, NKJV.

10 Genesis 16:1-4.

11 John 18:10.

12 John 10:27.

13 Genesis 6:13-22.

14 Acts 16:6-10.

15 Nehemiah 2:12; cf. 7:5.

16 Daniel 2:19-30.

17 Joshua 5:13-6:5.

18 1 Samuel 17:29, 45-47.

19 Genesis 50:20.

20 Luke 24:25-27; Revelation 13:8.

Chapter 9

1   Rachel Moore, "SNOW' JOKE Twitter Users Poke Fun at Snowflake Generation with List of 'Millennial New Year's Resolutions'", *The Sun*, 12-31-17, © News Group Newspapers Ltd. in England No. 679215.
    https://www.thesun.co.uk/fabulous/5241900/twitter-users-poke-fun-at-snowflake-generation-with-list-of-millennial-new-years-resolutions/

2   Jonah 1:12.

3   Matthew 12:34.

4   Matthew 21:12-15.

5   Matthew 6:24.

6   Exodus 14:10-12 / Joshua 24:14, 19-21 / 1 Kings 18:21.

7   Jonah 1:4.

8   Mark 6:52, ESV.

9   James 4:6.

10 Jeremiah 17:9-10, NLT.

11 From a Sermon by Christian Cheong, Sermon Central, 8-29-01, © 2003-2018 | Outreach, Inc.
    https://www.sermoncentral.com/sermon-illustrations/3815/billy-graham-we-re-suffering-from-only-by-christian-cheong

12 Jonah 4:10-11, NLT.

13 Rick Warren, Goodreads, © 2018 Goodreads Inc. https://www.goodreads.com/quotes/601712-our-culture-has-accepted-two-huge-lies-the-first-is

14 Tim Keller, Christian Quotes, © 2018 Telling Ministries LLC. https://www.christianquotes.info/quotes-by-author/tim-keller-quotes/#ixzz5Q9FyWaWr

Chapter 10

1 Tim Keller, Christian Quotes, © 2018 Telling Ministries LLC. https://www.christianquotes.info/quotes-by-topic/quotes-about-freedom/#ixzz5Q9ErgClO

2 Ravi Zacharias and Dennis Prager with Jeff Foxworthy, "The Death of Truth, The Decline of Culture Q&A", YouTube Video, 10-17. https://www.youtube.com/watch?v=RutMHp2ID1I

3 Matthew 6:21.

4 Romans 6:16.

5 John 3:18.

6 J. Maureen Henderson, "Why 'Do What Makes You Happy' Is The Dumbest Advice You Can Give Someone", FORBES, 2-29-16, © 2018 Forbes Media LLC. https://www.forbes.com/sites/jmaureenhenderson/2016/02/29/why-do-what-makes-you-happy-is-the-dumbest-advice-you-can-give-someone/#4d1f0cfc1501

7 John 4:5-17.

8 Jonah 1:5, ESV.

9 Jonah 1:8, ESV.

10 Jonah 1:12, NLT.

11 1 Corinthians 1:18.

12 Jonah 1:11.

13 Jonah 1:14-16.

14 Genesis 3:1-8.

15 Romans 14:23b.

16 Dave Stachowiak, "Four Ways to Lead in Times of Uncertainty", Coaching for Leaders, © 2018, Innovate Learning, LLC. https://coachingforleaders.com/lead-in-times-of-uncertainty/

17 Andrea Downing Peck, "GRIT", Costco Connection, 9-18, pp. 45-49, © 2018 Costco Wholesale, Issaquah, WA.

18 Ibid.

19 Jonah 4.

20 Barbara Kimmel, "Kouzes & Posner on Building Trust", Trust Across America / Trust Around the World, 8-29-15. https://www.trustacrossamerica.com/blog/?attachment_id=1005

21 Kathy Benjamin, "60% of People Can't Go 10 Minutes Without Lying", Mental Floss, 5-7-12, ©2018 Mental Floss. http://mentalfloss.com/article/30609/60-people-cant-go-10-minutes-without-lying

Chapter 11

1. John 16:33, ESV.
2. Thomas Sowell, "The Wisdom of Thomas Sowell", Aguanomics, 10-23-12. http://www.aguanomics.com/2012/10/the-wisdom-of-thomas-sowell.html
3. Matthew 12:36, ESV.
4. Romans 2:16, NLT.
5. Romans 1:19-20; 2:14-15.
6. Romans 1:20; 3:19.
7. Jonah 1:2, NKJV.
8. Matthew 13:20-21.
9. Jonah 1:5-16.
10. Kevin Kruse, "100 Best Quotes On Leadership", Forbes, 10-16-12, © 2018 Forbes Media, LLC. https://www.forbes.com/sites/kevinkruse/2012/10/16/quotes-on-leadership/#37cbe5c42feb
11. John 14:21, NLT.
12. Jonah 1:2.
13. Mark 10:21-22.
14. Andy Stanley, From the Sermon "Conviction vs. Preference", Preaching Today, Christianity Today, 8-05, © 2018 Christianity Today. https://www.preachingtoday.com/sermons/sermons/2005/august/0984.html
15. Genesis 12:1-3.
16. Jonah 1:2, NLT.
17. Genesis 19:16.
18. Romans 1:26-32.
19. Revelation 21:8.
20. Nicholas Cole, "7 Horrible Ways to Lead a Team (and the 1 Mistake Everyone Makes)", MEDIUM, 2-1-18. https://medium.com/@nicolascole77/7-horrible-ways-to-lead-a-team-and-the-1-mistake-everyone-makes-1fb33ffa8b5
21. Ephesians 6:4, NLT.
22. LIFEWAY Blog, "Pastors Are Not Quitting In Droves", Facts & Trends, 9-28-16, © 2018 LifeWay Christian Resources. https://factsandtrends.net/2016/09/28/pastors-are-not-quitting-in-droves/
23. Eric Geiger, "The Humble Leader", Christianity Today Blog, *The Exchange with Ed Stetzer*, 4-16-18, © 2018 Christianity Today. https://www.christianitytoday.com/edstetzer/2018/april/humble-leader.html
24. Judges 13:5.
25. Judges 16:5.
26. 1 Samuel 11:2-5.
27. 2 Samuel 12:10-14.
28. Attorney David C.. Gibbs Jr., "Conviction vs. Preference". http://www.freedomlaw.com/archives/oldsite/con_pref.html
29. Daniel 1:8, NKJV.
30. Daniel 6:23.

Chapter 12

1 Tim Harford as quoted on CLARITY.
   http://www.lessnoisemoreclarity.com.au/blog/few-of-our-own-failures-are-fatal-econo-mist-tim-harford.html
2 Seth Godin, "A Solution to Stalled", SETH'S BLOG, 9-10-18.
   https://seths.blog/2018/09/the-solution-to-stalled/
3 2 Samuel 12:7-13; Psalm 51:3.
4 Mark 6:51-52.
5 Hebrews 10:29.
6 Genesis 19:16.
7 Matthew 3:2.
8 Revelation 2:5.
9 Galatians 5:17, NKJV.
10 James 4:4, NLT.
11 Jonah 4:4-11.
12 Hebrews 11:6, NLT.
13 Jonah 2:2.
14 Jonah 2:4,8.
15 Jonah 2:9.
16 Jonah 4:2-3.
17 Jonah 4:11.
18 Newser Editors, "Good Role Models: 5 Most Uplifting Stories", Newser, 6-7-15, © 2018 Newser, LLC.
   http://www.newser.com/story/207697/good-role-models-5-most-uplifting-stories.html
19 Jonah 1:15.
20 Jonah 1:6.
21 Jonah 1:9-10.
22 Acts 1:8.
23 2 Corinthians 5:20; Acts 26:27-28.
24 2 Corinthians 5:10-11; Ezekiel 3:18-19; Romans 14:12; Hebrews 4:13; Luke 12:48; 1 Peter 4:4-5; Matthew 10:14-15.
25 Harry Radliffe II, "Proof That One Person Can Make A Difference", CBS News, 7-2-15, © 2018 CBS Interactive Inc.
   https://www.cbsnews.com/news/proof-that-one-person-can-make-a-difference/
26 Jonah 2:8-9.
27 Jonah 4:1.

Chapter 13

1 Lindy Lowry, "EGYPTIAN TEEN: 'MY FATHER'S DEATH FOR CHRIST MADE ME SEARCH FOR JESUS", Open Doors USA, 8-23-18, © 2000-2018 Open Doors USA.
   https://www.opendoorsusa.org/christian-persecution/stories/egyptian-teen-my-fathers-death-for-christ-made-me-search-for-jesus/
2 Acts 4:29-31.
3 Psalm 51:17, ESV.

4   Matthew 8:10; 15:28

5   Matthew 8:26; 14:31; 16:8.

6   Mark 4:40, Strong's Ref. #G3640.

7   Romans 4:20-22.

8   Matthew 9:20-22.

9   Matthew 17:14-21.

10   Hebrews 11:6.

11   Romans 10:17.

12   Hebrews 11:39.

13   Jonah 4:5-10.

14   Jonah 2:1.

15   James 1:6, ESV.

16   Mark 2:1-12.

17   "SPERM WHALE", National Geographic / Animals / Reference, © 1996-2015 National Geographic Society.
     https://www.nationalgeographic.com/animals/mammals/s/sperm-whale/

18   Genesis 1:21; Psalm 8:8.

19   Rose Eveleth, "Could a Whale Accidentally Swallow You? It Is Possible", Smithsonian.com, 2-25-13.
     https://www.smithsonianmag.com/smart-news/could-a-whale-accidentally-swallow-you-it-is-possible-26353362/#Q0okMfuDA6v9KAkt.99

20   1 Peter 3:7.

21   Psalm 84:11, NKJV.

22   Mark 5.

23   Luke 7:36-48.

24   Mark 5:40-42.

25   Acts 16:25-34.

26   Exodus 15.

27   Isaiah 37-38.

28   Romans 12:1.

29   Isaiah 55:8-9.

30   Geoff Colvin, *Talent is Overrated*: *What Really Separates World-Class Performers from Everybody Else* (New York: Portfolio Penguin Random House, LLC), © 2008, p. 188.

31   Jonah 1:5,14.

32   Exodus 4:8-9; Numbers 14:11,22; John 2:11,12:37.

33   Matthew 12:40.

34   Tony Robbins, "Are You Stuck", Blog, © 2018 Robbins Research International, Inc.
     https://www.tonyrobbins.com/mind-meaning/are-you-stuck/?utm_source=twitter&utm_medium=social&utm_campaign=Editorial&utm_content=Are%20You%20Stuck

35   Jonah 3:1-2.

36   "What can we learn from the life of Jonah?", Got Questions, © 2002-2018 Got Questions Ministries.
     https://www.gotquestions.org/life-Jonah.html

Chapter 14

1. Revelation 3:7, CJB.
2. Max Lucado, Excerpt from *God's Story, Your Story* in Zondervan Blog: "Closed Door Stories: Looking Back on God's Love", 10-5-11.
   http://zondervan.typepad.com/zondervan/2011/10/stories-closed-doors-gods-love.html
3. Sue Bohlin, "When God Says No: Reasons for Unanswered Prayer", Submitted by Probe Ministries, Bible.org, © 2018 Bible.org.
   https://bible.org/article/when-god-says-no-reasons-unanswered-prayer
4. Habakkuk 2:3.
5. Ecclesiastes 3:1; Galatians 6:9.
6. Daniel 6:11.
7. Jonah 3:5-8.
8. Jonah 3:9, NLT.
9. Mark 5.
10. John 11:4-5.
11. John 8:11.
12. John 4:16-18.
13. Matthew 26:46.
14. Matthew 27:50.
15. Chuck Frey, "Creative Lessons from one of the Most Inspiring Stories Ever Told: Acres of Diamonds", Innovation Management.se, © 2013 InnovationManagement.se.
    http://www.innovationmanagement.se/imtool-articles/creative-lessons-from-one-of-the-most-inspiring-stories-ever-told-acres-of-diamonds/
16. Matthew 24:36-44.
17. Luke 16.
18. Revelation 20:11-15.

Chapter 15

1. Victor Mather, "Bethany Hamilton, a Shark-Attack Survivor, Reaches an Unlikely Crest", The New York Times, 5-31-16, © 2018 The New York Times Company.
   https://www.nytimes.com/2016/06/01/sports/bethany-hamilton-world-surf-league.html
2. The inspirational quotes by Bethany Hamilton, Surfer Today, © 2018 SurferToday.com.
   https://www.surfertoday.com/surfing/8769-the-inspirational-quotes-by-bethany-hamilton
3. Luke 1:37.
4. Luke 15:15-20.
5. John 8:10-11.
6. Fox & Friends Interview with Brian Kilmeade, 9-25-18.
7. Hayden Bird, "'If Tom could, I think he would divorce him': 6 things we learned from the new Bill Belichick book", Boston Globe, 9-19-18, ©2018 Boston Globe Media Partners, LLC
   https://www.boston.com/sports/new-england-patriots/2018/09/19/belichick-book-brady-relationship-ian-occonnor

8   Genesis 7:16.
9   Acts 9:1-9.
10 Matthew 17:5; Philippians 2:5-11.
11 Kristy Etheridge, "After 'Unbroken': Billy Graham and Louis Zamperini", Billy Graham Evangelistic Association, 12-22-14, ©2018 BGEA.
    https://billygraham.org/story/louis-zamperini-billy-graham-and-a-life-changing-decision-the-rest-of-the-unbroken-story/
12 Deuteronomy 9:4, ESV.
13 Leviticus 18:20-25.
14 Adrian Rogers, "Four Lies That Ruined the World", Love Worth Finding, © 2018, Lightsource.com.
    https://www.lightsource.com/ministry/love-worth-finding/articles/four-lies-that-ruined-the-world-13313.html
15 David K. Li, "Mom of DC Stabbing Victim Forgives Daughter's Alleged Killer", New York Post, 9-21-18, © 2018 NYP HOLDINGS, INC.
    https://nypost.com/2018/09/21/
    mom-of-dc-stabbing-victim-forgives-daughters-alleged-killer/
16 Adrian Rogers, Sermon: "What Is the Unpardonable Sin? Part 2", Love Worth Finding, © 2018, Oneplace.com.
    https://www.oneplace.com/ministries/love-worth-finding/read/articles/what-is-the-unpardonable-sin-part-2-16256.html
17 Ibid, Hayden Bird, "'If Tom could, I think he would divorce him': 6 things we learned from the new Bill Belichick book", Boston Globe, 9-19-18, ©2018 Boston Globe Media Partners, LLC.
    https://www.boston.com/sports/new-england-patriots/2018/09/19/
    belichick-book-brady-relationship-ian-occonnor

Chapter 16

1   Jeff Foxworthy Quotes, BrainyQuote, © 2001 - 2018 BrainyQuote.
    https://www.brainyquote.com/quotes/jeff_foxworthy_452019
2   Mark 8:35 LB.
3   Romans 8:29, ESV.
4   Romans 8:28, NLV.
5   1 Corinthians 10:13.
6   Mark 6:48.
7   Judges 6:12-16.
8   2 Kings 14:25; Luke 11:32.
9   Matthew 14:29.
10 Jonah 4:2.
11 1 John 1:9.
12 Nick DeCola, "Does My Story Matter?", CRU, 3-7-16, © 1994-2018 Cru.
    https://www.cru.org/us/en/how-to-know-god/my-story-a-life-changed/does-my-story-matter.html
13 Greg Warren, Sermon: "The People Who Missed Christmas", Sermon Central, 12-13-03, © 2003-2018 Outreach, Inc.

https://www.sermoncentral.com/sermons/
the-people-who-missed-christmas-greg-warren-sermon-on-christmas-advent-64180

14 Hebrews 11:6; James 1:6.
15 Proverbs 16:32.
16 Ephesians 4:30-31.
17 John 8:11.
18 Jonah 3:5-9.
19 Matthew 25:34-40.
20 Will Maule, "Pro-Abortion Sen. Elizabeth Warren Quotes Bible to Slam Brett
    Kavanaugh: 'We're on the Moral Side'", FaithWire, 7-25-18.
    http://www.faithwire.com/2018/07/25/pro-abortion-sen-elizabeth-warren-quotes-bi-
    ble-to-slam-brett-kavanaugh-were-on-the-moral-side/
21 Emma Green, "Science Is Giving the Pro-Life Movement a Boost", The Atlantic, 1-18-18,
    © 2018 by The Atlantic Monthly Group.
    https://www.theatlantic.com/politics/archive/2018/01/pro-life-pro-science/549308/
22 Elizabeth Warren, Senate Newsroom, From the Full Text of a Speech Delivered on the
    Senate Floor: "Senator Warren Delivers Floor Speech Opposing Proposed 20-Week
    Abortion Ban", 1-30-18.
    https://www.warren.senate.gov/newsroom/press-releases/
    senator-warren-delivers-floor-speech-opposing-proposed-20-week-abortion-ban
23 2 Thessalonians 2:7b; 2 Timothy 3:1-3.
24 Jonah 4:5-11.
25 Seth Godin, 9-20-18 Blog "Diving Boards".
26 Emma Baty, "Gisele Bündchen Opens Up About Suffering Panic Attacks, Saying
    She Considered Suicide", Cosmopolitan Magazine, 9-26-18, ©2018 Hearst
    Communications, Inc.
    https://www.cosmopolitan.com/entertainment/celebs/a23473514/
    gisele-bundchen-panic-attacks-considered-suicide-new-book/
27 Jonah 4:3,8.
28 Jonah 4:9.
29 Robert Steven Kaplan, "Reaching Your Potential", Harvard Business Review, July-August,
    2008, © 2018 Harvard Business School Publishing.
    https://hbr.org/2008/07/reaching-your-potential

Chapter 17
1 Holly Black, "Red Glove", Simon and Schuster, 2012, p.146.
2 Samuel Rodenhizer, *Quotation Celebration*, Blog, 9-22-16.
   https://quotationcelebration.wordpress.com/2016/09/22/
   people-dont-resist-change-they-resist-being-changed-peter-senge/
3 Hebrews 3:12; Matthew 19:7-8.
4 Acts 24:25, NIV.
5 Revelation 13:15-18.
6 2 Corinthians 5:10-11, GNT.
7 2 Corinthians 5:20.
8 Matthew 20:28, NIV.

9   John 20:30-31.

10   2 Corinthians 4:5, NIV.

11   Luke 19:10, CEV.

12   2 Cor. 5:18, NIV.

13   Romans 3:10-18, 23.

13   Numbers 14:24, NIV.

15   Romans 12:1, GNT.

16   Tim Keller, Christian Quotes, © 2018 Telling Ministries LLC.
     https://www.christianquotes.info/quotes-by-author/
     tim-keller-quotes/#ixzz5Q9FyWaWr

17   Pamela Spinney, Reader's Digest, © 2018 RDA Enthusiast Brands
     https://www.rd.com/joke/social-media-irl/

18   Acts 4:18; 5:40.

19   Chris Kyle, American Sniper: The Autobiography of the Most Lethal Sniper in U.S.
     Military History

20   Jonah 4:5-11.

21   Nancy L. Clark, Reader's Digest, © 2018 RDA Enthusiast Brands.
     https://www.rd.com/joke/social-media-irl/

22   John 12:26, GNT.

23   1 Corinthians 15:56, GNT.

24   Rick Warren, "Ministry: How Real Servants Think", CBN, © 2018 The Christian
     Broadcasting Network, Inc.
     http://www1.cbn.com/ministry-how-real-servants-think

25   Bradford Manning, Blog: "HOW TO SPEAK YOUR TRUTH AND MAKE
     PEOPLE LISTEN", 2-15-18.
     https://twoblindbrothers.com/blogs/the-blind-spot/
     how-to-speak-your-truth-and-make-people-listen

Chapter 18

1   John Taylor, "A&M's Koda Martin transferring, joins dad, father-in-law at Syracuse",
     NBC Sports, 4-20-18, © 2018 NBC Universal.
     https://collegefootballtalk.nbcsports.com/2018/04/20/
     ams-koda-martin-transferring-joins-dad-father-in-law-at-syracuse/

2   Jonah 4:11, NLT.

3   Barbara Brown Taylor and David L. Bartlett, *Feasting on the Word: Year C, Volume 2:
     Lent through Eastertide*, (Louisville: Westminster John Knox Press, © 2009, p. 474).

4   Hebrews 1:1.

5   David Whitely, "Ten years later, Tim Tebow's speech echoes on", Orlando Sentinel,
     9-27-18.
     https://www.orlandosentinel.com/opinion/audience/david-whitley/os-ae-tebow-
     speech-david-whitley-0927-story.html

6   Acts 17:24-28, NKJV.

7   Luke 24:27 / John 5:46.

8   Romans 12:1-2.

9   Jeremiah 29:11, NKJV.

10 Brian Solomon, "Meet David Green: Hobby Lobby's Biblical Billionaire", Forbes, 9-18-12, ©2018 Forbes Media LLC.
    https://www.forbes.com/sites/briansolomon/2012/09/18/david-green-the-biblical-billionaire-backing-the-evangelical-movement/#40c8225d5807

11 "CEO's Prayer Saves a Business", Preaching Today, Christianity Today, © 2018 Christianity Today. Illustration from Suzanne Jordan Brown, "Prayer-Driven Enterprise," Pray! magazine (July/August 2006), p. 26.

12 Ibid.

13 Brian Solomon, Ibid.

14 Brian Moll, "Is God REALLY Speaking to You? 4 Questions to Help You Discern His Voice", 5-10-13, © 2018 Oath Inc. HuffPost MultiCultural/HPMG News.
    https://www.huffingtonpost.com/brian-moll/is-god-really-speaking-to-you-4-questions-to-help-you-discern-his-voice_b_3248509.html

15 "God Wants You To Succeed In All Things", Joseph Prince Ministries, © Joseph Prince Ministries 2018.
    https://www.josephprince.org/blog/articles/god-wants-you-to-succeed-in-all-things

16 Sean McDowell, "9 Important Insights about Generation Z" Josh McDowell Ministry, 12-8-16, © 2018 Josh McDowell Ministry.
    https://www.josh.org/9-important-insights-generation-z/?mot=J79GNF&gclid=Cj0KCQjw6MHdBRCtARIsAEigMxG0Bs1M_5IB57-9yYAd106dF46M1SlBsmJb-z7OcsdfabxDymLYzesIaArISEALw_wcB

17 1 Chronicles 5:26; 2 Kings 17:15-17.

18 Liberty in North Korea, "NORTH KOREA FAQS".
    https://www.libertyinnorthkorea.org/learn-faqs/?gclid=Cj0KCQjw6MHdBRCtARIsAEigMxGAChbll4O9z1u-aJz_p3eXapfiYPZ7QO7HBsQLY_37h3306xTDE9IaA-jbOEALw_wcB

19 Revelation 3:15-16, NLT.

CPSIA information can be obtained
at www.ICGtesting.com
Printed in the USA
BVHW040130091118
532574BV00015B/69/P